Born in Yorkshire Duncan was educated in Oxfordshire and at Trinity College, Oxford where he studied English. He spent his working life in education, most recently for 18 years as Head Master of Kingston Grammar School in London. He now works as an education consultant and has written widely on education issues and on teaching literature.

To Amanda,

Paradise Lost

A Drama of Unintended Consequences

How to read John Milton's poem in the 21st century

With best wishes,

Duncan

Duncan Baxter

28th February 2017

Matador
9 Priory Business Park,
Wistow Road,
Kibworth Beauchamp,
Leicestershire. LE8 0RX
Tel: (+44) 116 279 2299
Email: books@troubador.co.uk
Web: www.troubador.co.uk/matador

ISBN 978 1785899 027

British Library Cataloguing in Publication Data.
A catalogue record for this book is available from the British Library.

Typeset in 11pt Aldine401 BT by Troubador Publishing Ltd, Leicester, UK Printed and bound in the UK by TJ International, Padstow, Cornwall

Matador is an imprint of Troubador Publishing Ltd

For Neredah, Alexander and Sebastian

Who with patience, good humour and encouragement
have tolerated sharing the house with Milton

Preface

On being introduced to Milton's poetry at school I was immediately captivated by his erudition and ability to create fully credible biblical characters, as well as the variety and beauty of his sweeping verse. The more I read, however, it became clear to me that here was a complex and divided personality at work, whose poetry should be more widely read; it is this conviction which informed my teaching and this book.

I went on to study English at university, having chosen a college where the Tutor for English was a Milton specialist. Here the story takes a violent turn, as I came to disagree with my Tutor's view of *Paradise Lost*. Dennis Burden had published *The Logical Epic* in 1967 in which he opposed the fashion to criticise Milton's failure to 'justify the ways of God to men', arguing that the poem was founded upon a consistent, meticulously constructed argument which successfully defended God's treatment of mankind and the angels before and after their respective disobedience and rebellion. My view was and is that nothing could be further from the truth. This is not because Milton was deliberately setting out to criticise God or portray him as a tyrant but because Milton was not the stable and conservative Protestant of the caricature. Indeed, Milton had the capacity to hold two contrasting opinions simultaneously.

In *Paradise Lost* it was his ability to step into the shoes of his characters to present them with powerful conviction which led to unintended consequences. The power and success of the poem lie not in a justification of God's actions but in Milton's empathy with God's creatures in their expression of how difficult it is to live life to the full whilst obeying God's law. Yes Milton was clever, well read, technically outstanding and committed to the Parliamentary and Puritan causes but he fell out with everyone, even those on his own side. He often wrote that we should tolerate each others' views yet he was the least tolerant of men, but in *Paradise Lost* his temperament and training could not stop him from allowing his characters a fair hearing, which is where the trouble started.

When I showed an early draft of what was to become this book to my then retired Tutor, he was fully supportive, and with characteristic humility and encouragement wrote to me in July 2001: "As you may guess I don't come at the poem along that line but that is neither here nor there. I will make two sorts of point here; one about where the argument could be strengthened and the other on minor points of detail." I shall try to emulate this spirit in responding to those who may disagree with my view, and hope that Dennis, who died in March 2010, would have taken pleasure in the fact that I remain committed to unravelling the complex genius of John Milton. Milton provokes disagreement, so let us relish it!

Duncan Baxter

CONTENTS

Introduction

How best to engage with *Paradise Lost*

'Milton Studies Inc' is a multinational conglomerate, daily disgorging thousands of words; yet mention John Milton to first year students of English Literature or any reasonably well-read adult, and they will begin to turn pale, whilst unenthusiastically recalling being forced to study a couple of books from *Paradise Lost* at secondary school. These days it is less likely to be studied in school at all, whilst university students frequently do not relish the prospect of grappling with the notoriously difficult poet.

The quantity of scholarly material produced is not matched by the volume of enthusiasm generated by readers. Milton's work is more likely to be perceived as difficult (full of classical, historical and literary references unfamiliar to many readers, necessitating acres of footnotes), Latinate (comprising hard words and peculiar sentence structure), long (not easily digestible in bite-sized chunks) and dully moral because (as everyone seems to know) Milton was a severe Puritan. Dr Johnson's comment in his Life of Milton[1] concerning the poem's "want of human interest," and that reading *Paradise Lost* can be "A duty rather than a pleasure," was echoed by EMW Tillyard in his enquiry into Milton's Protestantism when he posed the question: 'Why would anyone wish to read an Evangelical Protestant?'[2]

Milton's reputation as a poet can also be damaged by what the great American historian and educationist Jacques

1 *Lives of the English Poets* publ 1779-1781

2 *The Miltonic Setting* Chatto 1966

Barzun called "the gangrene of specialism."[3] Milton's work is so full of learning that there is a treasure trove of allusion and minutiae to mine, together with a range of theological, political, autobiographical and philosophical angles to explore. All of this bears testimony to Milton's remarkable capacity to absorb learning, and reflects the magnitude of his achievement in synthesising so much in his poem. Displaying an uncanny prescience, however, Milton captured the plethora of activity which was to surround his greatest work and the technical language of theology and philosophy used by scholars:

> *Others apart sat on a hill retired,*
> *In thoughts more elevate, and reasoned high*
> *Of providence, foreknowledge, will and fate,*
> *Fixed fate, free will, foreknowledge absolute,*
> *And found no end, in wandering mazes lost.*
>
> (II 557-561)

On the other hand this also provides an apt description of the numerous complex and even contradictory ideas and topics explored in Milton's retelling of the familiar Genesis story.

Milton is such a monolithic figure that it is also possible to look backwards at causes (the influences that affected Milton's work) and forwards at effects (the influence of Milton on others). We may study Milton's antecedents in the classical and poetic worlds from Homer and Dante to Spenser, as well as Hebraic writings, and look forward to the massive impact he had on the writers who succeeded him, particularly in the Romantic period. Keeping things simple is of course not easily possible when dealing with such a complex writer, but the truth

3 See obituary of Jacques Barzun by Joe Holley, *Washington Post*, 26th October 2012: "In essays and a series of books on American education including *Teacher in America* (1945) and *The American University: How it Runs, Where it is Going* (1968) he inveighed against "the gangrene of specialism" in college offerings that he thought would cause the "individual's mind (to be) doomed to solitude and the individual heart to dry up.""

is that Milton Studies are now as far away from most readers as neurosurgery and string theory.

But what Milton has to say in addressing some of the biggest issues concerning our human condition, is too important to be left to the remote academic few. Shunting Milton's ideas into a university siding misses the point that at its heart *Paradise Lost* speaks to us today as much as it did to readers in the seventeenth century and the years between, about what it is to live on earth as human beings. Put simply Milton asks the reader to consider who we are, why we are here, where we come from, what if anything happens to us when we die and on what principles or authority we order our collective lives and morality. Pascal's cry: "Le silence eternal de ces espaces infinis m'effraie" ("The eternal silence of these infinite spaces [the heavens] terrifies me")[4] finds in Milton's dramatisation of the Fall a graphic exposition of the dilemmas and uncertainties which face us.

When facing the possibly daunting task of tackling this long and great work there is a choice of initial approaches. The reader may use either a microscope or a telescope. Should the microscope be chosen then every note and reference in the most comprehensive scholarly edition of the poem is examined, there being many pages where the footnotes occupy more space than the poem. The Miltonic equivalent of debating how many angels can fit on a pinhead may keep a reader happy for hours on end, but there is a danger of overlooking the vastness of the bigger questions Milton provokes us to consider. An alternative, therefore, is to look through a telescope and take the longer view, turning our eyes to the stars, where we find a bigger picture concerning both the human issues which Milton lays before us and questions relating to God himself. This approach converts what may appear to be no more than an over-elaborate retelling of the story of the Fall of man from the Book of Genesis into something brimming with insights about ourselves and the human condition. In an age when involvement in formal religion is said to be in decline yet people's appetite

---

4 Blaise Pascal (1623-1662) *Pensees iii 206*

has never been sharper to know more about the universe and mankind's place in it, Milton's poem is there for us. After we have engaged with the colossal human and spiritual questions with which Milton confronts us then is the time to deepen our understanding of his theme and appreciate the complexity of his style by examining the religious, philosophical, historical, literary, geographical allusions and concepts which enrich every page of this epic poem, further to understand Milton's place in the history of poetry and ideas.

On the spiritual plane there is the question of mankind's place in the scheme of the universe and what, if any, duty of obedience we owe to our creator. Perhaps surprisingly there are more human than divine matters dealt with in the poem. Among these is the basis for our understanding of good and evil within human nature and the principles on which society bases its moral order; there are questions of independence and interdependence within relationships and how this may inform authority structures in society. Finally, almost on a Shakespearean plane, Milton examines the nature of human love, the place of ambition, and whether we can ever distinguish between appearance and reality. None of these considerations is academic or remote. In his presentations of God, the Son, Satan, Adam and Eve, Milton confronted the dilemmas inherent in being human, albeit within a specifically Christian context.

This reading of the poem argues that it was Milton's artistic decisions which became a central influence on the unintended outcomes of the poem. Far from achieving his ambition of examining and explaining God's actions towards mankind, to "justify the ways of God to men"[5] paradoxically Milton elevates the stature of mankind by exposing the complex dilemmas which God places before us as human beings. By giving fuller personalities and voices to the protagonists in his dramatisation of the Fall Milton achieved something different from what he had intended. This may sometimes make reading the poem feel like studying the transcripts of interview notes from a police

5 *I 26*

investigation into a major crime. How could Milton succeed in justifying God's actions when the experience of reading the poem may lead us to question the character of God and total obedience to him? This may then lead us to ask whether God really is all good, whether Satan is all bad, whether Adam really is simply a weak husband and whether Eve is more than just an empty-headed, vain woman. Milton's audacious attempt to formulate a coherent and logical defence for God by enabling us to hear his voice and his commands and the reasons for them contrasts with the experiences of 'knowing' God portrayed by the medieval mystics, who claimed that truly to know God involved suppressing reason, letting go of the mind in order to sense God on another plane. It was by giving the protagonists voices that Milton created a drama which reveals a very different meaning from the one he intended.

This book aims to demonstrate that his decisions about style and technique led to unforeseen consequences, notably the subversion of Milton's intention to "justify the ways of God to men" leading to a radical questioning of God's relationship with mankind, which is timeless in its relevance. It is important not to be put off reading *Paradise Lost* by its length, apparent difficulty and the number of books and scholarly articles that have been written about it. We should respond to the protagonists as characters in a play, for this is how Milton presents them to us and how he originally envisaged his treatment of the Fall. By filling out the thinly described figures found in the Bible Milton provided a very different dimension in his version of events from that described in Genesis. Warming to the task of fuller characterisation, Milton created a drama of unintended consequences.

It is also possible to enjoy the music of Milton's poetry without being overwhelmed in scholasticism. The language of the poem moves in tidal surges, and so an ideal way to engage with it is to listen to it being read aloud or even performed on stage; after all, the blind Milton was forced to dictate it and therefore only ever heard the words being spoken. It is then possible to appreciate the lure of the classical names and stories which are woven into the narrative, and to concentrate on the way Milton treats the biblical figures as fully rounded human beings – a ruler, the leader of a rebellion and a couple trying to live their lives within God's law. Being selective about the amount of time initially taken to pore over every reference and image with their attendant notes pays dividends. The most productive approach is to start with the telescope and then turn to the microscope.

This book asks why *Paradise Lost* is such an enigmatic poem which simultaneously enthrals by its successes and fails because of the inner contradictions arising from its characterisation. A deeper understanding of the poem's inner tensions is gained by examining the poem as a work of art, analysing the creative decisions Milton took rather than just reading it as a piece of autobiography, theology or history. It is hoped that this critique will both contribute to the academic debate about what kind of poem it is, and stimulate the student or general reader who wishes to understand more about what makes *Paradise Lost* such an important work in the history of literature, which is as relevant today as it was in the seventeenth century.

I

Hunting for Milton

The enigma of Milton's mind

1

Autobiographical and historical readings of *Paradise Lost*

The 17th century was a time of extremes. The nation was divided on a scale hardly seen before or since. A king was beheaded, families were split by ideological divisions and the country collapsed into civil war. The political and religious imperatives which fuelled this crisis were never straightforward, despite the straight lines drawn in history books. Roundhead and Cavalier, Protestant and Catholic, Puritan and High Anglican are some of the groupings which merely hint at the jagged fault lines that created fractures between families, friends and fellow countrymen. They give little idea of the inner turmoil experienced by individuals whose religious faith and political beliefs were variously hidden, publically put on trial or privately tested. In addition, individual spiritual and political ideals frequently evolved as circumstances exposed the practical failings of their ideals and as experience limited the goals for which they strove.

As primary sources the poetry and prose of this period frequently provide powerful insights into writers' beliefs and opinions, deepening our understanding and helping to clarify some of the confusion. As a widely travelled and educated young man, a poet, pamphleteer, political apologist, vehemently Protestant and revolutionary believer, John Milton encapsulated the political passion, religious zeal and artistic ambitions of his century. There is, therefore, a strong temptation for the poetry of such a towering and complex figure to be read as a semi or even wholly autobiographical revelation about, amongst other things,

Milton's response to the failure of the English Revolution and the consequences for his own religious beliefs. As a rebel himself, Milton's relationship with his portrait of Satan is most often cited as evidence of his own predispositions in the poem. EMW Tillyard went so far as to say that *Paradise Lost* is really about "the true state of Milton's mind when he wrote it".[1]

However, for many readers throughout the ages Milton's poem has failed to convince that God is to be admired when Satan's apparent courage, inventiveness and charismatic leadership qualities make him a compelling figure. In looking for Milton behind his poetry critics fillet *Paradise Lost* in order to discover answers to some of the questions that have haunted readers for centuries. Why is God so severe? Why is Satan so mesmerizingly attractive? Why is it possible to sympathise with our disobedient ancestors? Scholars have attempted to construct a coherent personal theology for Milton from his poem or have used it as the basis for a psychological analysis of the man.

In the 20th century alone different readings of Milton's theology divided readers into opposing camps. Defenders of a conservative bent were led by CS Lewis in *A Preface to Paradise Lost,*[2] followed by critics such as Dennis Burden,[3] who defended the logic of Milton's argument in *Paradise Lost,* and Stanley Fish,[4] a more inventive but nevertheless conservative apologist for the success of Milton's justification of God. Reading the poem as double bluff he argues that Milton deliberately encourages the reader to read the wrong poem in order to experience the Fall for himself, but by flirting with this temptation to read the 'wrong' poem, he will eventually see the error of his ways, experiencing personal redemption. Following earlier 'Satanic' readings by figures such as Blake and Shelley, William Empson[5] heralded the 20th century objectors in his criticism of Milton's

1. *Milton* Part III chapter 1, Chatto & Windus, 1930
2. *A Preface to Paradise Lost,* Oxford University Press, 1942
3. *The Logical Epic,* Routledge, 1967
4. *Surprised by Sin*, Harvard University Press, 1967
5. *Milton's God*, New Directions, 1961

presentation of God, pointing out Milton's own struggle to accept God's 'ways' for himself. The 'New Milton' critics such as Michael Bryson[6] demonstrated Milton's own difficulties in accepting God's demeanour in *Paradise Lost*, arguing that Milton rejected the God who is perceived as a monarch in favour of the more loving Christ portrayed in *Paradise Regained*. To balance the radicals, David V Urban[7] fought back with a further defence of Milton's earlier defenders.

The argument of this book is that Milton wrote a poem which turned out to be different from the one that he or we might have expected. It may be both possible and enlightening to view the poem from a Milton-centric perspective; examining how tortured feelings of personal disappointment may have contributed to the theology of the poem and even the more sympathetic presentations of Adam, Eve and Satan against a stern and authoritarian God whose ways may be just but whose reasoning is frequently unfathomable. It is true that we should appreciate the catastrophe with which Milton had to come to terms. The republican cause had been lost, Cromwell's Protectorate was gone, and monarchy was re-established. Not only were Milton's books publicly burned, but he was arrested and imprisoned for some months in the autumn of 1660. This experience of political and personal loss may well be felt in *Paradise Lost*. Only a very few references in the poem give us clues about this. One such is when Michael is relating to Adam future events:

The conquered also, and enslaved by war
Shall with their freedom lost all virtue lose
And fear of God, from whom their piety feigned
In sharp contest of battle found no aid
Against invaders; therefore cooled in zeal

---

6. *The Tyranny of Heaven: Milton's Rejection of God as King,* Delaware Press, 2004

7. *Speaking for the Dead: CS Lewis answers New Milton Critics; or 'Milton Ministeries' strike back,* Milton Quarterly Vol 45, no 2, 2011

Thenceforth shall practise how to live secure,
Worldly or dissolute, on what their lords
Shall leave them to enjoy; for thee earth shall bear
More than enough, that temperance may be tried:
So all shall turn degenerate, all depraved,
Justice and temperance, truth and faith forgot;

(XI 797-807)

Tillyard goes too far when he writes: "Satan aspiring after a new world is Milton" though he may have empathised with Satan's desire for change.[8] Occasionally we are aware in the words of some of the characters of a sympathetic Milton, such as Adam's horror at the thought of men assuming authority over others:

O execrable son so to aspire
Above his brethren, to himself assuming
Authority usurped, from God not given:
He gave us only over beast, fish, fowl
Dominion absolute; that right we hold
By his donation; but man over men
He made not lord;

(XII 64-70)

Later in his life Milton came to disagree with this view, arguing from a more pragmatic, less idealistic point of view that people needed well educated leaders to steer them. Michael explains God's purposes during a revolution:

Since thy original lapse, true liberty
Is lost, which always with right reason dwells
Twinned, and from her hath no dividual being:
Reason in man obscured, or not obeyed,
Immediately inordinate desires
And upstart passions catch the government
From reason and to servitude reduce

8. Op cit Part III Chap 4

Man, till then free. Therefore since he permits
Within himself unworthy powers to reign
Over free reason, God in judgment just
Subjects him from without to violent lords;
Who oft as undeservedly enthral
His outward freedom: tyranny must be,
Though to the tyrant thereby no excuse.

(XII 83-96)

This directly relates to justifications for the revolution, attributing the facts of both unworthy kings and equally unworthy rebels to God's punishment on mankind after the Fall.

Reluctantly Milton was forced to accept that the republican experiment had failed because the English people had not yet shown themselves equipped to live under self-governance in a virtuous commonwealth. His early ideals had focused on freedom based upon self-discipline. In *Areopagitica* he boldly states: "If every action, which is good or evil in man at ripe years, were to be under pittance and prescription and compulsion, what were virtue but a name, what praise could then be due to well-doing, what gramercy to be sober, just and continent?" He put his trust in the good sense and self-discipline of individuals. He was vehemently opposed to any repressive regime, even a Puritan one. However, almost 20 years later when he published *The Ready and Easy Way to Establish a Free Commonwealth* in 1660 he was forced to concede that the people had lost the right to govern themselves through their own licentiousness. Paradise was indeed lost, at around the time he composed his great poem. In *Paradise Lost* Milton sought to educate his readers, to emphasise the importance of self-discipline and make them understand their relationship with God and each other in the hope that things would improve.[9] It is a theological argument arising from a political message, seen most vividly in Book XI where Michael paints a grim picture of the future, adding sternly: "From man's effeminate slackness it begins,/Said the angel,

9. See Christopher Hill *Milton and the English Revolution,* Faber, 1977

who should better hold his place/By wisdom, and superior gifts received" (XI 634-636).

A work of literature may then carry evidence of a writer's feelings at the time of composition within the political and religious context in which the poem was written. Milton's religious beliefs and the relationship between these and his response to the failed parliamentary revolution, as well as his feelings of exhaustion and disappointment and the catastrophe of his own blindness inevitably played their part in shaping the poem and are legitimate avenues of study. After all Milton was continually facing tensions between obedience to God and the messiness of human life, and between democracy and its reality in church and state. However, no matter how revealing a play, poem or novel may be about an author a work of literature is more than autobiography or statement of belief. A novel, poem or play is an artistic creation, an artefact; characterisation, structure and language all playing their parts in setting literature apart from an essay or treatise. *Paradise Lost* is not a political, religious or social document in the same category as Milton's prose works: it is hugely more than an historian's or a theologian's primary source. The importance of Milton as poet and dramatist needs to be appreciated in order that the status of the poem as a verse drama may be granted its rightful place.

2

Verse drama rather than historical document

During the process of writing, the creative act seems to have taken control of Milton, who warmed to the task of bringing biblical characters to life, to the detriment of his presentation of God and, therefore, to his plan to 'justify the ways of God to men.' What emerged was a densely woven picture of the difficulties faced by mankind in living moral lives. Theoretically the artistic choices made by a poet, dramatist or novelist combine to construct a means to distil and communicate the essence of a theme. The moving parts of this artistic vehicle, plot, structure, language and characterisation clearly affect our perception of the author's subject and consequently our understanding of it. Milton's artistic choices radically changed the meaning of his poem. The poetic and dramatic project assumed centre stage, overshadowing any political message we might expect to find, and radically changing the theological one. Milton did not set out to write a work of political theory or history, nor did he write a theological treatise although all three are enmeshed within the poem. His aim was to compose an epic poem on a Christian theme. Unexpectedly, however, the medium itself pushed aside the intended message, replacing it with a very different and, ironically, wholly revolutionary one. *Paradise Lost* was intended to be an epic poem, which it is up to a point through its narrative structure and many stylistic features, but the poem's significance is founded chiefly on characterisation and the verse drama which develops the Genesis account of the Fall.

The truth is that Milton had always seen himself first and foremost as a poet. He had put poetry aside temporarily in the

1640s in order to contribute to the political and religious causes of his times but regarded himself as an artist destined, through God's grace and supported by intense study, to deliver a great work in English. His almost Messianic zeal in wishing to speak about everything from education and freedom of speech to theology, the organisation of the church and the governance of the country was based on Protestantism and Republicanism. Most audacious of all, however, was his belief that he could unite this with his long-standing poetic ambitions to become God's spokesman, reminding people about God's ways in a manner that would bring them to a truer relationship with their maker and each other.

As scholars become increasingly embroiled in unravelling Milton's theology let us not forget that Milton began with the aim of writing an epic poem; the precise subject for which came later. It can be seen in the Trinity manuscript containing Milton's preparatory notes how he toyed with ideas from biblical and non-biblical possibilities. From an early age he had been confident about the power of poetry to do good well before he embarked on the great enterprise of writing a Christian epic in English, and his years of study gave him a broad knowledge of classical and other writings. Milton states that he is elucidating God's actions for mankind, whereas in fact there is a complex interaction between this and his poetic ambitions and his manner of thinking and communicating which heavily influenced the outcome of the poem. Many of Milton's hopes for the nation had failed to flourish during the 1640s so that his remaining ambition to write an epic poem in English without rhyme became even more important to him. The importance to Milton of experiencing the exhilaration of success in what was the first ambition of his life, overcame all other considerations including, ultimately, the Christian *apologia* itself.

The complexity of the political events and religious turmoil in the 17th century should not detract from appreciation of Milton the artist. Whilst complex theological investigations of *Paradise Lost* provide windows into understanding what Milton believed we should be asking more questions about the creative process itself, examining the artistic options which were open to Milton, and understanding their impact on his aim to persuade people to trust God, whatever happened. We can see from statements in both the poem and the prefatory Arguments that he knew exactly what he intended to say, but it was the artistic execution of the project that determined an outcome quite different from the intended one. Milton may have wished to justify the ways of God to a people who had lost their reason, but we should appreciate the force of other (unintended) ideas that issue from the lips of the principal characters when given the freedom to speak. It is these we remember rather than the repeated dogma of complete obedience to God.

Prior to relating to Adam the history of events in heaven Raphael perfectly sums up Milton's own ambitious enterprise in trying to describe the indescribable:

> *Yet for thy good*
> *This is dispensed, and what surmounts the reach*
> *Of human sense, I shall delineate so,*
> *By likening spiritual to corporal forms,*
> *As may express them best,*
>
> (V 570-574)

There are only a few times in the poem when the reader is aware that we are not hearing ordinary human beings. One such is when Milton recounts the reaction of the heavenly population to news of the Fall:

> *Soon as the unwelcome news*
> *From earth arrived at heaven gate, displeased*
> *All were who heard, dim sadness did not spare*
> *That time celestial visages, yet mixed*
> *With pity, violated not their bliss.*

About the new-arrived, in multitudes
The ethereal people ran, to hear and know
How all befell: they towards the throne supreme
Accountable made haste to make appear
With righteous plea, their utmost vigilance,
And easily approved; when the most high
Eternal Father from his secret cloud,
Amidst in thunder uttered thus his voice.

(X 21-33)

Shortly after this we gain a sense of how Milton envisaged God's communication with Adam and Eve:

the voice of God they heard
Now walking in the garden, by soft winds
Brought to their ears, while day declined, they heard,
And from his presence hid themselves among
The thickest trees, both man and wife, till God
Approaching, thus to Adam called aloud.

(X 97-102)

Mostly, however, it is real human voices we hear. By giving biblical characters human voices Milton unintentionally encouraged readers to relate to them and consequently judge them according to human standards. For example, given that God seems to know exactly what is going to happen in every situation, the Son's offer to sacrifice himself for the sake of mankind is arguably diminished, as the Father knew that the Son would react in this way. This begs the question of what real choice the Son had in the matter, and is a key issue with regard to the distinction between foreknowledge and predestination.

CS Lewis in *A Preface to Paradise Lost*[10] began the process of disentangling form from content: "The first question he (Milton) asked himself was not 'What do I want to say?' but 'What kind of poem do I want to make?'" Lewis goes on to

10. Op cit

highlight the question of choice from the options which an artist makes at the outset of the creative process. In the case of Milton it was the issue surrounding the range of epic, tragic or lyrical poems which was available to him as models, and the reasons behind Milton's final choice, which led him to write a 'Secondary epic'.

This decision was crucial; it built the body of the vehicle Milton used to convey his ideas: it was not, however, the only major artistic decision which was to have far-reaching repercussions for his subject. When adapting an existing narrative source consideration must be given to the additions and subtractions made by the author to the original, the development of characters and the emphasis given to particular ideas or emotions expressed by the participants. Was Milton's religious intention helped or hindered by allowing the protagonists to have their own voices, by creating an unparalleled quantity of debate, dialogue and soliloquy within the structure of an epic poem? And what is the effect of presenting complex theological matters in this dramatic form? Is Milton's theological ambition helped or hindered by his artistic choices?

The explosive revelation when looking at the way the poem is written is that Milton's choices led to the subversion of his declared purpose. Milton gives human voice to all the biblical protagonists in the most talkative epic ever written, yet the success of his characterisation leads to a hugely different product from that which may have emerged from a prose theological examination and justification of God's ways. In truth, how could Milton successfully fathom the unfathomable mind of God when mankind was deliberately placed in a position with restrictions on knowledge, lodged between animals and angels in the universal hierarchy? We should, however, also ask whether Milton's early belief in the power of poetry to teach fundamental lessons was achievable. In Milton's drama the very reasonableness of Adam's and Eve's love for each other; the reasonableness of concepts such as ambition and love compared with the unreasonableness of having to make seemingly cruel choices out of obedience to God raise issues for the reader which are at odds with his intended justification of God's goodness and emphasis on the use of reason. The stark conclusion of the poem is that obedience to God is everything. God cannot be wrong, and in spite of the assertions in the poem regarding the importance of using reason to reach a conclusion, any view that is contrary to God's will is deemed unreasonable.

The message of *Paradise Lost* is an intensely human (post-lapsarian) one; a message that by his choice of verse drama made Milton's thesis more complex than a narrative epic would have been expected to be. In its unravelling of the dilemmas faced by humanity, especially man's relationship with God, it makes for a more complex and provoking product. It led Milton to write the dramatic poem he had not intended.

There is a tension in *Paradise Lost* between Reason (Milton's brand of individual, biblical Protestantism) and his creative technique; in fact there is a fracture between intended content and style. This tension may have some origin in or bearing on Milton's despair at the failure of the Parliamentary revolution (God's revolution as he saw it);[11] may reveal a subconscious tension between what he knew was right and what he was feeling,[12] or a conscious encouragement of the reader to read the wrong interpretation so that he might eventually arrive at the correct one.[13] But the wholly autobiographical explanation ignores the influence of Milton's creative technique. The tension arises from Milton's artistic decisions; the technique of the poem, its very method, which creates its own strain. In order to appreciate the poem we need to see it for what it is rather than what Milton intended it to be. It is not a political document, though it may carry a sense of Milton's war weariness

11. Christopher Hill op cit and Andrew Milner: *John Milton and the English Revolution,* Macmillan, 1981
12. AJA Waldock: *Paradise Lost and its Critics*, Cambridge, 1961
13. JB Broadbent: *Some Graver Subjects: An Essay on 'Paradise Lost.'* 1960, and Stanley Fish, *Surprised By Sin*, Harvard, 1967

and disappointment. It does have a theological theme in that it was intended to bring the reader back to dutiful obedience to God and trust in his ways, despite signs to the contrary. But the outcome is not clear-cut. The conclusion has to be that it was impossible for this verse drama, and possibly for any poem, to treat with the intricate theological concepts which arise.

Rather than agonise about what the poem does not achieve we should celebrate Milton's presentation of mankind's complicated life on earth and how best to manage our existence. By dramatising the story and allowing his protagonists to express their emotions and thoughts as powerful, convincing and persuasive creations they take centre stage, elbowing aside their creator.

The current danger is that Milton Studies will become part of the Faculties of Theology and History. We must not forget that it is the literary technique of the poem which contributes to a dissonance. The craft of the poem, the medium itself, overwhelms the intended message. For *Paradise Lost* is no Puritan tract; it is an epic poem, satisfying Milton's ambition as a writer and, following the Renaissance belief in the power of poetry to teach truths, in this case obedience to God. By giving voice to feelings and ideas which are more convincing than the theological theory of the poem the scene is set for Milton to fail in his intention but to succeed in other ways.

As Milton wrote *Paradise Lost*, when so much that he had worked for ended in failure and disappointment, it is possible he was looking for a new certainty in his life. As a passionate reformer Milton clung to certainties which had guided him through his early and middle years. The aim of the poem was to remind people that they should adhere to the taxing but unchanging requirement for obedience to God's law. It is possible too that it was a reminder to Milton himself, but we cannot know this. One thing is certain: he did not set out to fail or confuse. His publisher encouraged Milton to add the Arguments to clarify the essential points of the poem, possibly because he did not think the poem was clear, but Milton believed he was supporting a belief in the absolute authority of God.

The themes of obedience and self-discipline were not, however, the things that dominated Milton's thoughts when he began considering options for what was to become *Paradise Lost*. Originally considering a drama, Milton could not escape his instinct to fulfil his poetic destiny to write an epic poem, though a Christian religion not a pagan one. As he planned which characters would take centre stage and how the poem would be constructed Milton's creative imagination, influenced by his education and experiences, led him to invent conversations and soliloquies for his protagonists, to put himself in their place and give them credible human voices. He imbued the drama with scenes which can be understood and felt by the reader, frequently strengthened by his knowledge of Jewish glosses on the Bible, and structured in such a way that, well known though the story of the Fall is, the highs and lows are presented with a fresh power. It is in this sense that Milton the poet, not Milton the theologian was at work.

Milton's power of empathy and his poet's expressiveness enabled him to give voice to contrasting arguments and passions in his characters. *Paradise Lost* is above all the dramatic poem of the human voice, as challenging and dynamic as any of the dramatic monologues by Robert Browning. CS Lewis was correct to stress the literary nature of the poem, the aggrandising of the vocabulary, the long sweeping sentences, the sequences of similes and classical allusions alongside biblical and classical material which inflated the Genesis story to epic stature. It is an expansive, breathless, rhetorical declamation dictated by Milton containing long stretches of stylised narrative. Yet all this is powerfully complemented by the sound of the human voice. Narrator and protagonists have distinctive voices but the *dramatis personae* drown the voice of the narrator's justification of God's ways by their clear speaking and frequently by their reasonableness. By contrast God is shown to be dismissive of the human concepts of love and ambition, relegating the reason he is so proud of having given mankind (and in which Milton trusted implicitly) to a secondary position behind obedience. Milton was presumptuous in thinking he could understand the mind of God. He was, however, triumphant in displaying his understanding of the mind of man.

The poem's *apologia* for God mutated into an enigmatic drama, a *Hamlet* of a poem; too full, too emotional, too human for it to be a theological justification to man of God's ways, and way beyond what Milton had intended. The poet's and dramatist's ambitions took over and created a dramatic poem of huge complexity, which challenges the reader to review the way human beings behave, how they relate to each other socially, politically and emotionally and how they fit into the great scheme of things. *Paradise Lost* is more successfully about what it is to be human than what it is to be God.

The argument of this appraisal of Milton's technique begins with a consideration of his determination to make his mark as a national poet and the foundations he put down in order to build his literary reputation. His zeal to be a teller of truths, even acting as an interpreter of God's mind, links with this ambition. He understands that the reading public will not always like what a writer has to say but nevertheless they must be told even unpalatable truths. Specifically, he promulgates the thesis that the life of the mind, enlivened by a good education, is vital to stimulate the growth of man's powers of reasoning. Thus equipped, argues Milton, man is capable of withstanding the temptations which surround him, in particular enabling him to demonstrate his obedience to God.

Consideration of how Milton's academic training and experience of political debate, his democrat's mindset that all viewpoints should be heard and his dramatist's talent to empathise with his characters is followed by an examination of how Jewish theology helped to augment his characterisation. Analysis of characterisation will show the effects of allowing the protagonists to speak so fully for themselves, ironically often at cross purposes to their creator. Finally, the consequences of

Milton's artistic decision to give voice to biblical characters are seen in a review of the problems this caused. Chief among these are the nature and power of human love and ambition, the usefulness of reason in decision-making and the clash between free will, foreknowledge and predestination.

II

Artistic ambitions

Milton's quest for greatness

3

Youthful ambition

Milton was seen by others and wished to see himself as a poet of renown. When his shorter poems were published in 1645 he was already 37 years old and fully engaged in pamphleteering, the bulk of the poems having been composed in his twenties, more than ten years earlier. He is praised in the Preface by the publisher Humphrey Moseley for being a worthy descendant of Spenser. Moseley goes on to claim confidently that "it is the love I have to our own language that hath made me diligent to collect, and set forth pieces both in prose and verse, as may renew the wonted honour and esteem of our English tongue."

The collection of poems shows Milton as a learned and courtly poet. He had collaborated with Henry Lawes in *Arcades* and *Comus*, which have a clear aristocratic link, and when he wrote *L'Allegro* and *Il Penseroso* Milton highlighted a life quite different from that of fractious party politics and religious turmoil which was later to occupy him. A Cambridge education, the years of private study reading widely in the classics and European travel seem to have prepared him for a life of poetic fame.

The ambitious young Milton had been published from an early age. *On the Morning of Christ's Nativity* was written in 1629 when he was just 21, *Comus* was first published by Lawes in 1637 and several other poems had seen the light of day before 1645, including translations of Psalms 114 and 136 when he was only 15. *On Shakespeare* had been contributed to the Second Folio of Shakespeare's plays, confirming Milton's growing standing on the literary scene. Consequently he was doubtless pleased to receive "the highest commendations and applause of the learnedst academics, both domestic and foreign" as cited by Moseley in 1645. Final corroboration of the point is found in the Preface to the Second Book of *The Reason of Church Government* where Milton recalls reciting his poems when he was in Italy, which "met with acceptance above what was looked for."

Milton's involvement in public affairs and controversies in the 1640s did not mean that he had forsaken his poetic ambitions. We know that his learned habits and love of immersing himself in poetry and drama were tinged with the ambition to be counted in the pantheon of great writers. It was this spirit that guided his artistic decisions for his epic poem, and which would take him beyond but build upon the youthful poems published in 1645 and again in 1673. In his Preface to the Second Book of *The Reason of Church Government,* written as early as 1642, Milton made clear what he was determined to achieve, and to paint a caricature of him only as a tortured Puritan and disappointed Parliamentarian using *Paradise Lost* as a 'cri de coeur' or form of catharsis, falls wide of the mark.

Milton clearly states that he wished to "leave something so written to aftertimes, as they should not willingly let it die," and expressed his determination "to fix all the industry and art I could unite to the adorning of my native tongue; not to make verbal curiosities the end (that were a toilsome vanity) but to be an interpreter and relater of the best and sagest things among mine own citizens throughout this island in the mother dialect. That, what the greatest and choicest wits of Athens, Rome, or modern Italy, and those Hebrews of old did for their country, I, in my proportion, with this over and above, of being a Christian, might do for mine." These are not insubstantial aspirations, and there should be no underestimation of the grandiose creative plans Milton had developed for himself.

Milton had no hesitation in asserting that poetry was the appropriate vehicle for his theme. He liked the poetry of Dante and Petrarch because it displayed: "sublime and pure thoughts,"[14] and he praised Spenser because he was a better teacher than Scotus or Aquinas. In *The Reason of Church Government* he considered which authors "shall be found more doctrinal and exemplary to a nation,"[15] concluding that poetry provokes "seeds of virtue and public civility;" must delight in order to teach, with Truth "elegantly dressed", and should encourage the reader to act for the good; poetry "giveth so sweet a prospect into the way, as will entice any man to enter into it." None of this would have been difficult for Sir Philip Sidney to appreciate. As far back as 1583 he had stated that poetry should: "move men to take that goodness in hand, which without delight they would flye as from a stranger."[16]

In *Areopagitica* Milton's appreciation of the virtues of poetry and music is used for a different argument: "If we think to regulate printing, thereby to rectify manners, we must regulate all recreations and pastimes, all that is delightful to man."[17] However, it was not to be so simple. To understand God to the point of justifying his ways was a huge undertaking, possibly harder. Finding the most appropriate poetic voice for this was to be Milton's greatest difficulty. Truth "elegantly dressed" seems potentially lightweight given the weight of his theme.

---

14. *Apology for Smectymnus* III Part I 303. All references to Milton's prose are from the Columbia edition of *The Works of John Milton* ed. FA Patterson et al, New York, 1931-8, and to *Paradise Lost*, the edition by Alastair Fowler, Longman,1968

15. III Part I 237-9

16. *An Apology for Poetry*

17. IV 317

4

Finding his poetic voice

RL Brett[18] argued that the Elizabethan tradition of Sidney was being modified in Milton's time. Brett states that Milton's use of classical literature and mythology could be fused with morality early in his career, in a form of Christian Humanism. This was replaced by the Platonic view that poetry was inferior to rational knowledge, and poetic style must, therefore, be plainer. Brett argues that *Paradise Lost* has a simpler style than, for example, *Comus*, and that Milton's style changed to an even plainer one after the description of the Fall – the "notes" are changed to "tragic," (IX 6) – because the grandeur of the early descriptions of Pandemonium had to change: "In the theme Milton chose for *Paradise Lost* history would be superior to fable and the life of the senses acceptable to the demands of reason. Here indeed was a subject that allowed Milton to be a Puritan theologian while remaining a Renaissance poet."

There are undoubtedly differences in style between Milton's earlier poems and *Paradise Lost* but they are not simply the result of fashion, and there is no evidence that Milton had changed his view about the efficacy of poetry on the minds of readers, or that "the demands of reason" affected the style so straightforwardly. The shorter poems are those of a young man keen to impress, as his link with Henry Lawes demonstrated, and he was determined to write in a style which would please a certain class of reader. It was frequently a courtly and deliberately poetical language that Milton employed in his earlier poems. He did, however, experiment with everything from the masque and translation

18. *Reason and Imagination – A study in form and meaning in four poems*, Oxford, 1964

to the sonnet and elegy, suggesting his determination to be not only visible as a poet but also to develop. The 1645 collection of poems contained in addition, no fewer than 87 pages of Latin poetry and 6 Italian sonnets.

Paradise Lost was Milton's crowning achievement and he had long before declared that to compose an epic poem was his ambition. Clearly an epic poem had stylistic conventions, just as the earlier courtly or poetical work had; it is, therefore, not surprising that we see the characteristics of that form which tend to be declamatory, grandiose and narrative in nature. It is not that *Paradise Lost* lacked a poetic style, for it clearly sits in the 'artificial' epic tradition, chosen because it was the form associated with the weightiest of human issues, involving travel through the universe and even relaying the voice of God. What Milton did was to attempt a fusion of the epic style with the argumentative or theological because he decided that the epic suited the grandeur and importance of the subject matter. The significant difference in Milton's epic was the inclusion of more theatrical dialogue than might have been expected. This created the conditions for tension between the thematic purpose of the poem and its stylistic treatment. There was a ticking time bomb which eventually exploded.

To address Brett's thesis directly, there is certainly variety in the poem. There are, for example, good reasons why Books I and II required an elevated style in order to open the epic on a suitably expansive pitch, and to portray the tragic sin and humiliating failure of the Fallen Angels. However, the evidence for a plainer style generally is not easy to find. The rhetorical devices and linguistic complexities are part of epic aggrandisement and are fundamental to *Paradise Lost*. The archaisms in *Lycidas* are similarly symptomatic of a mannered archaism consistent with a pastoral or poetical Spenserian form. On the other hand, the exchanges between Adam and Eve are written not simply to create Platonic simplicity but with a dramatist's ear for the discussion and disagreement between a man and a woman. Unadorned in language but with a power such that they could hardly be called simple because of their content, the couple struggle with the dilemmas facing them. Indeed, Milton's description of the passion between them confirms the view that he was adept at understanding this passion but also possessed the adroitness to communicate it. What he did not realise was that the skills he was employing were to be capable of overturning the theological argument he was propounding.

Of significance to the relationship between subject and style when assessing the effectiveness of *Paradise Lost* is the moment when Milton put poetry in its place. The earlier references to Milton's comments on the effectiveness of poetry came in the *Apology for Smectymnuus* and in *The Reason of Church Government* which were published in 1642. Contrary to his other comments about the suitability of poetry to teach and bear the weight of serious content he argued in 1644 that, when compared with logic and rhetoric, poetry was: "less subtle and fine, but more simple, sensuous and passionate."[19] Here we have the crux of the matter. The aim of *Paradise Lost* to: "assert eternal providence/ And justify the ways of God to men"(I 25-6) would be a hard task if a poetic drama did not turn out to be the form best suited for close argument. If the characterisation in such a medium is so successful that it supersedes the poet's intention, then something has happened during the creative process to upset the equilibrium between message and medium. Much of the success of *Paradise Lost* lies in the fact that it became a poetic drama with strong characterisation. Milton endowed his *dramatis personae* with recognisably human voices expressing complex emotions and inner tensions. He was generous enough to let them have their say; especially those persuasive characters who were expressing arguments in direct opposition to Milton's purpose and beliefs.

Milton's achievement in *Paradise Lost* was to create the epic work he had longed to write but he was drawn to the biblical protagonists as a dramatist might be. The resulting verse drama, though flawed in not living up to Milton's original aim of justifying the ways of God to men, achieved something both different, even greater.

19 *Of Education* IV 286

III

Missionary Zeal

Milton determined to tell it how it is

5

God's champion

Driven by his religious beliefs Milton knew exactly what he wanted to communicate in *Paradise Lost,* though stern and unpalatable to some the message might be. Whilst contemplating possible topics he repeatedly emphasised the superiority of a Christian theme above the stories of his classical forbears and did not shy away from the difficulties, including the unpopularity he might encounter as a writer pointing out eternal truths. There is no evidence to question the strength of Milton's personal commitment to the task of justifying the ways of God to men, nor any reason to suppose that he doubted the power of clear thinking to aid obedience to God.

In 1642 when he wrote *The Reason of Church Government* Milton did not appear to have foreseen problems in managing his dual role of national poet and God's champion. He did, however, temporarily put to one side his artistic ambitions over the next decade. It was the outspoken and radical spirit of the prose which he wrote in the 1640s that sat more naturally alongside his description of a writer in *The Reason of Church Government* than might have seemed the case in his earlier poems. However, the sonnets written after the 1645 edition of his poems was published, later included in the 1673 edition, demonstrated just how increasingly fervent and serious he was becoming in his poetry.

It is clear from the preface to Book II of *The Reason of Church Government* that Milton believed it was his duty to use whatever talents God had provided: "how and in what manner he shall dispose and employ those sums of knowledge and illumination, which God hath sent him into this world to trade with." Writers, the "selected heralds of peace and dispensers of treasure inestimable" would not necessarily find life easy, acting as "a very sword and fire both in house and city." He harks back to Jeremiah and "the irkesomeness of that truth which they brought was so unpleasant unto them, that everywhere they call it a burden." Undaunted he claims: "when God commands to take the trumpet, and blow a dolorous or a jarring blast, it lies not in man's will what he shall say, or what he shall conceal."

At this time Milton remained committed to the cause of Presbyterianism, which within two or three years he had come to challenge. He was, however, to be steadfast when he dedicated himself "by devout prayer…select reading, steady observation, insight into all seemly and generous arts and affairs," to the creation of a work "to imbreed and cherish in a great people the seeds of virtue and public civility, to allay the perturbations of the mind, and set the affections in right tune; to celebrate in glorious and lofty hymns the throne and equipage of God's almightiness, and what he works." Importantly "whatever in religion is holy and sublime, in virtue amiable or grave, whatsoever hath passion or admiration in all the changes of that which is called fortune from without, or the wily subtleties and refluxes of man's thoughts from within; all these things with solid and treatable smoothness to paint out and describe." He displays the passionate certainty of zealots, eager to "bestow, without any gain to himself, those sharp but saving words which would be a terror and a torment in him to keep back." Equally he did not wish to be labelled merely as a young man in a hurry, and dedicated himself to self-improvement.

Crucial evidence in helping the reader to understand the firmness of Milton's purpose is found in The Arguments written at the start of each book. These additions made at the request of Milton's publisher in order to clarify the narrative account of the Fall suggest Milton's ideas might be unpalatable, even be impenetrable without them. The early editions printed in Milton's lifetime (1667 and 1668) contained ten books but no Arguments, the latter appearing as one piece at the beginning of the fourth edition. It was not until the 1674 edition that the poem was divided into twelve books with the Arguments printed ahead of each.

Unequivocally Milton emphasised that man's sin was disobedience; a stern judgement taken directly from the Bible and definitely 'grave' rather than 'amiable.' Put simply the story to be told is about "man's disobedience and the loss thereupon of Paradise" (I) and Raphael is sent to "admonish him of his disobedience" (V). Submission to God is a repeated theme: Adam advises Eve that they should "Seek peace of the offended Deity by repentance and supplication," (X) and Eve wakes from a restorative sleep "to quietness of mind and submission" (XII).

Significantly this peacefulness only comes by virtue of total submission to God. Furthermore, a key element of man's sin is not only has he been disobedient, he has been presumptuous: "man hath offended the majesty of God by aspiring to Godhead" (III) and Raphael exhorts Adam "to search rather things more worthy of his Knowledge" (VIII). Satan is always painted as the ultimate cause of mankind's downfall. In Book III God sensibly "clears his own justice and wisdom from all imputation, having created man free," and states that man "fell not of his own malice as did Satan, but by him seduced." Punishment is duly meted out: the Fallen Angels are transformed into serpents and Christ's victory over evil is foretold (X) whilst Adam and Eve are expelled from paradise (XI).

Milton presented himself as a Christian poet, possessing confidence in his artistic talents and driven by a mission to speak the truth. With the conviction of a man in the prime of life, the 34-year-old poet and democrat had seen no problem in fulfilling his ambition. As an older man he confirmed this by making his intentions plain in the Arguments.

6

The meaning of 'Justify'

What Milton wished to achieve in *Paradise Lost* had already been referred to in the pamphlet *Of Education*.[20] In combining his belief in reasoned thinking and rigorous education with a description of mankind's Fall Milton was echoing his earlier words: "The end, then, of learning is, to repair the ruins of our first parents by regaining to know God aright, and out of that knowledge to love him, to imitate him, to be like him, as we may the nearest, by possessing our souls of true virtue, which, being united to the heavenly grace of faith, makes up the highest perfection." However, to understand Milton's mission in his presentation of God it is necessary to understand his use of 'justify', which underpinned his intention to "justify the ways of God to men" but which had a range of possible meanings. In essence he strove to turn man back to God by force of argument and not through an emotional experience.

Confusingly 'justify' had a contemporary theological meaning which has caused some readers to misunderstand Milton's intention. It is found in Section XI of the *Westminster Confession of Faith*, entitled 'Of Justification':[21]

I. Those whom God effectually calleth, he also freely justifieth: not by infusing righteousness into them, but by pardoning their sins, and by accounting and accepting their persons as righteous; not for any thing wrought in them, or done by them, but for Christ's sake alone; not

20 Published June 1644

21 A reformed confession of faith published in 1647 by the Westminster Assembly of Divines

by imputing faith itself, the act of believing, or any other evangelical obedience to them, as their righteousness; but by imputing the obedience and satisfaction of Christ unto them, they receiving and resting on him and his righteousness by faith; which faith they have not of themselves, it is the gift of God.

II. Faith, thus receiving and resting on Christ and his righteousness, is the alone instrument of justification; yet is it not alone in the person justified, but is ever accompanied with all other saving graces, and is no dead faith, but worketh by love.

IV. God did, from all eternity, decree to justify the elect; and Christ did, in the fullness of time, die for their sins and rise again for their justification; nevertheless they are not justified until the Holy Spirit doth, in due time, actually apply Christ unto them.

V. God doth continue to forgive the sins of those that are justified; and although they can never fall from the state of justification, yet they may by their sins fall under God's Fatherly displeasure, and not have the light of his countenance restored unto them, until they humble themselves, confess their sins, beg pardon, and renew their faith and repentance.

Here 'justification' and 'justified' share a specific theological meaning concerning faith in Christ which allows God to grant grace to the believer. It also appears in the *Westminster Confession* as the verb 'justify' but retains the essential sense of the noun and adjective. The point is that God calls individuals to be justified, whereby their faith is enlivened or illuminated, enabling them better to understand the ways of God through their faith in Christ. This state of being open to God's word and accepting his law in faith is a gift from God to the individual who is receptive to him. In his note to Book I line 26 Fowler follows this definition, though he does not mention the source. He does cite Cormican,[22] who argues that the word 'justify'

22 *The Pelican Guide to English Literature* Volume 3 'From Donne to Marvell' 1956 pages 175-6

"does not mean merely 'demonstrate logically' but has its biblical meaning, and implies spiritual rather than rational understanding." The *Oxford English Dictionary* definition of justification in this sense states the same meaning: "Protestant theologians regard justification as an act of grace in which God accounts man righteous, not owing to any merit of his own, but through imputation of Christ's righteousness, as apprehended and received by faith."

However, in his chapter on Milton Cormican pushes this definition to an extreme interpretation: "The criticism that Milton does not justify God's ways is based on a misconception of what Milton meant by God and what he meant by justification. It should be clear from the whole poem that, to Milton, God always remains the Great Mystery whose inscrutable ways can be comprehended only in the 'light' which is as yet inaccessible to men. And by justification Milton did not mean a merely logical demonstration which would prove an intellectual conclusion and bring God within the framework of the rational universe. He uses the word with the overtones it acquired from the New Testament usage, where it implies a divine, not a human or logical, understanding, a supernal illumination from the Holy Spirit whom he invokes for special guidance in his difficult task... If the ways of God can be justified, it must be through a purification of the heart rather than by the reasonings of the intellect. The poem is, among other things, a prayer addressed to the Deity from all mankind... We should then understand Milton as aspiring through his poem to prepare the hearts of men for the coming of the spirit whose great office is to lead men into truth about God and themselves."

Cormican proceeds to read the poem as a spiritual exercise expressed in verse. We are left with the notion that *Paradise Lost* in all its epic grandeur and enthralling dramatic conflict is a spiritual experience, an icon whose contemplation might take us to a higher level of spiritual understanding. However, the presence of God in *Paradise Lost* does not raise the reader's spiritual state through any of the conventional methods of religious writing. Our experience and knowledge of God is not that of natural theology, or what may be learned through study of the scriptures, or the revelations and physical sensations of God achieved by the mystics. None of these routes to God adequately explains what is happening in *Paradise Lost*, where Milton stresses the harsher realities of obedience and training of the mind through education as the route to accepting the mysteries of God's ways.

Certainly we do not experience a mystical sense of the presence of God, none of the longing for nearness to God or other sensations of him achieved on a deeper level of consciousness than the reasoning of the mind can evoke. Indeed, reason is always regarded by the mystics as of no use in the quest for perfect union with God. *The Fire of Love* by Richard Rolle[23] is part autobiography, part manual for the devout. It describes the mystic's love of and longing for God: "No creature can love God too much"[24] he asserts. Rolle feels a sensation of physical heat as a result of his spiritual experience: "…I felt my heart begin to warm. It was a real warmth too, not imaginary, and it felt as if it were actually on fire…the heat surged up."[25] God's fire is healing compared with the heat of sin: "in the coming of love the heart of the lover blazes up. Hotter than fire is this wonderful heat, which rejoices the mind so sweetly, and gives coolness and shade from the heat of sins."[26]

Neither is Milton writing in the manner of Thomas Aquinas[27] who wrote in the spirit of natural theology, using the process of reasoning and simple exemplars to communicate some of the hardest concepts, none more so than his five proofs for the existence of God. Whilst Milton elevated reason as the highest of man's powers he could do little more than repeatedly insist on the importance of using the mind to enable Adam

23 Written c1343 translated by Clifton Wolters, Penguin Classics 1972

24 Chapter 17

25 Prologue

26 Chapter 42

27 *Summa Theologica*

and Eve to make the correct moral decisions. What we witness is the drama of protagonists turning over options for action available to them, but in no sense is this written in the manner of Aquinas' limpid scholarly prose. Milton's writing is rooted in immediacy, the dramatic reality of characters searching to arrive at monumentally important decisions about how they should act. We experience instead a series of explanations in defence of a character's position, notably God's and Satan's, and in Adam, Eve and Satan dramatisations of characters examining possible alternative ways of acting.

In *Paradise Lost* our sense of God's presence can hardly be described as warm let alone hot, and abandoning our rational side in order to enter into a mystical union with him is far from Milton's approach. Our sense of God comes chiefly through his own words and of the Son, aided by messengers such as Raphael and Michael who provide explanations in support of God's actions. That is to say we learn about God through dramatic means. Milton takes the scriptures and fills out the spare narrative style of the Book of Genesis so fully that the sound of God and Satan is heard, whilst our human forbears speak in a manner that readers in any period of history could empathise with and comprehend.

Further evidence of Milton's difficulty in defending God by dramatic means and written about twenty-seven years later than Rolle's work, is *The Cloud of Unknowing*.[28] This highlights the unknowability of God, who is seen as an "unmade, ghostly thing". There is no point in our trying to use reason in order to reach or understand him because he is complete in himself and unknowable through ordinary means, though something of God may be knowable through Christ's love: "All rational beings, angels and men, possess two faculties, the power of knowing and the power of loving. To the first, to the intellect, God who made them is forever unknowable, but to the second, to love, he is completely knowable, and that by every separate

28 Author unknown. Composed c 1370. Penguin Classics first published 1961. Translated by Clifton Wolters

individual."[29] This mystic advises a series of meditative stages which culminate in yielding to the presence of God to experience "touches of God." God is Nought and Nowhere; No-thing, No-where but this 'unknowing' is actually Knowing him.[30] Milton did not advocate a renunciation of reason in favour of a mystical experience. Whilst he did not suggest we can know God, Milton defended God's position in order to persuade the reader that it is possible to understand what God demands of us by using our minds in obedient decision-making.

Of all English mystics it is Mother Julian of Norwich who illustrates most clearly what Milton was and was not doing in his presentation of God. Her *Revelations of Divine Love*[31] record and meditate upon sixteen 'shewings' or visions, which took place on the 8th May 1373. The visions derived from a desire for a near-death experience in which Julian would experience directly the passion of Christ and the love of God. Her visions enabled her to hear and see God directly: "Then, before he spoke to me, God allowed me to look at himself for a considerable time, and, as far as my simple mind could take it, to dwell on all that I had seen, and its significance."[32] She will not accept that God can be wrathful, and the vengeful God of the Old Testament has no place in her understanding of God's ways: "As I see it there is no anger in God, for our blessed Lord has eternal regard to the honour which is his due and to the benefit of all those who are to be saved."[33]

For Julian God represents pure love, which relates directly to man's inner need for God's loving presence. She examines man's threefold composition of "truth, wisdom and love," and "reason, mind and grace", together with his need for "love, longing and pity". In pursuit of this concept she discusses the

---

29 Section 4

30 Sections 68-70

31 Translated by Clifton Wolters. First published Penguin Classics 1966

32 Chapter 13

33 ibid

'Motherhood' of God,[34] and the homely nature of God's care for us, also interpreted as 'courtesy'.[35] So overwhelmed is she by God's love for man that she cannot understand why he allowed sin into the world at all.[36] Mother Julian's *Revelations* became influential among Christian believers looking for consolation, hope and the reassurance of an ever-present and caring parent. Although she attributes to man the faculty of reason it is rarely used to understand God and his ways. If Mother Julian is to be criticised for over-simplification, then Milton's boldness in facing these issues in dramatic form has to be acknowledged. Characteristically he did not duck a challenge and was prepared to wrestle with the presentation of God and allowing him to explain himself.

The experience of reading *Paradise Lost* is more akin to watching a play than experiencing spiritual enlightenment. Can we say that on reaching the end of *Paradise Lost* (in places softer in tone than the rest of the poem though it may be) we feel closer to God, understand him more or love him more? More likely it is the emotional power of Adam and Eve's very human repentance that stays in the mind. Neither the longing for God nor love of God described by the mystics can replace the questions about God raised by Milton; for many what remains is the crushing sense that we must obey. Rather than being a spiritual journey reading *Paradise Lost* involves uncovering layers of meaning, similar to uncovering hidden images of earlier drawings or paintings beneath the finished work of an Old Master. In Milton's defence of God there is more likely to be a feeling of questions unanswered and 'case not proved'.

The semantic spectrum of the word 'justify' is wide. From 'to administer justice fairly, to condemn or punish, absolve or acquit, to explain one's actions, to demonstrate or show, to explain, prove, excuse and defend', it is capable of multiple usages. It is difficult to understand why Milton

34 Chapters 58-63

35 See Chapter 51

36 Chapters 32-3

would have attempted to forgive, pardon or excuse God, for that would imply culpability on the part of God. The concept of predestination and the supremacy of the chosen seen in the *Westminster Confession* would surely be blasphemy when applied by man to God himself. For Milton to extend an act of grace from man to God would have been the ultimate presumption.

Milton's use of justify is, therefore, much closer to the sense of 'to show a person to be fair, right or reasonable, to support, maintain as true, to vindicate, aver or verify'. Thus a convincing interpretation of 'justify' encapsulates both expression of the justice or reasonableness of an action and the defence of something as right and proper. The *OED* quotes not only the opening lines from *Paradise Lost* but *The Reason of Church Government* (II iii): "How can they justify to have turned their domestic privileges into the bar of a proud judicial court?"

It becomes increasingly apparent that Milton began his great enterprise in order to remind readers about the nature of mankind's original sin and the subsequent need for repentance and obedience. The voice of the pamphleteer is never far away. He wished to replay the events of the Fall, lending support for and defence of God's actions. He had not, however, taken into account the impact his characterisation of God and other protagonists would have, to the detriment of this aim.

The tone and spirit of an epic poem is hardly suited to a devotional genre in the manner of Cormican's interpretation. Milton's focus was on giving voice to the protagonists in the narrative of man's Fall. As with any witness statements we question the motives and actions of the speakers and like jurors we decide whose words we trust. This creates the atmosphere of an inquest on why the disobedience occurred and whether the punishment was proportionate. It was not for Milton to give any form of grace or forgiveness to either man or God, and he had never written in a devotional manner. He shows us a fair trial where everyone, including God, is allowed their say to their advantage or disadvantage. He expects that by being reminded of the cause of our original sin and understanding

God's purposes we shall return to him. It was to be a reasoned argument in support of reason.

Milton was educated to use reason in the cause of faith, and so attempted to construct the most logical exposition on obedience he could muster. Here the word 'justify' in the sense of to put in order, to fit or arrange exactly, is relevant. More associated with typographical contexts, this sense reminds us that characterisation, dialogue, language and structure are intended by Milton to work together harmoniously in an orderly manner to display the reasonableness of God. However, as we deconstruct this artistic scaffold we find that the dramatic poem is not perfectly equipped to carry the weight of a theological treatise because the characters escape from Milton's control.

Awkward questions about God's ways are continually raised by other characters, his language and manner having the same effect. Milton's mission was to show that obedience brings freedom: God expects it and man owes it. But God's frequent demands for obedience raise questions concerning his motives, which can never be understood and therefore not defended. Furthermore Milton was a supremely creative artist who allowed his characters to have their say, often more convincingly than God. Milton wrote a drama rather than a spiritual exercise or a treatise: herein lies the source of the controversies.

IV

Poetry, drama and disputation

Artistic ingredients for an explosive mixture

7

The appropriateness of poetry

Milton's ambitions were then emphatically artistic as well as religious. In *Paradise Lost* Milton sought to fuse the red hot heat of his intellect with his theological zeal and poetic ambitions. The question remains how much he appreciated the limitations as well as the potential of poetry and its appropriateness for fine moral and theological argument. Did he appreciate the difficulty of the task ahead if poetry was to be his medium? If Milton both miscalculated the capacity of his medium to bear the weight of his theme and warmed to the task of creating extraordinarily convincing characters, then we have the origin of a poetic drama which took on a life of its own. The controversy surrounding *Paradise Lost* has an artistic as well as a theological explanation.

On one level the poem could be regarded as a tract, treatise or sermon; on another level it is a narrative poem written in epic style, but primarily it is a drama, a tragedy about the fall of the good – angels and humans. It is a tragedy because it concerns:

> *foul distrust, and breach*
> *Disloyal on the part of man, revolt,*
> *And disobedience:*
>
> (IX 6-8)

which brought into this world "a world of woe" (IX 11), echoing the very opening of the poem:

> *Of man's first disobedience, and the fruit*

Of that forbidden tree, whose mortal taste
Brought death into the world, and all our woe

(I 1-3)

It is epic because it deals with the biggest of all human issues, a story:

Not less but more heroic than the wrath
Of stern Achilles on his foe pursued
Thrice fugitive about Troy wall; or rage
Of Turnus for Lavinia disespoused,
Or Neptun's ire or Juno's, that so long
Perplexed the Greek and Cytherea's son;

(IX 14-19)

more worthy of epic status than "the wrath/Of stern Achilles", or "rage/Of Turnus for Lavinia disespoused": a "higher argument" (IX 42) altogether.

Milton searched for an "answerable style," (IX 20) with which to handle the ultimate theological question: how exactly is God just? Milton himself alerts us then to something it is all too easy to ignore, which is the originality of what he is attempting: "Things unattempted yet in prose or rhyme" (I 16). The poem concerns Christian theology but rapidly turned into something else.

As a comparison Aquinas' *Summa Theologica* presented proof of the existence of God but it covered just a page or two in a work containing several thousand pages. Aquinas adopted the tone of a scientific analysis, listing points in a spare style and landing on the conclusion as if he was working through a mathematical problem. His first 'proof' considers the Argument from Motion: *It is certain, and evident to our senses, that in the world some things are in motion. Now whatever is in motion is put in motion by another, for nothing can be in motion except it is in potentiality to that towards which it is in motion; whereas a thing moves inasmuch as it is in act. For motion is nothing else than the reduction of something from potentiality to actuality. But nothing can be reduced from potentiality to actuality, except by something in a state of actuality. Thus that which is actually hot, as fire, makes wood, which is potentially hot, to be actually hot, and thereby moves and changes it. Now it is not possible that the same thing should be at once in actuality and potentiality in the same respect, but only in different respects. For what is actually hot cannot simultaneously be potentially hot; but it is simultaneously potentially cold. It is therefore impossible that in the same respect and in the same way a thing should be both mover and moved, i.e. that it should move itself. Therefore, whatever is in motion must be put in motion by another. If that by which it is put in motion be itself put in motion, then this also must needs be put in motion by another, and that by another again. But this cannot go on to infinity, because then there would be no first mover, and, consequently, no other mover; seeing that subsequent movers move only inasmuch as they are put in motion by the first mover; as the staff moves only because it is put in motion by the hand. Therefore it is necessary to arrive at a first mover, put in motion by no other; and this everyone understands to be God.*

The tone is of a confidently controlled reasoned case. Aquinas presented a theoretical proof using the daily experience of the senses to open his thesis that motion presupposes a first mover. His example of fire is homely in its simplicity, yet encourages the reader to think of other examples, which might include the movement from day to night, from youth to age or winter to summer. Clearly easier to achieve in prose than verse Aquinas' argument possesses the calmness, balance and rhythm of meticulously articulated logic.

Milton knew this work[37] but did he understand the risk he was taking in using a poetic drama to defend God's actions? By presenting the very voice of God and demonstrating where

37 Mentioned by John T Shawcross in *John Milton: The Self and the World* p122, The University Press of Kentucky 1993. Milton commented on the style of Duns Scotus' commentary on the *Summa* in *Prolusion 3* quoted by Gordon Campbell and Thomas N Corns in *John Milton, Life, Work and Thought*, Oxford, 2008. Milton had cited Spenser as "a better teacher then Scotus or Aquinas," in *Areopagitica*

Adam, Eve and the Fallen Angels went wrong by means of soliloquy, dialogue and dramatic encounters could Milton ever achieve his goal? Instead of Aquinas' deftly chosen examples Milton presented a cornucopia of ideas and emotions. In his use of verse drama rather than prose Milton attempted to tidy up the loose ends of Christian theology by showing us God and applying logic to the human situation. This explains both the successes and the failures of the poem.

He certainly intended to turn us to God by force of argument. In addition, however, the control Milton wished to exert over the argument, the sense of a tightly executed legal defence, came face to face with three aspects of Milton's own personality which had grown out of the experiences of his life. These were his scholar's training in preparing arguments for examinations; his democrat's political instincts for tolerant debate, hearing all sides fairly, and his dramatist's ability to empathise with his characters. In addition, was his knowledge of theology and especially of Jewish glosses, which had attempted to bring bible stories to life for readers and which encouraged Milton to develop the Genesis narrative and characterisation. These were among the central features of his life and his creative method was shaped by them. Their legacy is the tangle of interpretations arising from the contradictions and conundrums which is *Paradise Lost*.

8

The scholar

Milton's experience of learning by debate, allowing each side in an academic argument to be heard in a formal disputation was central in influencing the force of the poem and its unintended consequences. University exercises consisted of spoken tasks designed to test both rhetorical skills and comprehension of classical learning, even when supporting a view with which the speaker disagreed. They centred on logic, ethics, physics, metaphysics and theology. As Barbara Lewalski points out: "In the final year as part of the exercises for the Baccalaureate, they were required by statute…to maintain two Latin theses on selected moral or metaphysical topics…against three opponents belonging to other colleges, and to serve as opponents on two such occasions."[38] Standing before a scholarly audience it would have been a common occurrence for Milton to hear all sides of an argument given an airing. The theatrical element in this would have appealed to the young man who in *Comus* had been instinctively drawn to staging a moral tale in the form of a masque. The dramatic emotions, the ebb and flow of the argument and the need to sway an audience were meat and drink to the scholar-artist.

Milton took to portraying the cosmic forces of Good and Evil confronting one another in *Paradise Lost* with ease as they parried opposing arguments, battering opponents with rhetorical devices and scoring hits with daring thrusts. From the artificiality of the devils' debate in Book II to Satan's

38 *The Life of John Milton: A Critical Biography*, Wiley Blackwell, 2000, new edition 2003

masterly speech volunteering to undertake the dangerous task of avenging their defeat and his attempted, then successful temptation of Eve; Eve's persuasion of Adam to be allowed to go off alone and later persuading Adam to eat the apple, to the painful decision he is forced to make between her and God we hear the roar of university sophistry. It is hardly surprising that it frequently seems as if the devil has all the best tunes and that God's sole argument concerning the need for good behaviour appears to be lightweight by comparison. God might be in the right but can he win the reader's vote?

Milton's membership of Christ's College from 1625 to 1632 was significant in the development of his mind and attitudes. The college was of the Reformist persuasion and Milton would have been at home in the radical atmosphere. He was a student rebel, disapproving of the mundane topics set for debate and study. For reasons that remain unclear he fell out with his tutor Chappell in his first year but he was swiftly transferred to Tovey, following a brief absence from college. It is clear that Milton retained a hatred of the university's teaching. This is clear in his *Seven Prolusions* in which he satirised the university.[39] He criticised the "vapid scholasticism" of the curriculum, particularly the set disputations on Aristotelian topics. The empty topics "have no existence in reality at all, but like unreal ghosts and phantoms without substance… obsess minds already disordered and empty of all true wisdom."[40] In the third *Prolusion* he went so far as to state that scholastic philosophy was useless, against the merits of divine poetry, rhetoric and history. Even while he was attending university Milton was determined to grapple with the most important issues of theology, morality and politics.

Yet the sterile exercises in academic argument and debate had a huge impact on his way of thinking, particularly his ability

39 Lewalski, op cit "The *Prolusions* are of several types: declamations or exercises in rhetorical persuasion (1, 2, 3 and 7) usually upholding one side of a topic in debate; disputations or exercises in logical argumentation (4 and 5); and a parody of these kinds (6)"

40 *Complete Prose Works* i 245

to present both sides of an argument convincingly. Here is a clue to the mind behind *Paradise Lost*. Milton never escaped the tension between the radical democrat, who believed in individual freedom in politics and religion, and the strength of his opinions communicated in an authoritarian, frequently intolerant manner. His insistence on obedience in the poem bears witness to this.

At St Paul's School Milton had been surrounded by the bustling environment of the Cathedral and the churchyard booksellers around it, and responded well to the teaching of Greek and Latin literature, sampling too the likes of Dante and Petrarch. He also began the study of Hebrew, probably in his final year at school, which became important for his subsequent reading of the Bible in Hebrew and the many commentaries on it. As with many industrious pupils and educated adults at the time he was alert to important ideas in what he read and kept a Commonplace Book containing his favourite quotations. Anna Beer interestingly cites the Aristotelian Commonplace Book in which headings were set up according to opposites such as joy and sorrow or justice and injustice.[41] These would have become useful in future debates and arguments, and have sown the seeds for the reasoned thinking and fair consideration of all points of view which were to become central to his approach in *Paradise Lost*. This period of academic delight was in stark contrast to what he was to experience at Cambridge, and helps explain why the so called 'Horton period' of study following his Cambridge years was so valued by Milton.

Here we reach the heart of Milton's approach to poetry. Scholarship, theology and poetic ambition combined with his experience of and commitment to rational debate helped shape the artistic infrastructure of *Paradise Lost*. In a heady mixture of influences and preferences we can see how Milton's mind turned to the option of a dramatic epic poem, where Biblical figures, even God himself, were handed scripts to read in the ultimate disputation between good and evil.

41 *Milton: Poet, Pamphleteer and Patriot*, Bloomsbury Publishing, 2011

9

The democrat

Superficially it seems indisputable to say that Milton was a democrat; his writings and his allegiance to the English Revolution appear to be incontrovertible evidence for this. However, his attitudes towards democracy and toleration were fluid and shifted, not only over the course of his lifetime but also depending on the context within which he wrote. This influenced his response to events taking place around him such as in foreign policy, theology, the conduct of the revolution and the structure of church organisation. He advocated tolerance, but not for everyone, and became impatient with the leaders of the revolution and exasperated at the failure of the English people to free themselves from the tyranny of monarchy. He could be illiberal and intolerant as much as he was radical and democratic.

However, Milton's experience of the cut and thrust of debate and pamphleteering doubtless ensured that he composed *Paradise Lost* in accordance with the spirit of free speech. Democracy, which was at the heart of the revolution's ideals, involved a revolution too in reading and the eruption of debate through pamphlets. Milton's involvement demonstrated his belief in the importance of education and the use of reason which should lie at the heart of religion. He wanted people free to read all opinions and use their powers of reasoning to distinguish between true and false arguments. Education was to be the foundation stone for democracy: "Milton aimed to create revolutionary readers, those who would be able to read and understand the coercive nature of many printed opinions.

The revolutionary reader would be well armed to see through the manipulations of future politicians."[42]

Milton's view that only liberty could make morality possible is at the core of Milton's ideals, even if there were times, especially in his later years, when this stretched his patience, owing to the inability of people to exercise their freedom in a manner of which Milton approved. Indeed, if we wish to argue that *Paradise Lost* is about the English Revolution then the democratic ideal of hearing all sides of an argument is as relevant as any other issue. However, by giving his characters credible human voices Milton provided them with a considerable degree of autonomy, which affected their roles in supporting his justification of God's ways. They are endowed with so much energy and space to clarify and defend their own ways to God that much of their powerful questioning of God's plans means they do not always play the role destined for them. As star prosecution witnesses Adam, Eve and to a degree Satan paradoxically do sterling work for the defence.

The spirit of the age is characterised by a written war of words and Milton played a pivotal role in both attacking and defending points of view in support of the Protestant, Parliamentary and other causes. We need look no further than Milton's prose works to see his keenly felt views or grievances as he both promulgated new ideas and supported or countered opinions expressed in other tracts. He can be surprisingly vulgar and arrogant when making fun of his targets. In *Colasterion* he refers to an opponent as a "fleamy clodd" and talks down to him because he was a 'Serving man,' expressing incredulity that he could have any finer feelings at all. Milton's lack of tolerance is often breathtakingly apparent. He advocated tolerance in matters of press freedom, the composition of an 'invisible' church, where there were no institutions but a body of the faithful tolerant of each other's beliefs, and believed in political democracy but his belief in religious liberty did not for example

42 *Milton and the Revolutionary Reader* by Sharon Achinstein, Princeton University Press 1994 pp224-5

extend to Roman Catholics, especially the Irish.[43] Nicholas von Maltzahn[44] has argued that Marvell rather than Milton in fact became "the norm of the liberal tradition". Loewenstein develops the idea, believing that while Milton was not good on toleration he was better on liberty of conscience, which is expressed through *Paradise Lost*.[45] This is certainly true for example in Milton's description of 'the hell within' as opposed to 'the paradise within' where he states that we create our own inner environment. His views were more elastic than the rigid Puritan and Parliamentarian image might suggest but he was capable of vehemently expressing condemnation of opposing views whilst subscribing to a belief in the validity of views expressed by all believers.

The *Anti Episcopal tracts* of 1641-2 launched Milton onto the public stage. A celebrated saga began with the treatise *Of Prelatical Episcopy, and whether it may be deduced from the Apostolical times by virtue of those testimonies which are alleged to that purpose in some late Treatises; One wherof goes under the name of James Archbishop of Armagh*, being an answer to *An Humble Remonstrance to the High Court of Parliament in defence of Episcopacy* by Joseph Hall, Bishop of Norwich, to which five ministers had retorted under the pseudonym of Smectymnus[46] in March 1641, led by Milton's former tutor Thomas Young. The febrile climate of the day can be judged by the sequence of publications which followed. Next month came Hall's reply in his *Defence of the Humble Remonstrance*. This provoked Milton in July to the publication of a bad-tempered pamphlet called *Animadversions upon the Remonstrant's Defence against*

43 See *Milton and Toleration* Essays edited by Achinstein and Sauer, Oxford University Press 2007, Introduction

44 Ibid p 6

45 See *Treacherous Faith* by David Loewenstein, published Oxford University Press 2015

46 The word is formed from the initials of the authors' names: Stephen Marshal, Edmund Calamy, Thomas Young, Matthew Newcomen, William Spurstow

Smectymnuus (1641). *A Modest Confutation* of Milton's attack, probably written by Hall's son, emerged in the following February and in March Milton retorted with *An Apology against a Pamphlet call'd A Modest Confutation of the Animadversions of the Remonstrance against Smectymnuus*. Early in 1642, after the dust had settled, *The Reason of Church Government urged against Prelaty* continued in more measured tones Milton's battle for liberty as a necessary precursor of self-discipline: "For there is not that thing in the whole world of more grave and urgent importance throughout the whole life of man than is discipline." That discipline had to be self-imposed: "If he exhort this, I hear him as an angel, though he speak without warrant; but if he would compel me, I know him for Satan."[47] No one was going to push Milton around.

Areopagitica – A speech of Mr John Milton for the Liberty of Unlicens'd Printing, to the Parliament of England (published on 24th November 1644) was especially relevant to the theme of individual self-discipline and free will in *Paradise Lost*, which is almost the poetic version of the pamphlet. Milton tried to demonstrate that only tyrannies imposed censorship of the press. At this point his confidence was high concerning the possibility that man could grow towards moral freedom, though he realised that none of this would work without a willingness on the part of individuals to take on the responsibility of making reasoned judgments for themselves. This is where he was to face a dilemma regarding the deliberations of Adam and Eve, for in attempting to use their reason to debate Eve's desire to work apart from Adam they disobey God, raising the question of the effectiveness of reasoning when faced with a God who insists on obedience. What happens when using our reason as best we can, we reach the wrong conclusion or where there is no place for reason at all, only obedience?

The tenor of Milton's prose writings was then belligerent, radical, obdurate and at times inconsistent. Possessing great belief in the power and rightness of his arguments he was

47 *The Reason of Church Government*

sufficiently confident to write on matters ranging from education, divorce, the constitution of the church and laws of censorship to theological issues including the nature of the Trinity, mortalism[48] and free will. However, his epic poem presented the ultimate challenge of combining a cause to be justified with a creative undertaking. It is here that a more complex Milton is found. He retained his belief in man's free will based on Arminianism rather than the predestination preached by Calvin as expressed in the *Westminster Confession* and granted freedom of speech to all characters. Ultimately, however, it was upon the morality of strict obedience to the law of the Old Testament that Milton concludes the story of *Paradise Lost*.

Milton experienced a: "highly conflicted, strained and volatile" relationship with his country, which vacillated between "national pride and disappointment, between natural hope and doubt."[49] Between 1651 and 1655 Milton proudly signed his name Joannis Miltoni, Angli, in the title page to his *Defences* yet later: "after having allured me by her lovely name (patriotism) has almost expatriated me, as it were."[50] His ambition to encourage: "combative debate and the plurality of opinions, including clashing ones, necessary for a civic nation in the making of the truly free"[51] seemed dashed and was displayed in the Infernal Debate in Book II, which captured the twisted democracy Milton had witnessed. Milton had hoped to develop: "a defence of nationhood, dependent less on a codified judicature and legal positivism than on natural law equated with

48 The view that the soul sleeps or dies until the general resurrection of the departed. For analysis of Milton's complex views see *Milton and the manuscript of De Doctrina Christiana* by Gordon Campbell, Thomas Corns and John Hale, Oxford University Press 2007 and *Milton Studies 45* 2005, paper by Albert Labriole

49 *Early Modern Nationalism and Milton's England*, Essays edited by D Loewenstein and P Stevens, University of Toronto Press, 2008, Introduction Page 3

50 Ibid page 3

51 *Areopagatica. Complete Prose Works* ii:539

the law of God."[52] He planned for: "a climate for toleration, inquiry and the hazarding of truth in a free nation"[53] which ended in the failure of popular self-governance in favour of yet another elite.

The mighty Protestant nation had been "chosen before any other" so that "out of her as out of Sion should be proclaimed and sounded forth the first tidings and trumpet of Reformation to all Europe."[54] Instead the nation returned to slavery and servitude. He identified the Jews with bondage and servitude[55] which would be extinguished with the appearance of Christ: "For Milton slavery was both a sign and a consequence of moral degeneration" and "Much of Milton's writing was concerned about the difficulties and temptations of subjection. In *Eikonoklastes* Milton accused Englishmen of being "by nature slaves," "not fit for that liberty which they cried out and bellowed for." Just as in the story of the Fall Adam and Eve allow base appetites to dominate their powers of reasoning so the nation fell down and allowed itself to be dominated by the decadence and authority of the Restoration court and kingship. Shoulson goes so far as to find parallels between the destruction of the Temple and loss of the Rabbis' political power within the Roman Empire and the restoration of the monarchy and the disempowerment of more radical Protestantism.[56] The theme of loss is common to both *Midrash* and *Paradise Lost*; exile from Eden parallels the Jewish theme of exile.

Coping with the frailties of others was Milton's toughest challenge and is frequently responsible for his inconsistent views as his exasperation spilled over. It was frustrating and

---

52 *Milton, Toleration and Nationhood* by Elizabeth Sauer, Cambridge University Press 2013 page 78

53 Ibid page 98

54 *Complete Prose Works* ii: 552

55 See "The Rise of Asia and with them the Jews": Israel, Asia and England by Rachel Trubowitz in *Milton and the Jews* Essays edited by Douglas A Brooks, published 2008, Cambridge University Press

56 *Milton and the Rabbis: Hebraism, Hellenism and Christianity* by Jeffrey S Shoulson, Colombia University Press 2001

incomprehensible to Milton that the revolution had not turned out as he had hoped but in *Paradise Lost* acceptance of events confirmed that there was no democracy where God's law was concerned: obedience is all. Is this the conclusion of a tired, blind man whose revolution had failed, where the people had shown themselves unfit for the enormity of the undertaking or was it that Milton had to concede with patient acceptance that it was not yet in God's plan for this alternative society to be born? This is a psychological and historical way of approaching the poem. What is clearer to see is Milton's democratic approach to the presentation of character in the form of verse drama. His characters are frequently persuasive and the reader has to be cautious not to be persuaded by illogical or self-serving 'reasoning' yet there are many questions concerning God's actions and his relationship with mankind which cannot be so easily dismissed. Satan is capable of deluding himself and others; the debate in Pandemonium shows how democracy may be subject to manipulation with "words clothed in reason's garb,"[57] and we must be wary of Satan's and Eve's attempts to sway an audience in their respective attempts to persuade. The conundrum is how much of their arguments we might accept as reasonable points or questions deserving answers, rather than simply being against God's commands. In both its literary technique and its conclusion perhaps *Paradise Lost* was to be a new departure in more ways than one.

57 II 226

10

The dramatist

Milton's knowledge of plays and drama came from many sources but acting and attending the theatre appear to have figured relatively little in his life. This is not because Milton was as opposed to theatrical entertainment as some of his Puritan colleagues but that the opportunities were few, the quality of what existed was variable and the closure of theatres inevitably threw Milton back into books. Had events turned out differently it is not inconceivable that Milton may have participated more in the dramatic world of his times. Anne Baynes Coiro sees evidence of Milton's identification with Cambridge playwright Thomas Randolph and potential aspirations for a career in London theatre.[58] His father was a trustee of Blackfriars Theatre and in the 1630s he sketched out ideas for tragedies on the Fall, Sodom, Abraham and Isaac. His notes in the Trinity manuscript demonstrate that he considered the practical aspects of staging, thus setting the foundation for *Paradise Lost* and *Samson Agonistes.* Milton clearly had no problem in permitting Dryden to prepare a stage version of *Paradise Lost.* Milton valued Shakespeare, and his (anonymous) contribution to poems in praise of Shakespeare, published in the Second Folio (1632), turned on the theme of how the best monument to a writer is in his readers' minds rather than stone memorials:

58 *Anonymous Milton: or a Maske Masked* in *ELH (*English Literary History) 71 2004 pp 609-629. See also *Milton the Dramatist* by Timothy J Burbery, published by Duquesne University Press 2007

Thou in our wonder and astonishment
Hast built thy self a live-long Monument[59]

Milton's Satan bears striking similarities to Shakespeare's Iago in his inner torment and finding an outlet for his envy and frustration through destruction. Other Elizabethan and Jacobean drama would have been known by Milton but the quality of university drama does not appear to have been high. Barbara Lewalski comments that if Milton: "was in Cambridge in March (1632) he may have seen King Charles and Queen Henrietta Maria and viewed the two English comedies presented for their entertainment, *The Rival Friends* by Peter Hausted of Queens' (a crashing failure), and *The Jealous Lovers* by Thomas Randolph of Trinity (a great success)."[60]

Lewalski continues: "In 1642 Milton spoke harshly of collegiate playacting, countering charges that he attended theatres in London by denouncing the authorized but demeaning plays performed at the university by ordained or prospective ministers. He admits attending those, sometimes, but only as a scoffing critic." Lewalski quotes Milton: "*...they thought themselves gallant men, and I thought them fools, they made sport, and I laughed, they mispronounced, and I misliked*."[61] Significantly, however, Lewalski notes: "Yet even in the year Puritans closed the theatres, Milton distanced himself with a subjunctive – "if" – from the ordinance making stage plays unlawful."[62] He was certainly not against instrumental music, singing and dancing[63] and was familiar with Mystery plays, as the draft options in the Trinity manuscript[64] indicated, incorporating allegorical figures and personifications in abundance.

Arcades and *Comus* testify to Milton's willingness to work in

59 *On Shakespear* 1630

60 Op cit Chap 2

61 'Apology' *Complete Prose Works i* 887-8

62 ibid

63 *Areopagitica* op cit

64 Op cit

(albeit a highly stylised) dramatic mode, which chiefly revolved around dance and spectacle, though they were not without moral purpose. The former was 'Part of an entertainment presented to the Countess Dowager of Derby at Harefield, by some noble persons of her family' and is in truth more a graceful compliment to the Countess set in the elegant verse of the pastoral style with songs, against the backdrop of the great house. It was performed by her grandchildren and other visitors. The Protestant Countess had shown great fortitude in supporting the family of her eldest daughter, following the execution in May 1631 of her daughter's second husband for sexual abuse of his wife and stepdaughter. There is a clear moral dimension, which is never directly mentioned in the masque. Milton walked a tightrope by writing the masque, for such entertainments had been denounced by Puritan commentators for the way they brought the immorality of court life to the people.[65] Milton managed to adopt a middle way by creating a masque that could be seen as respectable.

The Genius' final song is an exhortation to the visitors to leave behind the world of Arcadia (court and/or town life) and to gaze on the Countess and her estate as the repose of equanimity and probity:[66]

Nymphs and shepherds dance no more
By sandy Ladon's lilied banks,
On old Lycaeus or Cyllene hoar,
Trip no more in twilight ranks,
Though Erymanth your loss deplore,
A better soil shall give ye thanks.
From the stony Maenalus,
Bring your flocks, and live with us,
Here ye shall have greater grace,

---

65 See the two contemporary Puritan commentators quoted by Lewalski (op cit) in Chap 3: Lucy Hutchinson's *Memoirs of the Life of Colonel Hutchinson* ed Julius Hutchinson, London 1968, and William Prynne's *Histrio-Mastix: or, The Players Scourge and Actors tragedy* 1633

66 *Arcades* III Song

To serve the Lady of this place.
Though Syrinx your Pan's mistress were,
Yet Syrinx well might wait on her.
Such a rural queen
All Arcadia hath not seen.

If in *Arcades* Milton made tentative steps towards balancing art and morality, in *Comus*, more accurately *A Masque presented at Ludlow Castle 1634*, he attempted an even more overtly moral piece, though the presentation of the drama is dull by comparison with the story of man's Fall, which Milton was to imbue with more energy and humanity, though in *Comus* there are some indications of what was to follow. Courtly masques containing dance, song, drama and spectacle had originated as dumb-shows performed by masked dancers. In Milton's version of the genre he decorously produced an entertainment of pleasure and compliment to the Earl of Bridgewater and his family written in such a way that it could be performed by the younger members of the family.

The moral issues are the triumph of virtue and the praise of temperance; both would be at home in *Paradise Lost*, though in *Comus* Milton praises the young lady's virtue but does not develop the matter further; it would have been inappropriate to discuss the virtues of "Sun-clad power of chastity"[67] and the "serious doctrine of Virginity"[68] in too much detail. The tone of the Elder brother is suitably simplistic when he expresses confidence in the power of his sister's virtue:

'Tis chastity, my brother, chastity:
She that has that, is clad in compleat steel,

(419-420)

There is potential too for a whole volume to be written about the Spirit's line: "Vertue may be assail'd, but never hurt."[69]

67 l.781

68 l.786

69 l.588

The tone is pastoral and elegant but also displays a moral seriousness, particularly in the two debates which take place; one between the brothers and the other between Comus and the Lady. Although lacking the dramatic tension that such conversations have in *Paradise Lost* it was the 26-year-old Milton's apprenticeship in presenting such debates in verse, in accordance with his view that poetry was capable of teaching moral truths, thus giving him the confidence twenty years later to embark on his epic poem. There was singing and dancing, and potentially stunning tableaux but it was Milton's only attempt to incorporate a deep truth within a verse drama, before *Paradise Lost*. He was clearly constrained by the venue, the youth of the actors and the nature of the occasion but it was his first draft on the theme of obedience to a higher law whilst praising Lady Alice's[70] innocence and resolve and her brothers' concern for their sister.

Neither a morality play nor a court masque *Comus* is in the main pastoral and graceful but it contains a moral seriousness and some satire. It has to rely on poetry for its effects but does not possess a fully worked out psychology for each protagonist; a masque would not have been the vehicle for that level of realism and the youth of the actors could not have credibly sustained it, though the portrayal of Comus is more than just the 'devil in disguise' of a family entertainment. Significantly Comus lies when he says he wishes to take the lady to the cliché of a rural idyll, which instead turns out to be a debauched urban court. It is as if Milton is here practising for the presentation of Satan's guiles. Comus has all the debating weapons to hand as he attempts to persuade the Lady to give way to a more luxurious lifestyle, citing the point that the Creator made all these good things for us to enjoy, and it would be impertinent not to take them up:

> *If all the world*
> *Should in a pet of temperance feed on Pulse,*

70 The Earl's daughter who plays the part of The Lady

Drink the clear stream, and nothing wear but Freize,
Th'all-giver would be unthank't, would be unprais'd,
Not half his riches known, and yet despised

(719-723)

Similarly: "Beauty is nature's coin, must not be hoarded, /But must be current"[71] could well have been spoken by Satan when tempting Eve.

The central message was that life at Ludlow represented an ideal of rectitude which was missing at court. Sabrina here represents the fundamental goodness of the rural haven, and although Comus is not defeated, merely thwarted, the parameters of morality are established.

What happened then to Milton between 1634 and the 1650s to enhance his understanding of both drama and human nature? Close contact with political characters of the day, their machinations and commitment to the 'Good Old Cause,' experience of a country riven by disorder and disagreement and his engagement in tract and pamphlet warfare on contentious issues. He inhabited an arena in which there was an incessant atmosphere of claim and counterclaim so Milton had to grow up fast, though it has to be said that his acerbic wit and critical tongue had long been in evidence in his student writing and Prolusions. As the revolution subsided, the scholar possibly more at home in the library than the cockpit of national affairs, was replaced by a writer ready to return to his life-long ambition to become the poet of a national epic who was now supported by years of unique experience: he had lived through and survived the country's only civil war. He had also travelled through Europe, from where he returned on hearing news of the civil war, worked as a tutor and began writing tracts; importantly he was married to Mary Powell in 1642 after which he endured a topsy-turvy married life. Just as he planned to marry someone else in 1645 Mary returned to him and in subsequent years gave birth to his first children.

71 Lines 738-9

By 1652 Milton had become completely blind and Mary died following childbirth. Each of these and other experiences added to Milton's knowledge of how men and women act in domestic and extreme circumstances, broadening his understanding of what people from different backgrounds to his own hoped for and feared in their everyday lives. All was distilled through the horror of civil war, the failure of which must have concentrated his mind on where the whole enterprise and its conclusion fitted into the great scheme of things.

This is not to say that *Paradise Lost* is simply about the civil war, that Milton is on Satan's side or that it is about Milton's private emotions as he saw his dreams for the future of his country vanish. However, his experiences provided a richer understanding of how people react in life-changing situations and he could appreciate how in real life education, the power of reason, and the life of the mind had to be translated into situations requiring practical as well as principled solutions. This is the experience that underpinned his portrayal of Adam and Eve and allowed him to see under the skin of Satan.

If it was a matter of principle for Milton to give freedom of speech to his protagonists it was Milton's creative imagination which was instrumental in making the *dramatis personae* of *Paradise Lost* come to life in a way he did not foresee. His natural inclination to allow characters to state opinions or ask awkward questions found expression through the imagined world of drama. Milton's imagination has long been a source of interest. Coleridge asserted that "Milton had a highly imaginative, Cowley a very fanciful style,"[72] and frequently used examples from Milton to illustrate the theory of association and the way the imagination could become the agent of reason. In this regard and in many other ways Milton became an unexpected hero to the Romantic poets.[73]

---

72 *Biographia Literaria* chap 4

73 See *Paradise Lost and the Romantic Reader* by Lucy Newlyn, Oxford, 1993

In Milton's own world view, as with everything else, it is Reason which has to control the wanderings and imaginings of the mind:

> *But know that in the soul*
> *Are many lesser faculties that serve*
> *Reason as chief; among these fancy next*
> *Her office holds; of all external things,*
> *Which the five watchful senses represent,*
> *She forms imaginations, airy shapes,*
> *Which reason joining or disjoining, frames*
> *All what we affirm or what deny, and call*
> *Our knowledge or opinion; then retires*
> *Into her private cell when nature rests.*
> *Oft in her absence mimic fancy wakes*
> *To imitate her; but misjoining shapes,*
> *Wild work produces oft, and most in dreams,*
> *Ill matching words and deeds long past or late.*
>
> (V 100-114)

There is in this analysis a well known attempt to understand the workings of the brain, as found, for example, in Burton's *Anatomy of Melancholy*. Fancy gathers images via the five senses, but left to her own devices fancy can run amok, producing the insane images of dreams. Under the firm control of reason, these images create our thoughts and opinions. Later, however, Milton used this analysis not to describe the poetic imagination but to understand the way a human brain must rationalise and harness individual images into concepts, as opposed to the angelic mind which operates intuitively, by-passing these processes, as Raphael explains to Adam:

> *flowers and their fruit*
> *Man's nourishment, by gradual scale sublimed*
> *To vital spirits aspire, to animal,*
> *To intellectual, give both life and sense,*

Fancy and understanding, whence the soul
Reason receives, and reason is her being,
Discursive, or intuitive; discourse
Is oftest yours, the latter most is ours,
Differing but in degree, of kind the same.

(V 482-490)

Milton's understanding of his own kind of poetic imagination is not, however, highly developed. It was Hazlitt's concept of the sympathetic imagination, known to us as empathy, which turned out to be a more accurate description of Milton's method in *Paradise Lost*.

Hazlitt propounded the theory of empathy before the word was invented, (it is not recorded in the *OED* until the early twentieth century), when he wrote: "I can only abstract myself from my present being and take an interest in my future being in the same sense and manner in which I can go out of myself entirely and enter into the minds and feelings of others" (Works I 39),[74] and: "Imagination is another name for an interest in things out of ourselves, which must naturally run counter to our own" (Works XX 170). Hazlitt used this ability as a criterion for judging the effectiveness of actors, (Works V 185 and 303), claiming that this ability was what made Shakespeare: "the least of an egoist of anybody in the world." (Works XI 92). It was but one step from Milton's natural inclination to look at all sides of an argument to Hazlitt's statement: "This is the true imagination, to put yourself in the place of others, and to feel and speak for them." The imagination is superior to abstract reasoning, because it combines or amalgamates experiences into "intuition."[75] The result of applying this process to his retelling of the Fall of

74 References to *The Complete Works of William Hazlitt* ed PP Howe, Dent, 1930

75 See I 124, XII 257 and XX 10

man, was a dramatic poem as complex as *Hamlet* and in its format as thorough as Browning's *The Ring and the Book*. Like Browning Milton knew that in a reasoned debate or trial all sides of a question had to be aired in order to arrive at what Browning termed the "white light" of truth.

Dramatic characterisation was the essence of Milton's artistic, as well as intellectual method. It is what forces us to face the difficulty of squaring his justification of God's ways with his method of characterisation and all its consequences. When we hear convincingly portrayed characters speak about fundamental issues which face mankind we are inclined to understand their positions. According to Milton's theory of reasoning, however, we should be harder on ourselves, and judge them by God's rigorous standards. Crucially it is the tension between Milton's insistence on our obedience to God's laws and the questioning of these laws which emerges from the reasonableness of the counterarguments that lies at the heart of the poem's failure to achieve its ends.

It is Milton's artistic method based on his belief in free speech, which accounts for the poem's fractured theme. Theological reasons alone are not the cause of the problem. Both the failure of the poem to achieve its stated aim and its success in achieving something different, stem from his intellectual and artistic approach. This tension arises because on one side is a religious poem espousing the use of reason to live a life of obedience to God, and on the other is the dramatic reconstruction of a crime scene, where the witnesses are allowed to speak for themselves.

Hebraic sources may also have provided Milton with examples of literary, legendary and ethical interpretations of the scriptures from which Milton drew. These glosses on biblical stories, which presented people and events in a more fully human manner and setting, may have acted as exemplars, giving Milton the confidence to develop his own account of the Fall. Just how many of these works he knew and how accurate the Latin translations of the texts were is uncertain. They would certainly have given Milton both ideas on which to build and the encouragement to believe that it was possible to convey the inner emotions, thoughts and torments of thinly drawn biblical characters so as to bring them dramatically closer to and thus more comprehensible to the reader.

11

The theologian

Milton had not previously written anything as psychologically forensic as his depiction of the Fall. In *Paradise Lost* his protagonists take centre stage by their utter humanity. It is possible that his knowledge of Hebraic writings or glosses on biblical texts, which presented familiar Old Testament characters in novel, non-biblical ways containing additional material with which to enlarge and clarify biblical passages with more 'human' details, played a part in supporting Milton's plans. Just how far this is the case is a matter of dispute between Hebrew scholars. It is likely that whether or not Milton knew some of these works in their original language, or in Latin translations or merely by reading and hearing of them from other scholars (Protestant theologians of the time are known to have been familiar with them) these glosses supported Milton's inventiveness. From portraying recognisably human figures in credible human situations to providing some of the narrative detail such as Satan entering the body of the serpent in order to tempt Eve, the Hebrew tales to a greater or lesser extent would have supplied Milton with both raw material and the confidence to proceed with his poem. Ultimately, Milton's protagonists became his finest achievement, even though they frequently complicated, even circumvented his aim of clarifying God's ways.

There has been disagreement among biographers concerning when and how much Hebrew Milton learned. Lewalski[76] comments that: "In *Ad Patrem* Milton specifies

76 Op cit Chap 1

French, Italian and Hebrew (possibly including Aramaic and Syriac) as the languages he then learned in addition to his schoolboy Latin and Greek." All this was achieved by his father's generous funding of private tutors in order to supplement his school curriculum. This would have provided Milton with the opportunity to read some of the Old Testament in Hebrew. Indeed in his own version of a school curriculum, following an already gruelling day of study Milton suggests:

> *"Sundays also and every evening may now be understandingly spent in the highest matters of theology and church history, ancient and modern: and ere this time at a set hour the Hebrew tongue might have been gained, that the Scriptures may be now read in their own original;*[77]

It is known that at Cambridge Milton tutored an Anglo-American dissident theologian called Roger Williams in Hebrew in exchange for lessons in Dutch. Just how proficient Milton was and if he could have read Hebrew glosses on the Bible, known as *Midrash*[78] is unclear. The question of Milton's indebtedness to such works is clouded by confusion over Milton's level of knowledge and difficulties in isolating which texts he may have known, depending on their linguistic complexity and when they might have been available to him. It may have been that ancient ideas had been handed down through generations of literary and theological writings,

---

77 *Of Education* 1644

78 *Midrash* (plural Midrashim, adjective midrashic): compilations of legal (halakhic) and homiletic (aggadic) expositions of biblical texts. Milton was strongly influenced by *Aggadah* (plural Aggadot), the non-legal homilies or glosses on biblical passages. *Halakhah* are the legal rules regulating all aspects of Jewish life. The *Masorah* (adj masoretic) is the body of notes found in the margins of Rabbinical bibles. The *Talmud* is the collected record of academic discussions of generations of scholars. The *Torah* is the Pentateuch and all the material deriving from it.

including Protestant writers and preachers without special knowledge of Hebrew. [79]

It was not until the early twentieth century when, for example, the German scholar Louis Ginzberg published his translation of *aggadic* literature that this material became more widely appreciated.[80] Around the same time Harris H Fletcher investigated Judaic literature for possible Miltonic sources, culminating in two books arguing that Milton borrowed from the Hebrew medieval commentaries which surround the text in the Rabbinical Bible.[81] Golda Werman, a modern scholar, has condemned much of the earlier work carried out on this subject, arguing that: "In most cases the critics fail to convince their readers because their scholarship is not credible; they do not have the training necessary to read *midrashic* sources in the original, nor are they capable of evaluating such translations as exist."[82] Werman accepts that Milton may well have known the work of John Selden, a scholar whom he admired, though she is critical of aspects of Selden's scholarship.[83] It is, however, possible that only Selden had the scholarship required for Rabbinical Hebrew, though Werman states that Selden's work does not account for all Milton's borrowings.[84]

The complexities and specialist knowledge required to unravel what debt Milton owed to Jewish sources (very much the microscope approach) should not distract us from appreciating that whether it was from direct knowledge of *Midrash*, translations of them in Latin or references made by

79 See Jeffrey Shoulson *Milton and the Rabbis*, Colombia University Press, 2001

80 *The Legends of the Jews* Published 1908-1938. Available from The Project Gutenberg: www.gutenberg.org/ebooks

81 *Milton's Semitic Studies* (1926) and *Milton's Rabbinic Readings* (1930)

82 *Milton and Midrash* by Golda Werman, The Catholic University of America Press, Washington DC, 1995 p 4

83 Op cit p 5

84 See Jason P Rosenblatt *John Selden: Renaissance England's Chief Rabbi*, Oxford University Press, 2006

contemporary Protestant theologians which Milton may have read or heard there are some striking parallels between passages and episodes in *Paradise Lost* and this material. The texts provided interpretations and additional literary material about people and events, supplementing the Genesis account with material concerning the motivation and behaviour of the protagonists. At the very least Milton took inspiration from them which prompted his own imagination to develop his narrative. Close examination shows that some of the confusions inherent in Milton's characterisation may derive from some of these borrowings. *Paradise Lost* may even be seen as Milton's own *Midrash* on the Book of Genesis, as he developed situations and added depth to characterisation. Ironically, as well as enriching his message they also contributed to its unravelling by allowing the introduction of ideas and emotions which challenged his own thesis too convincingly.

How then did Milton, who probably had just sufficient Hebrew to read or listen to the Old Testament being read to him, gain access to *midrashic* material? One of the most vehement arguments for Milton's indebtedness to this material comes from Werman[85] who argues that the answer is simply there were copies of these works in circulation in the years leading up to and during the time Milton was writing *Paradise Lost*, most of them being Latin translations.[86] Werman's line by line comparison of Milton's poem with potential sources demonstrates his possible borrowings, a practice which he began much earlier and goes back as far as a considerable number of Talmudic passages and technical *masoretic* terms in his prose tracts, almost as if he were quoting directly from the original. However, "These practices have led some critics to assume that the poet had no need for secondary sources. A close inspection of Milton's use of this

85 Op cit

86 For example: Johannes Buxtorf the Elder's *Lexicon Chaldaicum Talmudicum at Rabbinicum* published 1640; Christopher Cartwright's *Mellificum Hebraicum* published 1649; John Lightfoot's *Horae Hebraicea et Talmudicae* published 1658 onwards

material, however, demonstrates that he had such a narrow understanding of the principles he cites that it is inconceivable that he read his Jewish sources in the original."[87] There were particular works which Werman argues had a major influence on Milton's methods of characterisation, though it is important to identify what Milton himself brought to this task. As Werman says: "… to furnish his epic with suitable material with which to flesh out the austere biblical plot, Milton became a creative *midrashist,* making novel use of the ancient methods and contents of *Midrash* while adding his own and very original voice to the borrowed materials."[88] His debt to Hebraic sources may be hard to fathom but the originality of Milton's creative imagination was to be transformed by the addition of dramatic immediacy and in the way issues raised by the characters rebounded on Milton's plan.

Werman's thesis provides an example of how Milton may have been influenced. In its detailed analysis Werman's argument is unparalleled in Milton scholarship. It may be accurate or it may simply be indicative of the kind of material that influenced Milton but it provides an insight into the long history of developing the story of the Fall which preceded Milton. Werman argues that by far the most significant was the 8th century *Pirkei de-Rabbi Eliezer* translated into Latin by Willem Vorstius.[89] Werman cites this work as the chief inspiration for Milton's Invocations to the heavenly muse in Book I; descriptions of angels and their lives in Book III and ideas concerning Satan and the Fallen Angels. These include Satan as the chief angel, his envy, desire and pride; the reigning evil angel called 'Serpent';[90] the Fallen Angels' war with God arising from their jealousy at the creation of man and use of Beelzebub to suggest they provoke God by tempting man; even the Fallen Angels turning to dust derived from the Rabbi. The

87 Ibid page 31

88 Ibid page 92

89 Leiden 1644

90 See I 34-44

important conversation between God and Adam on loneliness and the need for a partner is attributed to the Rabbi, as are views on marriage in Eden and prelapsarian sex, which traditional Catholic thinking asserted had not taken place and which Werman argues lay at the heart of many of Milton's views on love and marriage. Details of Eve's seduction by Satan are said to provide the structural outline of Book IX. Among the most significant borrowings were Satan using the serpent as disguise, the description of Eve as the easier of the two potential targets and her torment at the thought of Adam with another woman. Adam's furious responses to Eve's sin, followed by sorrow at his loss of innocence in nakedness, are similarly attributed to the Rabbi.

The other significant borrowing is the notion of the place of work in prelapsarian Eden. This raises the question as to whether Milton intended his description of life in the garden to be realistic or metaphorical. The question which has frequently puzzled readers is that if the garden was perfect what would there be for Adam and Eve to do? The Rabbi's solution is an allegorical interpretation where work in the garden is intended to educate Adam and Eve in order that they gain an understanding of God and his ways, particularly regarding their duty and obedience owed to him. In this way their efforts to cut back the abundant growth in the garden parallels their effort to control their own temptation in Book IX. There becomes, therefore, a moral purpose to work in the garden, in the absence of a practical one. Of other possible borrowings from the Rabbi even the narrative of future events in Books XI and XII, especially the Nimrod episodes, may have derived from this source.

Three other possible sources were translated into Latin by Francis Tayler who, between 1649 and 1654 published the *Targum Yerushalmi*, an Aramaic paraphrase of the Pentateuch;[91] *Pirkei Avot*, a non legal tracate of the Mishnah[92] and *Avot de-*

91 London 1649

92 The *Mishnah* is the legal codification of the oral rather than written law, compiled about AD 200

Rabbi Nathan, a tract of the Talmud commenting on *Pirkei Avot.*[93] Lastly is *Ze'enah U-Re'enah*, based on a Hebrew commentary on the Pentateuch but written in everyday Yiddish by Jacob ben Isaac Ashkenazi to assist those who found the higher register of Hebrew too difficult. This was translated into Latin by Johan Saubert.[94] These texts were known to Protestant theologians so it is possible Milton was aware of them, even though in later life his reading lists are not included in his Commonplace book. According to Werman the number of direct parallels, particularly to the first mentioned, could not be mere coincidence.

An important concept Milton gleaned from The *Targum Yerushalmi* was another example of the garden as a moral place. The narrative in Genesis 2.15 simply states: "And the Lord God took the man and put him into the Garden of Eden to dress it and to keep it." This is developed in the *Targum* into: "And the Lord God took the man from the mountain of worship where he had been created, and made him dwell in the Garden of Eden, to do service in the law, and to keep its commandments." The conclusion is that Milton borrowed the concept of work in the garden as metaphor for serving God and obeying his commands.

Immediately following the Fall God asks: "Where art thou?"[95] This is one question God should never have to ask. In the *Targum* God is given more words: "Is not all the world which I have created, manifest before Me, the darkness as well as the light? And how did you believe in your heart that you could hide from before Me? Don't I see the place where you are hidden? Where are the commandments that I have given you to obey?"[96] These points lead to a discussion of God's omniscience and omnipotence; indeed God is given many more speeches in the *Targum*, a device similarly employed by Milton.

The *Avot de-Rabbi Nathan* repeated the use of Invocations

93 London 1654

94 Published 1660

95 Genesis 3.9

96 Werman pages 81-82

and comments on the place of work in the Garden in addition to the serpent's love for Eve. Milton also has the serpent envy Adam for having a beautiful wife with whom to share his life. This emotion reaches its zenith when he is so overcome by Eve that he almost neglects his task:

> *Such pleasure took the serpent to behold*
> *This flowery plat, the sweet recess of Eve*
> *Thus early, thus alone; her heavenly form*
> *Angelic, but more soft, and feminine,*
> *Her graceful innocence, her every air*
> *Of gesture or least action overawed*
> *His malice, and with rapine sweet bereaved*
> *His fierceness of the fierce intent it brought:*
>
> (IX 455-462)

Eve's form of address to Adam opens another possible attribution. In the prelapsarian state Eve referred to Adam as 'my master': "'All the things about which my master admonished me are false,' for at first Eve addresses Adam only as 'my master'." Werman wonders if this provided Milton with the idea that Eve should address her husband formally before the Fall ("My author and disposer", "My Glory, my perfection," "Offspring of heaven and earth and all earth's Lord") whereas after the Fall he is simply Adam.[97] Milton's borrowings are therefore possibly details of vocabulary as well as of topic.

Jacob ben Isaac Ashkenazi's commentary on the Pentateuch, *Ze'enah U-Re'enah,* is seen by Werman to contain similarities with the previous works. These include the serpent's lust for Eve, the difference between pre and postlapsarian sex; Adam's earlier yearning for a helpmeet; the physical nature of angels' needs, together with their jealousy at man's creation, particularly his possession of free will, based on the Genesis comment: "God created man in his own image."[98]

97 Werman pages 88-89

98 Genesis 1.27

Of particular note are ideas concerning the exact nature of God's command: "But of the tree of the knowledge of good and evil thou shalt not eat of it,"[99] and the notion of repentance at the end of the poem. God commands Adam clearly about not eating the fruit but when Adam tells Eve he changes the words, claiming that God said: "But of the fruit of the tree which is in the midst of the garden, God hath said, ye shall not eat of it, neither shall ye touch it, lest ye die."[100] Milton and the midrashist both see the addition of the command not to touch the tree as a negative because Eve's use of this change directly leads to the Fall. Unlike the *Midrash* Milton did not have the serpent push Eve's hand against the tree but had the serpent claim he had both touched the tree and tasted the fruit and did not die. The same point about this addition to God's words had been made in the *Avot de-Rabbi Nathan* with the comment: "Therefore it is said: If a man puts an excessive hedge around his words, he shall not be able to stand by his words. Furthermore, it is said: Let no man add to what he hears."[101] Likewise in *Pirkei de-rabbi Eliezer* the serpent persuades Eve to eat the fruit with a trick by touching the tree without any harm coming to him to prove that the same applies on eating the fruit. Milton also used this point regarding touching the tree which Genesis does not mention in the moment of the Fall, when he has the serpent say: "Look on me, /me who have touched and tasted, yet both live," (IX 687-8).[102] The Rabbis were at one in emphasising that obedience involves adherence to the letter of the law, and adding terms to the law is not necessarily an advantage.

Werman makes a major point regarding Milton's inclusion of Adam and Eve's repentance, which forms no part of the Genesis account but is found in *Ze'enah U-Re'enah*. Milton has God tell the Son that he offers repentance to penitent sinners: "I will clear their senses dark, /What may suffice, and soften

99 Genesis 2.17

100 Genesis 3.3

101 Quoted Werman page 87

102 See Werman pages 62-4

stony hearts/To pray, repent, and bring obedience due." (III 188-190). Werman argues that Adam and Eve's penitence (X 1086-1096) is accepted by God, that Satan is without hope because he refuses to repent (IV 79ff) and quotes from the *Midrash* to show Milton's indebtedness to it: " From all of this we see that when a man repents, God shows him good will. For He commanded the Jews to bring a sacrifice on the day of the New Moon, in order to compensate the moon after diminishing it in size and brightness. Because of this the Torah calls the New Moon offering a repentance offering to God."[103]

Midrashic material may then have assisted Milton to make the story of Adam and Eve more credibly human and his selection of what to incorporate should have enabled him to control the poem's argument. At the least his poetic and dramatic imagination may have been inspired by these ancient stories, whether they were known to him in the detail which Werman assumes or through Milton's memories of texts he had heard and the writings of other Protestant scholars who knew them. How then did he lose control of his most important characters so that they simultaneously enrich the poem while detracting from its aim? The answer lies in a combination of Milton's academic approach, his democratic principles, his dramatist's imagination and the hard to quantify but palpable influence of theological scholarship, in addition to the personal, religious and political turmoil he had experienced.

103 Quoted Werman page 108

12

Drama not theology

Milton had always conceived the Genesis story as a drama. The Trinity MS shows four sets of notes with cast lists in which Milton's thinking evolved towards fully rounded characterisation and away from medieval allegory. In addition to a Chorus of Angels Milton's first draft contained named 'characters,' Michael, Lucifer, Adam and Eve. Apart from the serpent the remainder were personifications and allegorical figures; Heavenly Love, Conscience, Death and Faith, Hope and Charity, complemented by Mutes representing Labour, Sickness, Discontent and Ignorance "with others." To these the second draft added Justice, Mercy and Wisdom; Fear is a further Mute and Hesperus the Evening Star may have been a stage device. Significantly Moses appeared as a major character at the top of the list.

Milton's third draft gained the title *Paradise Lost* and was plainly a drama divided into five acts. It opened with a monologue by Moses informing the audience that they "cannot see Adam in this state of innocence by reason of their sin." The practical limitations of presenting a drama with nude scenes having been dealt with the remaining acts simply outlined the lists of participants. We are, however, beginning to see here the makings of a drama. There was a core of 'characters' beginning with Michael, Lucifer, Adam and Eve, Moses being added in place of Michael. However, there were 19 allegorical figures plus the Chorus, Heavenly Love and Evening Star, contributing to a more static and medieval picture of the expulsion from Eden. The Chorus would have had a large role in explaining the issues and adding information such as Lucifer's rebellion and fall, and the number of allegorical figures grew significantly. It would have been possible, according to the classical concept of *decorum,* for such figures to be one-dimensional 'types' whilst still contributing to the unravelling of a complex situation and/or issue. Samson's visitors in *Samson Agonistes* are one-dimensional, as they have walk-on roles as elements of Samson's self-analysis, though the anguish of Samson's mental journey is no less complex and powerful for this. However, in his notes on *Paradise Lost* Milton appeared to be searching for a vehicle to convey a more human tragedy.

Eventually he retained the title of the version named *Paradise Lost* but in the single paragraph prose narrative of what is called *Adam's Banishment*, then amended to *Adam Unparadized,* is something that approached more closely the final plan. There remain signs that Milton retained an interest in the stage mechanisms he had employed in *Comus,* such as the descent of Gabriel at the beginning and the appearances of Conscience, Justice, Faith, Hope and Charity, as well as a masque displaying "all the evils of this life." Nevertheless the emphasis focused on the thoughts, words and emotions of the protagonists.

Now set in Eden the Chorus explains that Gabriel is present to keep a watch on Paradise, and through the interplay between Gabriel and the Chorus we hear about the rebellion in Heaven and the creation of Paradise. We can imagine Lucifer's appearance at this point in a moment of highly charged drama, and the seeds of Milton's dramatic epic poem were sown with Lucifer who "bemoans himself" and stating his desire for revenge. There is to be a clash with the Chorus, who, after Lucifer's departure, give details of his rebellion and fall. Maintaining the momentum Lucifer returns and seems to gloat over what he has done to man.

A new act then unfolded with the arrival of Adam and Eve in a postlapsarian state covered in leaves. Justice and Conscience have something stern to say to them, and clumsily an angel informs the Chorus about the temptation of Eve by Lucifer.

Significantly we then see more evidence of the beginnings of Milton's final version as Adam and Eve blame and accuse each other for what has happened. Once again echoes of *Comus* appear with 'shapes' in a masque, which display for Fallen man "all the evils of this life." In the spirit of the ending of *Paradise Lost* itself, Mercy comforts man, calling in Faith, Hope and Charity to instruct him, leading to acceptance of his lot and eventual repentance.

There is increasing dramatic energy, a growing interest in the psychology of the protagonists and a shape to Milton's summary plans, which laid the foundations for *Paradise Lost*. Importantly Milton's final words in this paragraph are "Compare this with the former draft". All the time he was looking to develop and improve upon his ideas, the characterisation becoming more subtle as he dispensed with allegorical figures.

There remained, however, trappings of the courtly masque about all the versions. Ironically however, justification of God's ways may have been easier for Milton had he presented them in this simpler way. A theological defence is less likely to sound ambivalent or contradictory when biblical narrative is expressed in the barest language by simple figures. Milton was bound by the requirements that the narrative had on our views about the characters and there was always the danger that fuller characterisation might distort the thesis of Milton's poem as he became drawn to allowing them a fair hearing to express their thoughts and feelings. By contrast in his final version Milton was not afraid to use simpler figures and complex characterisation side by side. The debate of the Fallen Angels in Book II, is a showcase for points of view rather than complex characterisation, whereas Satan's Machiavellian speech offering to take responsibility for the fight-back sheds light on his inner self in a more psychologically complex and credible characterisation.

13

The architecture of a play

In his biography of Milton WR Parker quotes a meeting between Milton and John Dryden in February 1674. Dryden asked Milton if he might be allowed to turn *Paradise Lost* into "an heroic opera" in rhyming couplets. Milton supposedly replied: "Well, Mr Dryden, it seems you have a mind to tag my points, and you have my leave to tag them. But some of them are so awkward and old-fashioned that I think you had as good leave them as you found them."[104]

It may have been difficult to convert to rhyme but the poem possesses the essential ingredients of drama, comprising all the characteristics of a drama in five acts with twelve scenes. Acts I and II occupy Books I-IV, where the purpose of the poem is made explicit and the locations of the drama are established. There is an introduction to the protagonists, establishing their strengths and weaknesses, whilst the central plot is initiated with the journey of Satan to earth and the dream which he induces in Eve. This is the ominous beginning of the war Satan will wage on God via Adam and Eve. Having whetted our appetite for Satan's successful temptation of Eve, Milton slows the pace in preparation for the crisis itself.

Books V-VIII constitute the third act, where the crisis is withheld while the historical background of the war in heaven, the expulsion of the Fallen Angels and the subsequent creation of paradise and mankind unfold through the discussion between

104 WR Parker *Milton: A Biography*, Oxford, 1968 Vol i 634-5. For the source see vol ii 1148. Dryden wrote the rhymed play *The State of Innocence and Fall of Man* (1671) but music was never composed and the libretto never performed

Adam and Raphael. The episode of Eve's dream at the beginning of this Act skilfully whets our appetite for the subsequent climax but we are held in suspense for some time. In addition, there is clear dramatic irony in the confident words of the angels in heaven following the creation of the earth, as told by Raphael:

> *Who can impair thee, mighty king, or bound*
> *Thy empire? Easily the proud attempt*
> *Of spirits apostate and their counsels vain*
> *Thou hast repelled,*
>
> (VII 608-611)

Warning bells for the future sound loudly:

> *Who seeks*
> *To lessen thee, against his purposes serves*
> *To manifest the more thy might: his evil*
> *Thou usest, and from thence createst more good.*
> *Witness this new-made world, another heaven*
> *From heaven gate not far,*
>
> (VII 613-618)

This prefigures what is about to occur, in addition to emphasising the underlying concept of the 'fortunate fall' that is central to the story. The climax in Act IV is dramatically the strongest, containing a huge amount of dialogue in the longest books of the poem. The denouement of Act V passes quickly in the last two books which relate the consequences of the crisis for the future of the earth, heaven and hell.

Aware that the reader knows the outcome of the narrative before starting to read Milton incorporated all the classical touches, such as beginning *in media res* and including a long retrospective section in the middle, slowing down the pace, making us wait for the climax of man's Fall and the terrible consequences. How the story is told provides variety to the familiar narrative and creates an appropriate level of reader engagement. It is unsurprising that there has been a number of successful adaptations for the stage of parts or the whole of the poem. Each set piece, ranging from the Infernal Debate to Adam and Eve's dialogue concerning Eve's desire to work alone, Satan's subsequent temptation of Eve and Adam and Eve's meeting following the successful temptation is able to operate as a single dramatic entity.

Analysis of the dramatic structure has, however, created disagreement over interpretation as well. David Hopkins[105] makes acute observations concerning the mechanism by which the poem operates but finds a curious link between structure and meaning. Hopkins examines the poem as a narrative, which has to be read as a whole like a drama and not in extracts. He argues: "It achieves its objective of 'justifying the ways of God to men' not by deductive reasoning or theological dogma, but by conducting us through an experimental process which conveys to us both the goodness of the divine dispensation which it imagines and the perils of rejecting that dispensation." The shape of the poem is certainly conceived as a whole but this conclusion is too close to that of Stanley Fish,[106] who sees the work as a spiritual exercise. It is difficult to see a direct link between the structure and the meaning of the poem, which surely derives from the words Milton attributed to his characters. Milton's characterisation is the most important link between style and content, as the outcome of characterisation precipitates the failure of the poem to achieve its aim but is central to the achievement of a different though successful outcome.

In *Paradise Lost* Milton united the epic and the domestic. Issues of universal significance, epic journeys, titanic forces, the battle between good and evil fought between God and Satan with their attendant angelic forces, Sin and Death, all expressed in an expansive and allusive style sit alongside the human dimension encompassing love, marriage, ambition, duty, obedience, the nature of authority and hierarchies. Yet Milton had a dramatist's eye for detail. *Paradise Lost* arose naturally from his interests and talents. Its failure to make us love God also derived from some of the same sources.

---

105 *Reading Paradise Lost*, Wiley-Blackwell, 2013

106 *Surprised by Sin* op cit

The poem as a play

	Book length in lines	Stage	Action	Dramatic Phase
ACT I		Introduction 1	Statement of Theme. Hell	EXPOSITION
	I 798		Milton's purpose explained and description of Hell	
	II 1055		The Infernal debate and Satan's journey	
ACT 2		Introduction 2	Heaven and earth	
	III 742		God and the Son. Satan takes directions from Uriel	
	IV 1015		Description of Eden	
ACT 3		Retrospective	Events leading to the current situation	DELAY ACTION TO BUILD TENSION FOR CRISIS
	V 907		Eve's dream. Raphael tells Adam about Free Will and Satan	
	VI 912		The Battle in Heaven	
	VII 640		The creation of the Earth	
	VIII 653		Raphael explains cosmology. Adam tells of his and Eve's creation	
ACT 4		The crisis	The quarrel, Eve's temptation, Adam's Fall	CATASTROPHE
	IX 1189		Eve is tempted and Adam follows. Adam and Eve quarrel	
	X 1104		Sin and Death build a causeway to Earth. Satan returns to Hell	
ACT 5		Consequences of the crisis	The future is foretold with the hope of redemption through Christ	DENOUEMENT
	XI 901		The Son intercedes with God on behalf of Man. Michael foretells mankind's future	
	XII 649		The Son's role foretold. Adam and Eve leave Eden reconciled	

14

The characterisation of a play

Persuaded by his experience of academia and politics, together with his insistence on tolerance and a dramatist's feel for imaginative identification with his characters Milton allowed his characters to speak fully for themselves. His skill lay in letting characters say what was in their minds but he also demonstrated how language may be used to mislead and persuade.

The dramatic intensity of the poem derives from the moral pressure experienced by the protagonists, especially Adam and Eve, alongside the sense of danger and conflict which is ever present. The conflict may be the inner torment of despair or the agony of making decisions between impossible options such as love of God or love of a spouse. The cosmic battle between good and evil exists at different points on a continuum, ranging from the battle in heaven, Satan's pursuit of mankind through Eve, Adam's disagreement with Eve and the inner conflicts experienced by Satan, Adam and Eve as they try to work out their destinies, to the staged positioning which takes place in the Infernal Debate of the Fallen Angels. All this derived from Milton's decision to give voice to the protagonists' words and thoughts, which is a long way from the Genesis narrative where blame is the sole ingredient of the story – Adam blames Eve, Eve blames the serpent, Satan blames God and God blames everyone:

> *Who told thee that thou wast naked? Hast thou eaten of the tree, whereof I commanded thee that thou shouldest not eat?*
>
> *And the man said, The woman whom thou gavest to be with me, she gave me of the tree, and I did eat.*

> *And the Lord God said unto the woman, What is it that thou hast done? And the woman said. The serpent beguiled me, and I did eat.*

Here the force of the message derives from simplicity of language. The Christian narrative is straightforward: mankind is disobedient. Eve should have obeyed both God and her husband and Adam should have been a stronger leader. Their failure to obey forces God to show himself to man in the human form of Jesus, who dies on the cross as recompense for our sin, rising from the dead to demonstrate God's continuing love for his people. The devil is wicked and should never have questioned God's authority. Every time a theologian or writer begins to unravel and develop the simple narrative, in whatever form, the powerful simplicity is lost, leading to more questions and doubts about the core issues.

Consequently, Milton's drama complicated the Christian message. By raising questions about alternative courses of action; by exposing contradictory ideas within the narrative and by the inclusion of the protagonists' strong emotions, insecurities and dilemmas the message of powerful simplicity which he tried to justify became clouded. What he did prove was that in practice living a human life on earth is not as simple as it sounds in theory. The complexity of human existence is graphically highlighted by attributing to the protagonists the thoughts and reactions of human beings facing life-changing decisions. God is cast as an autocratic ruler with the Son as his adoring child keen to inherit the throne; Eve raises entirely reasonable questions about how and when she and Adam are to develop and grow as people; Adam suffers the torment of being given the gift of love for his wife which he may then be forced to sacrifice when pressure to obey God is demanded, and Satan possesses strengths, which as an angel we would expect, but he rebels, begging the question about the origin of sin in creation.

It is worth bearing in mind that Milton's artistic aims, as expressed in *The Reason of Church Government,* make explicit his ambition to make full representations of his subjects and characters: "whatsoever in religion is holy and sublime, in virtue amiable or grave, whatsoever hath passion or admiration in all the changes of that which is called fortune from without, or the wily subtleties and refluxes of man's thoughts from within; all these things with a solid and treatable smoothness to paint out and describe." The last comment here warns us that we shall hear more in his poem than we have read in the Bible.

Eschewing 17th century stagecraft and courtly drama what Milton finally wrote was a Christian dramatic poem, epic in scale and tragic in tone. Indeed he fulfilled the ingredients for drama identified by Aristotle as spectacle, poetry, character and plot.[107] He gave to God, the Son, Satan, Adam and Eve human voices on a scale not seen in classical epics. It is unsurprising that so many dramatic adaptations for the stage and radio have been successfully produced. Milton imagined what the protagonists might have said but the consequence of this decision was to affect the poem irrevocably. This was to the advantage of Satan, Adam and Eve, who may be said to emerge as more sympathetic characters as we understand the dilemmas they raise, but to the disadvantage of God and the Son.

By presenting conversations and stand-offs between characters which mimic the academic and political disputations with which Milton was daily familiar, and the depth of characterisation which he would have known in Elizabethan and Jacobean drama, he did not write the poem he had planned. Instead, by enabling us to face the complexities of issues such as marriage, the nature of human society, obedience and Godhead we travel a thornier yet more satisfying road. Milton's achievement is all the greater for these unintended consequences.

---

107 *On the Art of Poetry*

15

The effects on his message of writing a verse drama

Milton's ambition to be the nation's epic poet was certainly in tune with the breadth and depth of the poem's narrative, and its elevated style which was matched by his powerfully imaginative descriptive technique. However, the control Milton wished to exert over the argument, the beauty of an elegantly structured defence, collided with his desire to write a poem which vividly dramatised the characters, bringing them to life on a fully conceived human dimension. His planned assertion of the reasonableness of obedience to a just God, conflicted with his more recently discovered but highly developed dramatic imagination. It was as if Milton did not foresee that he would be drawn ever closer to his dramatist's instinct to fill out the Genesis story of the Fall. By allowing characters to have their heads, Milton unleashed ideas that he could not control, leaving the reader with a barrage of competing ideas about the justness of God's ways. We know we should resist the temptation to question God's justice and his plan for mankind. That Milton does not convince every reader shows how successful drama may possess an uncanny power to persuade.

Two examples demonstrate some of the issues with which readers must grapple. Firstly, there is the problem of unquestioning obedience to God and free will. Raphael explains to Adam:

> *Our voluntary service he requires,*
> *Not our necessitated, nor can we find, for how*

Can hearts, not free, be tried whether they serve
Willing or no, who will but what they must
By destiny, and can no other choose?

(V 529-34)

In his note to these lines Alistair Fowler comments: "Raphael's emphasis – and the emphasis throughout *Paradise Lost* – on obedience, may at first seem coldly moralistic. But a steady and passionately committed discussion of free will and predestination in *De Doctrina I 3* soon suggests that obedience is for Milton bound up with the value of freedom. Only if God wishes obedience as a sign of faithful love can man's freedom of will have significance." He quotes from *De Doctrina*: "The acceptableness of duties done under a law of necessity is diminished, or rather is annihilated altogether, inasmuch as freedom can no longer be attributed to that will over which some fixed decree is inevitably suspended."[108] Religious orders throughout the ages have similarly argued that freedom comes through obedience.

However, we should not mistake *Paradise Lost* for a religious artefact to be meditated upon and used as a gateway to a new relationship with God. Milton's life and character indicated that this is not what he intended; he wanted a thinking readership which would come to make the right choices of their own volition. Milton may have had in mind that freedom through obedience was what he advocated but what occurs in the poem does not easily convince that obedience is the liberating concept Milton would have us believe. If it is art and not theology, *Paradise Lost* should be regarded as a dramatic poem and we should read it as we find it, appreciating the nuances of characterisation and dialogue, which frequently raise fundamental questions about God's ways.

Secondly, Milton advocated tolerance and the right of believers to access the scriptures without any priestly intermediary. Milton dealt with this in *De Doctrina i 3*. He wrote: "…it is evident that

---

108 Columbia xiv 141

the use of the scriptures is prohibited to no one; but that, on the contrary, they are adapted for the daily hearing or reading of all classes and orders of men..." He proceeded to argue that the scriptures were "in themselves so perspicuous, and sufficient of themselves...through what infatuation is it, that even Protestant divines persist in darkening the most momentous truths of religion by intricate metaphysical comments, on the plea that such explanation is necessary; stringing together all the useless technicalities and empty distinctions of scholastic barbarism, for the purpose of elucidating those scriptures, which they are continually extolling as models of plainness?"

He stressed that: "Every believer has a right to interpret the scriptures for himself, inasmuch as he has the Spirit for his guide..." and that "It is not therefore within the province of any visible church, much less of the civil magistrate, to impose their own interpretations on us as laws, or as binding on the conscience; in other words as matter of implicit faith." Tolerance was vital: "If, however, there be any difference among professed believers as to the sense of scripture, it is their duty to tolerate such difference in each other, until God shall have revealed the truth to all." For Milton this meant that: "the 'pillar and ground of the truth' has not uniformly been the church, but the hearts of believers, which are 'properly the house and church of the living God.'" Milton should therefore accept that not to agree with his interpretation of the Bible is our prerogative.

Milton's belief in Protestant individualism shone brightly through *De Doctrina.*[109] Written with the certainty of a young man recently returned from Italy, *De Doctrina* expressed the idealism which led Milton to believe in political democracy and a Protestant church comprising a congregation of independent believers. However, the author of *De Doctrina* is not universally accepted to be Milton and towards the end of his life he wrote

---

109 Milton's authorship of *De Doctrina* has been questioned. See Lieb *De Doctrina Christiana and the Question of Authorship* in *Milton Studies* 41, 2002

with rancour about the English people's inability to carry out the political revolution because they possessed neither the guts nor the brains. In fact Milton's view of democracy evolved to the point where he hardly seemed to be a democrat at all.

His repeated insistence on submission and obedience to the rules throughout *Paradise Lost* is tough to accept without understanding his concept of freedom through obedience. Confusingly Milton's certainty concerning obedience may clash with our right (even according to Milton himself) to hold alternative interpretations of the Bible. However, Milton's certainties are repeated: obedience is everything. Milton's own voice and insistence on obedience throughout the poem may even make him sound as authoritarian as his God. As his protagonists raise questions about God's ways the more insistent Milton becomes in order to prove that God's ways are just.

No matter how firm Milton's views appeared to be in prose about free will, obedience, foreknowledge and predestination, in writing a verse drama his *dramatis personae* unearthed questions about and objections to these fundamentals which just will not go away. The spotlight is on mankind rather than on God – our desire to know more, our yearning to discover our origin and purpose, and our frustration at having our dreams and aspirations constrained by our inability to know more about ourselves and our place in the universe. Even the Arguments which were designed to clarify the poem's intention are unable to hint at what riches await as we explore the layers of meaning.

V

The Voices

16

The Controller

Throughout the poem we sense the presence of a controlling poet marshalling evidence, sifting arguments and attempting to tidy up loose ends within a meticulously crafted epic structure. In Milton's quest for the perfectly articulated justification, logic and structural coherence were paramount, and a style commensurate with the task was required. However, he allowed his characters space to express their thoughts and emotions in a spirit of tolerance, consequently creating a more complex and thorough dramatisation than might be expected.

In his personal statements at the beginning of Books I and IX Milton highlighted the nature of the challenge he had set himself. He reminds us that the treatment of his theme is original: "my adventurous song", which deals with: "Things unattempted yet in prose or rhyme." He searches for an "answerable style," (IX 20), with which to handle the ultimate theological question: 'how exactly is God just?' Control of his medium is what we would expect from a poet possessing a missionary zeal to bring the English people back to trust in God.

Firm management led Milton to exert control over the epic grandeur he evoked, as he painstakingly structured the narrative to suit his argument, simultaneously incorporating the devices of epic poetry. He provided changes of pace and location to provide variety, which was especially important given that the narrative was so well known. He took pains to create a sense of place, which frequently comes to us via secondary images taken from classical literature, history and geography.

It is, however, in characterisation, dialogue and soliloquy that Milton excelled. He is frequently better with presentation of character than of place. A good example of a simile used to illustrate character occurs when Satan is tempting Eve; the guile of a politician's smooth tongue being the apt image:

As when of old some orator renowned
In Athens or free Rome, where eloquence
Flourished, since mute, to some great cause addressed,
Stood in himself collected, while each part,
Motion, each act won audience ere the tongue,
Sometimes in highth began, as no delay
Of preface brooking through his zeal of right.

(IX 670-676)

Not all Milton's images are 'thrown back into the distance;'[110] many possess a force and immediacy, but it is in characterisation that the full extent of Milton's imaginative powers is found.

Paradise Lost is a drama of the human voice, including Milton's own voice as narrator. Behind the drama Milton the director strove to be in control; sometimes he tried too hard to manage the performance but he is always the inventive force behind the production. He could not have been clearer about his aims and spared nothing in his efforts to make the epic style fit his theological argument. Everything from the ordering of the narrative to creating the hugeness of an epic poem without sacrificing moments of softness and calm carry the imprint of his hand. Managing the infrastructure and organisation of an epic came relatively easily to a poet such as Milton, who had accumulated the necessary knowledge to embark on the toughest literary enterprise. However, it is characterisation which contains the seeds of controversy.

Performing as a ventriloquist, he captured the distinctive voices of his protagonists, handling dialogue, grand speeches and soliloquy with precision. But his characters got away from

110 Coleridge op cit

him. He was so successful in his imaginative identification with them, so comprehensive and liberal in allowing them to express themselves that they are more compelling than the presentation of God and steal his show. Milton's control is firm in the matter of structure, epic aggrandisement and in creating variety through narrative ordering and tone but he had less success in reigning in his characters and utilising them to contribute to his theme of unquestioning obedience.

It was an extraordinarily complex creative process but the relative success of each component varies, and readers will have their own preferences. Milton had the huge task of managing the synthesis of classical learning and biblical allusion with the characteristics of epic poetry, which he then infused with emotionally charged dialogue, grandiose public speaking and intensely passionate human emotion within a tightly constructed drama. Descriptions of epic journeys through the universe, parallels drawn with heroic deeds of classical literature, similes drawing the reader's mind to parallel literary, historical or biblical events, sometimes even domestic ones: all play their part. Milton's 'Grand Style' provided the 'white noise', the epic backcloth against which the human drama is performed.

The heart of the poem's impact is based upon intense dialogue and soliloquy, where individuals or groups face making momentous decisions. It is when the poem is read aloud, heard and even watched as drama, that its energy, passion and humanity come together. It is then that the vibrancy, immediacy and universal significance of Milton's presentation of the human condition is brought to life.

17

Milton's own voice

Milton decided to involve himself as narrator to establish his identity as a seer, driven by a vision of himself as God's spokesman. He spent a lifetime defending causes and in *Paradise Lost* he is uncompromisingly insistent on the requirement for obedience to God. *Paradise Lost* is a religious poem but it is not devotional in the way that a poem by Herbert is. It is a massively learned, cerebral poem possessing a clearly stated objective, the voice of the pamphleteer arguing and persuading in defence of God. Despite this the sound of his characters drowns their creator's voices, who escape his control.

Using a form as stylised as an epic was a risk for a poet who wanted to write a convincing justification of God. Milton was greedy for fame as an epic poet, but he simultaneously possessed a religious mission and could not resist inserting vitriolic attacks. The assumption of a monkish habit in order to sneak into heaven: "Dying put on the weeds of Dominic, /Or in Franciscan think to pass disguised;" (III 479-80) found an echo in an attack on church corruption:

> *Then shall they seek to avail themselves of names,*
> *Places and titles, and with these to join*
> *Secular power, though feigning still to act*
> *By spiritual,*
>
> (XII 515-518)

and the nonsense, in Milton's view, of designated places of worship:

To teach thee that God attributes to place
No sanctity, if none be thither brought
By men who there frequent, or therein dwell.

(XI 836-838)

His special contempt was reserved for all things Roman Catholic, beginning with the orders of monks: "eremites and friars/White, black and gray, with all their trumpery." (III 474-475) leading to the vituperative:

Cowls, hoods and habits with their wearers tossed
And fluttered into rags, then relics, beads,
Indulgences, dispenses, pardons, bulls,
The sport of winds: all these upwhirled aloft
Fly o'er the backside of the world far off
Into a limbo large and broad, since called
The Paradise of Fools,

(III 490-496)

He refers to the way in which many Sectarians supported themselves by a trade or profession in contrast to over-indulged priests or "lewd hirelings" (IV 193). Later Michael foretells that:

Wolves shall succeed for teachers, grievous wolves,
Who all the sacred mysteries of heaven
To their own vile advantages shall turn
Of lucre and ambition,

(XII 508-511)

Death's causeway "wondrous art/Pontifical," (X 312-13), is an ironical play on the Pope's official title, and while eating lunch with Adam and Eve Raphael manages a swipe at the doctrine of transubstantiation:

but with keen despatch

Of real hunger, and concotive heat
To transubstantiate;

(V 436-438)

As narrator Milton highlighted significant issues such as his comments on the God-given differences between men and women which underpinned the authority vested in Adam:

Not equal, as their sex not equal seemed;
For contemplation he and valour formed,
For softness she and sweet attractive grace,
He for God only, she for God in him:

(IV 296-299)

His introductory lines and invocation in Book I are the first of many references to the great poetic company with which Milton wished to be numbered. He alerts us to the enormity of the task he has undertaken: "what in me is dark/Illumine, what is low raise and support;" (I 22-3). The invocation to Light at the start of Book III allows a similar opportunity, this time more personally by reference to his blindness, which may aid concentration on finding God: "these eyes, that roll in vain/To find thy piercing ray, and find no dawn;" (III 23-24). He adds weight to his poetic qualifications by drawing parallels between his fate and those of Thamyris, a Thracian poet, Maeonides, Homer himself and the prophets Tiresias and Phineus, firmly placing himself in the line of notable Greeks.[111] However, the moment leads to some of the most lyrical verse in the poem:

Thus with the year
Seasons return, but not to me returns
Day, or the sweet approach of even or morn,
Or sight of vernal bloom, or summer's rose,
Or flocks, or herds, or human face divine;
But cloud in stead, and ever-during dark

111 III 34-36

Surrounds me, from the cheerful ways of men
Cut off, and for the book of knowledge fair
Presented with a universal blank
Of nature's works to me expunged and razed,
And wisdom at one entrance quite shut out.

(III 40-50)

The beautiful phrase, "human face divine" provides a clue to Milton's view of his own role as interpreter of the divine for the benefit of the human. At the opening of Book IV his emotional involvement in Adam and Eve's Fall cannot be contained as he wishes he could have warned them about the temptations to follow.[112]

His most important intervention is at the start of Book IX, which pulls the narrative back to the human:

foul distrust, and breach
Disloyal on the part of man, revolt,
And disobedience:

(6-8)

He claims the subject to be more heroic than "Wars, hitherto the only argument/Heroic deemed," (28-29). Milton was conscious of the need to keep the reader's eye on the argumentative thrust. As Eve leaves Adam to work alone Milton could not, however, contain himself, intervening vigorously:

O much deceived, much failing, hapless Eve,
Of thy presumed return! Event perverse!

(IX 404-5)

Milton's voice is heard too in the occasional human detail, such as the opening of Book XII: "As one who in his journey bates at noon," and the mist that "gathers ground fast at the labourer's heel/Homeward returning,"(XII 631-2), or Satan's approaching

112 IV 1-8

the earth "And like a weather-beaten vessel holds/Gladly the port, though shrouds and tackle torn;" (II 1043-4), together with references to historical or contemporary journeys and figures, not least of which is Galileo. The effect is to provide some respite to the reader and a connection to reality.

On one level all seems well with the success of Milton's thesis: the wicked are punished and Adam learns his lesson: "Henceforth I learn, that to obey is best"(XII 561), and we have been instructed about the limits of what we are allowed to know:

> *Enough is left besides to search and know.*
> *But knowledge is as food, and needs no less*
> *Her temperance over appetite, to know*
> *In measure what the mind may well contain,*
> *Oppresses else with surfeit, and soon turns*
> *Wisdom to folly,*
>
> (VII 125-130)

> *the rest*
> *From man or angel the great architect*
> *Did well to conceal, and not divulge*
> *His secrets to be scanned by them who ought*
> *Rather admire;*
>
> (VIII 71-75)

Adam says all the right things and God is firmly in charge.

There is, however, frequently the sense that Milton tried too hard with his logic, for example pinning down details concerning angels in an effort to convince us. Among these is their self-healing ability:

> *for spirits that live throughout*
> *Vital in every part, not as frail man*
> *In entrails, heart or head, liver or reins,*
> *Cannot but by annihilating die;*

Nor in their liquid texture mortal wound
Receive, no more than can the fluid air:

(VI 344-349)

And:

Since now we find this our empyreal form
Incapable of mortal injury
Imperishable, and though pierced with wound,
Soon closing, and by native vigour healed.

(VI 433-436)

Their eating habits:

And to their viands fell, nor seemingly
The angel, nor in mist, the common gloss
Of theologians, but with keen despatch
Of real hunger, and concoctive heat
To transubstantiate;

(V 434-8)

And not least, angels' sex lives:

Let it suffice thee that thou know'st
Us happy, and without love no happiness.
Whatever pure thou in the body enjoy'st
(And pure thou wert created) we enjoy
In eminence, and obstacle find none
Of membrane, joint, or limb, exclusive bars:
Easier than air with air, if spirits embrace,
Total they mix, union of pure with pure
Desiring; nor restrained conveyance need
As flesh to mix with flesh, or soul with soul.

(VIII 620-629)

Day and night in Heaven are described as being different to the earthly equivalent:

There is a cave
Within the mount of God, fast by his throne,
Where light and darkness in perpetual round
Lodge and dislodge by turns, which makes through heaven
Grateful vicissitude, like day and night;

(VI 4-8)

By contrast the contours of earth mimic those in heaven: "(For earth hath this variety from heaven/Of pleasure situate in hill and dale)," (VI 640-1).

When Adam tells Raphael about his and Eve's creation we might have expected Raphael to know this already, given his position in the heavenly hierarchy. In order to give Adam a reason for telling the tale Milton is forced to invent a situation; like a schoolboy Raphael admits that he does not know about the creation of man because he was away that day:

For I that day was absent, as befell,
Bound on a voyage uncouth and obscure,
Far on excursion toward the gates of hell;
Squared in full legion (such command we had)
To see that none thence issued forth a spy,
Or enemy, while God was in his work,

(VIII 229-234)

He adds an awkward qualification to prevent God from seeming weak:

Not that they durst without his leave attempt,
But us he sends upon his high behests
For state, as sovereign king, and to inure
Our prompt obedience.

(VIII 237-240)

This makes matters worse, as God now appears to have sent Raphael away merely because he could: it is another test.

Of course an epic has to be all-inclusive but in his attempt to use human logic in God's defence Milton was forced into occasionally jarring moments. Indeed, by insisting on the corporeality of angels, particularly in their eating habits, he was going against the views of Protestant theologians. On the other hand, there are situations where apparently prosaic explanation is legitimately required, such as the question of whether there are seasons in paradise:

> *Raised of grassy turf*
> *Their table was, and mossy seats had round,*
> *And on her ample square from side to side*
> *All autumn piled, though spring and autumn here*
> *Danced hand in hand,*
>
> (V 391-395)

This echoes the classical view that the seasons in paradise were simultaneously present.

There are then moments when the sound of Milton's voice is to be welcomed, even if on occasion he seemed to be trying too hard. His repeated references to his position in a line of distinguished poets and prophets are also more than egoism, assisting him to give the Christian epic its due literary and theological place.

Milton's voice insisting on mankind's duty of obedience to God is, however, more than matched by the contrary sound of others' voices. In his portraits of Adam, Eve and Satan, in stark contrast to the simpler allegorical figures, Milton faced truths about humanity which were not dealt with as straightforwardly as exhortations to use reason and obey God might suggest. Milton's stretched plane of reality began with allegory and caricature and culminated in complex and compelling protagonists. His debt to Hebraic and other sources may be apparent, but so is the originality of his creative imagination. Paradoxically, however, Milton's humanising of the heavenly angels, God and the Son opens difficulties for his aim, as these figures raise matters which do not help the argument of the drama. Satan, Adam and Eve on the other hand benefit from being allowed to put forward their questions and anxieties about God and his universe, though the reader must remain vigilant in assessing their reasoning and motivation.

18

Allegorical figures

Sin, Death and Chaos are extraordinary allegorical figures, neither humans nor spirits. At first glance their inclusion stretched the already taut plane of reality on which Milton was working: king of the uncreated world, the monstrous figure of Sin, and Death, progeny of the brutally incestuous relationship between Satan and Sin. They have precedents in the monsters of epic narratives and mythology, and highlight the almost palpable awfulness of wickedness; Milton did, however, make these figures his own. Their relationships break all taboos and subvert all morality but because he presented them as grotesque distortions rather than human figures, in contrast to his protagonists and even angels, Milton retained control over them and their roles.

In a different context Chaos might have been presented as an ancient drunken lord, a crumpled Sir Toby Belch wearing a skewed crown greeting Satan as he journeys from Hell to Earth.[113] Whilst it might have made an effective comic turn in a miracle or morality play Milton's Chaos, along with "eldest Night" (II 894), Orcus, Ades, Demogorgon, Rumour, Chance, Tumult, Confusion and Discord,[114] is a powerless, confused parody of a monarch, an: "anarch old/With faltering speech and visage incomposed" (II 989-990). Milton managed to make Chaos sound like a grumpy old man. He complains that his territory is being denuded by the building works undertaken by God in creating Hell and Earth but expresses a willingness to

113 In fact it is Death who wears "The likeness of a kingly crown" II 673

114 II 962-967

assist a traveller and is respectful of Satan's courage in leading a rebellion and making the journey through his lands, describing Satan as "That mighty leading angel" (II 991). He does, however, relish the prospect of the "Havoc, spoil and ruin" (II 1009) which will be his gain should Satan's mission prove successful.

Sin is first described at II 648:

> *The one seemed woman to the waist, and fair,*
> *But ended foul in many a scaly fold*
> *Voluminous and vast, a serpent armed*
> *With mortal sting:*

but the full impact is deliberately withheld, as she is not named until II 760. Horror is created by the accumulation of grisly detail, but the all too human horror of incest, with the revelation that Satan has challenged his own son/grandson, is a powerful image which is also delayed.[115] The contemporary reference to witches[116] adds the spice of seventeenth century concerns, together with geographical allusions to the Arctic sky and Caspian storm, whilst mention of Circe, Scylla and Hecate overlays the mythological dimension. Similes serve to help describe the indescribable, as well as Satan's reaction to his son: "like a comet burned, /That fires the length of Ophiucus huge/ In the Arctic sky," (II 708-710).

Unsurprisingly the description of Sin's birth[117] stuns the population of Heaven: "amazement seized/All the host of Heaven;" (II 758-9). This daughter/lover speaks in the manner of a gangster's moll, gloating at the prospect of being on the arm of her husband/father. She shares Satan's hatred of God, who sent her to Hell's gates, whilst her parody on obedience to her father seals her character. Satan has swiftly got her measure and offers her what he knows she will want; he is correct:

115 II 727-8

116 II 665

117 II 752-758

Thou art my father, thou my author, thou
My being gavest me; whom should I obey
But thee, whom follow? Thou wilt bring me soon
To that new world of light and bliss, among
The gods who live at ease, where I shall reign
At thy right hand voluptuous, as beseems
Thy daughter and thy darling without end.

(II 864-870)

Hardly to describe Death's appearance at all seems an effective solution:

black it stood as night,
Fierce as ten Furies, terrible as hell,
And shook a dreadful dart; what seemed his head
The likeness of a crown had on.

(II 670-673)

This parody of the Lord of Misrule is very powerful. Unlike Chaos Death has no respect for what Satan achieved in heaven "in proud rebellious arms," (II 692) but sees himself as superior to Satan in approaching Hell's gates "Where I reign king," (II 698). Death is a bully, made all the more horrific because he is attacking his own father. His language is all aggression; he is only pacified by the promise of the prey that will come his way should Satan be successful in corrupting mankind, "upstart creatures," (II 834). Like his mother/sister he also has his price.

This and other episodes featuring the pair enable us to appreciate the human depths of Milton's characterisation of Satan, Adam and Eve, but provide an important variety of mood, pace and scene that was essential to the epic dimension. Sin and Death are related to figures from mystery and miracle plays but the layers of texture which Milton adds through his descriptive techniques prevents them from becoming a comedy subplot. Theologically the description of Sin appearing from Satan's head is a parody of the relationship between God and the Son, though missing out the theological problems which surrounded that relationship, but the overt descriptions of incest, violence and horror build a powerful momentum.

Most important is the light all this sheds upon the character of Satan. In the middle of Heaven, amidst the Heavenly Host, he gave birth to Sin and proceeded to have an incestuous relationship with her. Heartless to the point of not recognising his own daughter, he is doomed to pick a fight with his own son like a character from Greek tragedy. Satan's wile continues beyond the Infernal Debate in his quickly determining how to calm both Sin and Death through the pretence of having their interests at heart in the manner of the good husband/father/grandfather he is by promising Death more fodder and freeing both of them from "this dark and dismal house of pain," (II 823).

Milton's images of Sin and Death could only successfully inhabit the world of an epic poem. Apart from Chaos it is hard to imagine their presentation on stage, their only reality being in Milton's mind. They are saved from pantomime simplicity by serving God's purposes in the future punishment of mankind and having theological significance though their emotions and language are those of types. Importantly the sickening subversion of conventional relationships represented by Sin, Death and Satan highlights by contrast the depth of Adam and Eve's love for each other.

19

Angels

Paradise Lost is full of angels, their inescapable presence being set alongside the two human characters. The Fallen Angels and the Heavenly Host together with the messengers and functionaries who maintain the momentum of the narrative are essential to Milton's story. His success in portraying the human pair sits alongside the challenge of portraying angels. Milton's difficulty in presenting angels highlights the complex task he faced in writing a poem in which he was able to bring the human figures credibly to life whilst also successfully creating allegorical types such as Sin and Death. Creatures possibly lacking any known substance were a greater challenge. Not only are there problems regarding the appearance of angels but also considerable theological challenges. What is the precise status of angels when they appear to sit between man and God? Can they have personalities? What do they do all day if they are not out on a mission? Do they eat? Do they have sexual relations? Do they ever disagree with one another, or with God? How is it that some angels joined the rebel force when others did not? What is the origin of evil?

Questions regarding the status and role of angels had been under discussion long before Milton attempted to portray them.[118] Traditional Roman Catholic teaching had its origins as far back as the 6th century Syrian Dionysius who focussed on

118 See *In the Anteroom of Divinity: The Reformation of the Angels from Colet to Milton* by Feisal G Mohamed, University of Toronto Press 2008 and *Milton's Angels: The Early Modern Imagination* by Joad Raymond, Oxford University Press 2010

the ninefold hierarchy of angels and their place in an ordered creation. Recent Protestant theologians on the other hand had questioned the need for angels to mediate between man and God, relying instead on the Bible, God's grace and the faith of believers.[119] Milton is, however, unable to manage without them. Angels start a rebellion, build an alternative home when they are expelled from heaven, plot revenge, talk to humans (in the case of Satan by first inserting himself into the body of a serpent) bring messages from God, act as the historians of heaven by telling Adam about earlier events and offer consolation to Adam and Eve as they are escorted from Eden having been presented images of the future. It was a formidable mountain for a poet-dramatist to climb and Milton found different solutions to suit each set of circumstances, while sometimes finding himself in a tangle in mediating between their 'divine' and 'human' characteristics.

Fallen Angels

In the caricatures presented in the Infernal Debate, we see three personifications of Anger, Sloth and Greed alongside slick political machinations of the leaders. The speakers in the ironically named conclave are cartoon politicians and Milton exerts masterful control over the scene. He is successful chiefly because although what the speakers stand for is clear he does not delve too deeply into their personalities, rather it is what they stand for that matters most. Milton seems at ease with the technique he adopted, managing this plane of reality skilfully, and does not complicate matters by deviating from caricature or personification into realism. It is hard not to see in the speeches the influence of both university and political debate, though the deftness of Milton's handling of this technique demonstrates that his light touch was packed with insight, adding variety to

119 On the work of Colet and Hooker for example see Mohamed op cit.

the poem whilst skilfully preparing us for future events. An important source for this section of the poem, which connects with the general influence of Hebraic material on the poem, is John Selden.[120] Milton used Selden's historical information concerning ancient gods[121] but steadfastly adhered to a critical presentation of such pagan ideas by not giving the three personifications in the debate any hint of sympathy through a fuller characterisation, which may have tempted the reader to agree with them.

In answer to the announcement of the debate's title: "Whether of open war, or covert guile," (II 41) against God and his new creation Milton identifies three clear standpoints. Moloch the warrior immediately asserts: "My sentence is for open war", (II 51). He portrays himself as a plain-speaking, practical warrior. Despite his plea for honour and revenge there is a clear sense that the tired and wretched Fallen Angels do not have the appetite for further hardship.

Belial picks up this theme, disguising his innate cowardice and sloth by suggesting they make themselves as comfortable as possible where they are, against the insurmountable forces of Heaven. His "tongue dropped manna" (II 113) and in carefully crafted mellifluous tones his words represent the political ploy of gaining the votes by giving the electorate what they want. Milton concludes that this view merely recommends "ignoble ease and peaceful sloth" (II 225). Milton describes Belial's argument as: "words clothed in reason's garb" (II 226), highlighting an example of wrong reasoning, or points made in an apparently convincing manner with each morally weak. However, Belial merely states the obvious, that they should stay where they are and keep their heads down as God planned. Belial is lazy but confusingly he is also correct in acknowledging God's powerfully unstoppable watch over them.

Mammon's view takes this argument to its next stage by

120 See Jason P Rosenblatt op cit Chapter 3 'Selden and Milton on Gods and Angels'

121 *De Diis Syris ('On the Syrian Gods')*published 1617

painting a picture of false grandeur; by staying in Hell they can live a life which apes their former glory: "This desert soil/Wants not her hidden lustre, gems and gold;/Nor want we skill or art." (II 270-2). Mammon was in fact:

> *the least erected spirit that fell*
> *From heaven, for even in heaven his looks and thoughts*
> *Were always downward bent, admiring more*
> *The riches of heaven's pavement, trodden gold,*
> (I 679-682)

In a corruption of faith in God he uses reason in a twisted way by claiming that God may yet be found in Hell: "How oft amidst/ Thick clouds and dark doth heaven's all-ruling sire/Choose to reside, his glory unobscured," (II 263-265).

Beelzebub seems to save the day, firstly by his mere presence:

> *in his rising seemed*
> *A pillar of state; deep on his front engraven*
> *Deliberation sat and public care;*
> (II 301-303)

But this is soon revealed to be a sham. In turning to Satan as their rescuer, therefore absolving the rest of all responsibility and risk, he reveals the entire debate as a contrivance leading to this moment: "his devilish counsel, first devised/By Satan, and in part proposed" (II 379-380). The appearance of democracy was a charade, a hellish masque performed by the wicked and orchestrated by Satan. Beelzebub demolishes all three previous arguments for the shallow responses they were intended to be. The peace the devils want is unattainable, for Heaven is impregnable and Hell was always intended by God as a punishment: "our dungeon, not our safe retreat" (II 317). "War hath determined us" (II 330) strikes an appropriately bellicose chord, yet magically this would be at no risk to the Fallen Angels: "What if we find/Some easier enterprise?" (II 344-345). The suggestion that they should corrupt mankind, the newest of God's creations, seems a more attainable goal, satisfying the desire for revenge, yet the electorate can both assuage its conscience and accept something that carries no danger to them. Beelzebub then slips in the final blow: "But first, whom shall we send/In search of this new world?" (II 402-403). The Fall of man is sealed.

Like Milton, Satan is the arch controller. The superficiality of the first three speakers gives way to Satan's offer to take full responsibility for their futures without danger to the devils. The true cunning lies in Satan's avoidance of impractical ploys by his proposal of a middle way, taking something from all the other arguments and thus acceptable to the masses for its simplicity. Beelzebub and Satan understand their audience. Both use flattery. Beelzebub calls them by their former names: "Thrones and imperial powers, offspring of Heaven,/Ethereal virtues" (II 310-311), while Satan congratulates them on making a good decision:

> *Well have ye judged, well ended long debate,*
> *Synod of gods, and like to what ye are,*
> *Great things resolved.*
>
> (II 390-392)

Yet Satan has been behind the entire pantomime, providing hope: "I give not Heaven for lost," but painting such a terrible picture of the arduous and dangerous nature of the task that no one else would step forward to volunteer.

Satan achieves his goal, his own ambition well on the way to fulfilment:

> *Toward him they bend*
> *With awful reverence prone; and as a god*
> *Extol him equal to the highest in Heaven.*
>
> (II 477-479)

The scene shows Milton at his best. His understanding of how the electorate responds to dire situations, knowledge of their instinctive reactions at such times, deft presentation of political manipulation using sharply drawn caricatures or personifications contribute to the success of this set piece. As the precursor to Satan's temptation of Eve it alerts us to what we may expect later: Milton was building his defence of God.

The Heavenly Host

'What do angels do?' is a question that may nag the reader throughout the narrative, and it is to Milton's credit that while he does not provide answers that from a terrestrial standpoint make complete sense, we do learn more about some angels when they are involved in particular tasks or errands. Paradoxically, however, it is the all too human characteristics and frailties which Milton attributes to them that make them interesting, even problematic. In contrast to his allegorical figures and personifications it is the more humanly credible weaknesses and mistakes of these angels which makes their status as angels harder to understand and occasionally distorts what Milton is trying to say. As we read the poem we sense that the closer Milton brings us to his characters, the more we delve into their minds and actions the denser the writing becomes; the more he attributes human characteristics and foibles not only to angels but also protagonists including God, the Son and Satan, the more complex, even argumentative and critical is our reaction to the view Milton wishes us to take. His ability to create characters from biblical figures resulted in a distortion of what he plans to say and this extends to angels.

Unless they are acting as God's messengers the Heavenly Host rarely has a function apart from praising God, and even some of their missions seem pointless. Angels simply soak up the grandeur of God himself:

Thus while God spake, ambrosial fragrance filled
All heaven, and in the blessed spirits elect
Sense of new joy ineffable diffused:

(III 135-137)

The heavenly aroma is all-pervading, as seen in Raphael's introduction:

Like Maia's son he stood,
And shook his plumes, that heavenly fragrance filled
The circuit wide.

(V 285-287)

Their eating and sexual habits are simply on a higher spiritual level than man's: "Food alike those pure/intelligential substances require," (V 407-8), which Raphael proves by sharing a meal with Adam and Eve, yet he proceeds to explain the Platonic movement or a scale of being from earthly to heavenly. In Heaven food is even easier to find than in Eden, for the:

trees
Of life ambrosial fruitage bear, and vines
Yield nectar, though from off the boughs each morn
We brush mellifluous dews, and find the ground
Covered with pearly grain:

(V 426-430)

As far as sex is concerned, despite Raphael's very human blush at the thought: "with a smile that glowed/Celestial rosy red, love's proper hue," (VIII 618-619) he coyly explains that angels enjoy sexual relations but without the inconvenience of anything physical, "easier than air with air," (VIII 626).

Angels support God's actions with choruses of approval but demonstrate a collective personality by showing disagreement or remaining silent when not one of them steps forward to volunteer for the role ultimately taken by the Son. Milton is occasionally forced into awkwardness, as when Adam has to tell Raphael about the details of mankind's creation because Raphael missed the announcement when he was away on an errand:

> *say therefore on;*
> *For I that day was absent, as befell,*
> *Bound on a voyage uncouth and obscure,*
> *Far on excursion toward the gates of hell;*
>
> (VIII 228-231)

Angels are capable of feeling anger, such as in the war with the rebels:

> *Rage prompted them at length, and found them arms*
> *Against such hellish mischief fit to oppose.*
>
> (VI 635-636)

though the dice are already loaded against the enemy and they had no need to feel anything: "(behold the excellence, the power/Which God hath in his mighty angels placed)" (VI 637-638). They are able to throw away their arms and rip up hills, which they proceed to hurl at the rebels.

Milton had trouble with the angels' reluctance to volunteer to save mankind, which is required in order to enhance the reputation of the Son who is able to step forward:

> *He asked, but all the heavenly choir stood mute,*
> *And silence was in heaven: on man's behalf*
> *Patron or intercessor none appeared.........*
> *.........................had not the Son of God,*
> *In whom the fulness dwells of love divine,*
> *His deepest mediation thus renewed.*
>
> (III 217-226)

When the Son's offer and position have been ratified by God, there is cheering from the Heavenly Host:

The multitude of angels with a shout
Loud as the numbers without number, sweet
As from blest voices, uttering joy, heaven rung
With jubilee, and loud hosannas filled
The eternal regions: lowly reverent
Towards either throne they bow

(III 345 – 350)

The awkwardness remains, however, suspended between the requirement for the Son to step forward and the semi-humanising of the angelic host. A parallel to this has already been seen in Pandemonium as the Fallen Angels similarly bow to Satan following his volunteering to undertake a task they had not desired:

Towards him they bend
With awful reverence prone; and as a god
Extol him equal to the highest in heaven:

(II 477-479)

Joy in Heaven that a volunteer has been found leads to a quiet life for the angels:

Thus they in heaven, above the starry sphere,
Their happy hours in joy and hymning spent.

(III 416-417)

There may be a hint of relief here, and there is a contented return to glorifying God. By contrast, in Hell:

Thence more at ease their minds and somewhat raised
By false presumptuous hope, the ranged powers
Disband, and wandering, each his several way
Pursues, as inclination or sad choice
Leads him perplexed; where he may likeliest find
Truce to his restless thoughts

(II 521-526)

Whilst the Heavenly Host had seemed equally backward in coming forward they are content to praise God, whilst the Fallen Angels have to occupy their minds, filling in time to quell their "restless thoughts" with Olympic-style games, music, poetry, philosophy, or exploration, the latter vividly described in an expansive example of Milton's epic style.[122] A fickle group, the Fallen Angels are easily led, so long as a leader provides them with security and no involvement for themselves. Milton's point, however, is that Fallen Angels will never revive their earlier state of contentment. Yet Milton's semi-humanising of the Heavenly Host may lead us to wonder about the nature of contentment in Heaven, how exactly the minds of angels work and the nature of their existence, which were it not for the drama and action of the rebellion would seem static, even idle to human eyes. These are the questions Milton risks us asking.

Abdiel

Abdiel seems to be the one angel with attitude, though like the other angels who speak for God he is only given the argument of obedience. The one voice to be heard standing up to Satan when he is stirring the angels to rebellion, Abdiel supports the promotion of the Son, so hated by Satan. However, Abdiel's defence is that this was the "just decree of God," (V 814). This demonstrates a laudable defence of God in the face of Satan's questioning of God's right to make such decisions. Milton's presentation of this moment might be criticised for the way he presents the elevation of the Son into an all too familiar human form of nepotism. Abdiel's obedience is correct, but Satan had a point when he complained earlier of the unexpected announcement by God of the Son's new role, "Strange point and new," (V 855) though it is not made clear whether or not Satan may have harboured such thoughts previously. Of course Milton's point is that we are not supposed to know everything

122 II 570-628

about God's motives but the scene takes on an historical setting of rebellion with which Milton was clearly familiar:

> *...us eclipsed under the name*
> *Of king anointed, for whom all this haste*
> *Of midnight march, and hurried meeting here,*
> *This only to consult how we may best*
> *With what may be devised of honours new*
> *Receive him coming to receive from us*
> *Knee-tribute yet unpaid, prostration vile,*
>
> (V 776-782)

Abdiel's opposition, though correct: "Unshaken, unseduced, unterrified," (V 899) is too easily subverted by Satan in front of the other rebels into appearing an act of acquiescence, even though it is hard to see what else Milton could have him say, at this the earliest (in the chronology of the narrative) mention of obedience in the poem. Oddly, Abdiel seems to know what he is not in a position to know: "Decrees/Against thee are gone forth without recall;" (V 884-5), adding to the sense that those who speak for God have some of the weakest lines. Alternatively Abdiel could be lying. This opens a whole new hornets' nest of issues concerning the origins of evil, for if Abdiel is deliberately telling a lie then Satan is not alone in his deceit.[123] The explanation may be more simply that Milton is trying too hard to create the dramatic spirit of such an encounter and attributes to Abdiel an all too human threat or boast to support his act of defiance against Satan. Curiously, on his return to Heaven at the beginning of Book VI Abdiel rushes in eager to tell the latest news concerning the rebels, when to his surprise he finds the heavenly army already fully briefed and preparations for war well underway. His thunder having been stolen his spirits are raised by the warm reception he receives: "with joy and acclamations loud," (VI 23) as he is led to the sacred hill to be presented "Before the seat supreme" (VI 27) where he is praised

123 See Joad Raymond op cit

by God for his steadfastness "in word mightier than they in arms;" (VI 32).

This is an interesting cameo which highlights the larger issue of the theological consequences of Milton's imaginative identification with the scene and the personality of Abdiel. Not least of these is the matter of whether or not angels really can possess such personalities as that shown by Abdiel.

Functionaries and Emissaries

Other than the heavenly army Raphael, Michael, Gabriel and Uriel are the angels who have definite roles. Raphael and Michael allow Milton a means of passing messages from God to man, especially in providing God's insurance by reminding Adam about obedience, free will and the sin of eating fruit from the Tree of Knowledge. They also enable him to set the Fall in context by filling in the history of the rebellion in heaven and the creation of the universe, in so far as Adam is allowed to know about it, and finally to map out future events. More straightforwardly Gabriel and Uriel hold specific responsibilities for security.

Occasionally angels are given seemingly pointless tasks. There was no need for Raphael, for example, to check that no spy was being sent from Hell during the creation of earth because God would have known this: "Not that they durst without his leave attempt" (VIII 237). Some jobs seem to be given merely as a time-filling exercise or a test of angels' obedience:

> *But us he sends upon his high behests*
> *For state, as sovereign king, and to inure*
> *Our prompt obedience.*
>
> (VIII 238-240)

Here God seems more concerned with exercising his ability to command his subjects just because he can or testing their obedience than in providing satisfying or meaningful roles for them.

In terms of characterisation the functionaries and emissaries are the least satisfactory in the poem, which seems odd given the importance of their roles and the huge amount of narrative responsibility given to them. They have their distinct characteristics and do make mistakes but they are conscious of being answerable to God and attempt, not always successfully, to achieve God's aims. We cannot but sympathise with Adam, for example, whose questions to Raphael about creation and the universe remain unanswered because of the limitations placed by God on them both. We are also confronted by Milton on occasion trying too hard to ascribe human characteristics to the leading angels, which unfortunately leads either to their appearing silly or producing inconsistencies, thereby raising questions concerning God's creation and his plans for it. Faisal Mohamed[124] argues that all four of these angels fail to perform competently. To some extent this may be true but we should also understand the way Milton's imagination was at work. Angels should be perfect but if they are to some degree presented as if they are real people then they will behave accordingly. Extending and deepening the natures of angels with some human attributes does, therefore, frequently rebound on Milton's plans.

Raphael

Our initial impression of Raphael is of a supremely elegant, almost regal figure. Hierarchy is important in Heaven. His wings shade his "lineaments divine" (V 278) and another pair provides "regal ornament" (V 280). The middle pair of wings have "colours dipped in heaven" (V283) and as a leading Archangel Raphael exudes the fragrance earlier associated with God: "And shook his plumes, that heavenly fragrance filled/ The circuit wide" (286-7). The surrounding angels know

124 In *The New Milton Criticism* edited Herman and Sauer, Cambridge University Press 2012

him to be important and "in honour rise" (V 289). On seeing this creature Adam immediately calls Eve to come and see for herself, instructing her to prepare some food for their guest. Indeed Raphael is a "godlike guest" (V 351).

Raphael has the hardest task, given that he must prompt Adam regarding his duty as Eve's guardian, and of his duty of obedience to God:

> *God made thee perfect, not immutable;*
> *And good he made thee, but to persevere*
> *He left it in thy power, ordained thy will*
> *By nature free, not overruled by fate*
> *Inextricable, or strict necessity;*
>
> (V 524-528)

Mohamed's argument[125] that Raphael is a failure because Adam does everything he is told not to exaggerates the point. Raphael puts forward what he has been instructed to: "let it profit thee to have heard/By terrible example the reward/ Of disobedience;" (VI 909-10) and it is Adam's choice whether or not he obeys. It cannot be true to say that Raphael begins well by stating that man may proceed by stages to the level of angels because he then destroys this by saying it all hinges on obedience, prompting Adam to ask for clarification on that point (V 512-14). Equally it seems if anyone is to blame here it is surely Milton, whose aim throughout is to emphasise obedience and it is a natural juncture for Raphael to do this. Nor can it be fair to accuse Raphael of not alerting Adam more fully to Satan's plot against him. True God instructs Raphael:

> *tell him withal*
> *His danger, and from whom, what enemy*
> *Late fallen himself from heaven, is plotting now*
> *The fall of others from like state of bliss;*
>
> (V 238-241)

125 ibid

and it is also true that it is as a result of Adam's questioning that Raphael tells the story of the rebellion but it is not certain that he would never have mentioned this without Adam's question. Raphael reveals that Satan is a threat and is: "now plotting how he may seduce/Thee also from obedience," (VI 901-2). Adam is also warned again: "take heed lest passion sway/Thy judgment," (VIII 635-6). Providing more detail would have been like giving Adam the examination question plus the answer before the test had started. Adam and Eve must be on the alert at all times; that is Milton's point and Raphael eventually does as he had been instructed. Faisal's objection to the fact that Raphael appears to ignore Eve in his meetings with Adam is not relevant to the outcome. It is clear from the outset that God regards Adam as the responsible head of the family even though it is Eve who eventually has to face Satan in the guise of the serpent. She also prefers to hear things from Adam (VIII 52-3). On the other hand Raphael's coyness regarding sex may be an endearing touch but adds little to the story of the Fall or much to our understanding of angels.

He has then to recount the story of the revolt in Heaven and answer Adam's questions but in this he is hampered by being allowed to tell only what God has decreed is within man's limits to know. In fact the purpose of the narration of the revolt in heaven, other than extending the narrative to include a battle in epic style, seems intended as a warning to Adam, as Raphael chillingly concludes Book VI with the lines:

> *let it profit thee to have heard*
> *By terrible example the reward*
> *Of disobedience; firm they might have stood,*
> *Yet fell; remember, and fear to transgress.*
>
> (VI 909-912)

In neither case does Raphael ask the questions which only Satan seems to have the courage to voice. Such matters as why God allowed the Fallen Angels to revolt and where they fit into the grand scheme of things does not occur to him. Along with the other functionaries Raphael seems to be trying hard, reading painstakingly from a script lest he should say the wrong thing but occasionally not being perfect, which is what we might have expected of an angel. This makes his narration of earlier events seem bland, though presumably factually accurate, and it is little wonder that Adam asks questions about matters he soon learns are beyond his comprehension. The lines:

> *knowledge is as food, and needs no less*
> *Her temperance over appetite, to know*
> *In measure what the mind may well contain,*
>
> (VII 126-128)

epitomise the crushing of Adam's thirst for knowledge and Eve's ambition to be creative in planning their work, which are two of the unintended human consequences of Milton's poem. Raphael takes the opportunity to point out the differences between Heaven and earth, such as the fact that day and night exist in Heaven, but only: "for change delectable, not need" (V 629). This is a detail unnecessary in the context of the narrative but demonstrates Milton's determination to control his material, leaving no stone unturned. However, when Raphael says to Adam that he is about to tell him things: "perhaps/Not lawful to reveal," (V 569-70) this is untrue, for he never strays beyond his remit. We do not know how far Raphael's knowledge extends, particularly in the matter of Adam and Eve's Fall. If he has foreknowledge then we may sympathise with his delicate task.

Gabriel

Gabriel's role is to be the guardian of Eden. However, Milton's portrait shows him to be a not very effective guard and his inclusion precipitated a dilemma for Milton. Satan is of course successful in penetrating Eden and tempting Eve, so any guard is going to appear either inattentive or inefficient or both. The human dimension of the angel, seen best in his conversations with Satan, is therefore doomed from the first.

Gabriel is given words which merely prompt what Milton wished us to hear from Satan and Gabriel's character suffers as a result of this function. Gabriel asks why Satan came, which elicits the forceful response:

> *thou hadst in heaven the esteem of wise,*
> *And such I held thee; but this question asked*
> *Puts me in doubt.*
>
> (IV 886-888)

This highlights the pointlessness of the question, since escape from Hell's torment was obvious to Satan: "Lives there who loves his pain?" (IV 888). If Gabriel's next query concerning why Satan travelled alone is an attempt to aggravate Satan the response merely allows him to speak glowingly of his personal courage and public service but in so doing Milton is able to demonstrate the high opinion of himself which Satan has, or at least the reputation to which he aspires. Again Milton sacrifices the impression we have of Gabriel on the altar of exposing Satan.

Gabriel then has an opportunity to taunt him further by accusing Satan of moving from one explanation to another:

> *pretending first*
> *Wise to fly pain, professing next the spy,*
> *Argues no leader but a liar traced,*
>
> (IV 947-949)

Satan refers to himself as a "faithful leader" (IV 933) to which Gabriel responds with fierce and angry words. The ongoing exchange appears to be sterile but Milton's objective is to allow an opportunity for Satan to condemn himself through his own words. Mohamed[126] pushes his view of Gabriel too far when he writes that Gabriel witnesses Satan at Eve's ear as she sleeps and accuses him of being there "to violate sleep" (IV 883) and thus, according to Mohamed, mistaking his purpose. However, we do not know precisely what Gabriel means by 'violate'; it could be to disturb Eve's sleep but he could also be referring to an attempt to tempt Eve, it is not clear. Mohamed is correct in stating that after Gabriel points to the heavenly scales Satan understands their meaning and flees:

> *Satan, I know thy strength, and thou know'st mine,*
> *Neither our own but given; what folly then*
> *To boast what arms can do, since thine no more*
> *Than heaven permits, nor mine*
>
> (IV 1006-1009)

but Gabriel and his troop make no effort to stop him, thus allowing Satan to return to Eden.

To display Satan's guile and bravado was the reason for the encounter. There is little doubt that God had ordained the moment. Gabriel becomes the instrument by which this statement of God's victory and Satan's defeat is made and Gabriel is the classic functionary whose character is sacrificed to his function.

Michael

Michael is also charged with making Eden secure but importantly escorts Adam and Eve from there and provides consoling words about the future:

> *If patiently thy bidding they obey,*
> *Dismiss them not disconsolate; reveal*
> *To Adam what shall come in future days,*
>
> (XI 112-114)

126 Op cit

for God wishes them to leave "sorrowing, yet in peace" (XI 117). The tone is established by Michael's change in appearance from Archangel "but as man/Clad to meet man;" (XI 239-40), though he carries a sword and spear.

His tone is important, for he seeks reconciliation: "patiently resign/What justly thou hast lost;" (XI 287-8) he advises Eve. He is clear about their sin but tries to calm them with the prospect that God will not desert them but always be present: "in valley and in plain." Michael intriguingly combines the roles of warrior and consoler. Despite his difficult task and warrior's reputation, Michael is a rare symbol of hope and consolation, his calming tone beyond that of God. He advises them how they may lead better lives following: "The rule of not too much, by temperance taught" (XI 531). His other significant moral aphorism: "Judge not what is best/By pleasure," (XI 603-4) reinforces the Puritan morality with which the poem ends. Michael's success is heard in Adam's conclusion "to obey is best," (XII 561). Adam is congratulated by Michael who, attempting to bolster Adam's sagging morale, says: "This having learned, thou hast attained the sum/Of wisdom;" (XII 575-6). His final point regarding the new Paradise: "A paradise within thee," (XII 587) is the last and best piece of consolation, being one example in the poem of how poetry may indeed convey moral truths, but of a very specific brand. In fact in much of the moralising at the close of the poem we detect the voice of Milton himself, using Michael as a vehicle for his aphorisms, which detracts somewhat from the presentation of Michael as a distinct character. Not only carrying the voice of God, he bears the voice of Milton and any attempt at characterisation is superseded by the necessity of function.

Uriel

The Archangel Uriel is not found in the Bible. He comes from the Hebraic tradition, appearing three times in 2 Esdras,[127] his name in Hebrew meaning flame or fire of God. Milton makes him the "regent of the sun", a "glorious angel", "The same whom John saw also in the sun:" (III 622-3).[128] In later Rabbinical tradition he became one of the seven Angels of the Presence and one of four commanders with authority of the south.[129]

Despite his description as the "sharpest sighted spirit of all in heaven" (III 691) the evidence we have in the poem would not justify this summary. Uriel does not see through Satan's disguise as a 'meaner' angel and his ploy of asking his way to earth in order to wonder at the glories of mankind. This was a strangely obvious thing for Uriel to miss and he offers no excuse: "Mine eye pursued him still, but under shade/Lost sight of him;" (IV 572-3). This is odd, given that Death and Sin immediately recognised him as he approached them on his journey from Hell to earth.[130]

Apart from creating an additional detail when Satan asks for directions his only other significant action is to inform Gabriel that there is an intruder on earth.[131] However, his chief contribution is to explain that man cannot detect hypocrisy:

> *For neither man nor angel can discern*
> *Hypocrisy, the only evil that walks*
> *Invisible, except to God alone,*
>
> (III 682-684)

His point regarding man's inability to detect deception superficially provides a defence for Eve's failure to detect the

127 4:1, 5:20 and 10:28. Esdras is a variant of the name Ezra and the book was regarded as a part of the apocrypha, preserved in Latin as an appendix to the Vulgate version

128 See Revelation 19:17

129 The others being Michael, Gabriel and Raphael

130 II 688-734

131 IV 564-575

wiles of Satan disguised as a serpent. This appears to complicate Milton's argument concerning the proper use of reason to help determine our actions, given that neither angels nor men can detect deceit. However, it allows Milton to reinforce his point that obedience to God's law should be sufficient to withstand such wiles, and even when apparently reasonable arguments are put which might involve breaking God's command we should nevertheless remain steadfast. It does not, however, make life any easier for man or angels. Here again Uriel's function may well be at the expense of consistent characterisation.

Milton's chief angels have clear functions, though their behaviour may seem inexplicable at times. Significantly his imagination or 'sympathetic identification' with these figures led him to ascribe to them words and actions which are prone to raise awkward theological or practical questions, occasionally blowing the poem off course. Endowed with some personality albeit oddly awkward at times, they may, though not always, perform clear narrative functions making them appear to be more Milton's functionaries than God's. It is in the fuller characterisation of his protagonists, however, where Milton's successes and failures are shown on a truly grand scale.

20

God and the Son

God

The challenge of portraying God

The presentation of God in a verse drama was Milton's hardest task. By allowing God to speak Milton enabled us to hear his self-justification, however, his tone and inconsistencies in his statements force us to judge him, to the detriment of the poem's aim.

God is Milton's Achilles heel. An omnipotent and omniscient God should not have to explain himself or require the services of functionaries to find information or act as look-outs; does not need a brigade of soldiers to see off rebels or humans to cultivate Eden. Why was mankind required to repopulate heaven, given that before the rebellion there seemed no dearth of angels, who were presumably created more easily? Why complicate matters by creating flawed mankind who must progress by degrees to angelic stature? We want to know who and what God is but in speaking like a human Milton could do little more than present a crude portrait. The problem of Milton's God is, indeed, the problem of God.

Modern critics have attempted to explain away the unprepossessing nature of God as seen in *Paradise Lost*. Inspired by Empson[132] Victoria Silver[133] envisaged literary sleight of hand by Milton, arguing that he provokes us to revise our human and fallen understanding of God as a superhuman, simply bigger and better than us. Basing the argument on the

---

132 Op cit

133 *Imperfect Sense: The Predicament of Milton's Irony*, Princeton, 2001

theology of Luther's "hidden God" we are encouraged to come to a new understanding of an unknowable God. Taking over the baton Michael Bryson[134] believes Milton deliberately created an unjust and unlikeable God who "is not a figure who inspires love, loyalty or even admiration." The Old Testament "God as a King was, for Milton, to imagine God as if he were the Devil." According to Bryson Milton shows us how we imagine God but not how he is, encouraging us to re-imagine God as he appears in the form of Christ in *Paradise Regained*.

Both these ingenious explanations of God's unpleasant demeanour seek to excuse Milton for what he has written. They assume that Milton was writing a literary mystery thriller for a 17th century audience sufficiently astute to understand his mind games; indeed Bryson claims Milton's statement that he required a "fit audience" for his poem was because only an intelligent reader could spot and then dismiss the picture of God as king. Imposing 21st century literary inventiveness on Milton's epic requires some stretching of the imagination. Alternatively it is entirely feasible to envisage a scenario where Milton came to realize that his portrait of God presented an unbalanced picture, thereby encouraging him to write *Paradise Regained* as a counter balance.

Presenting God was made harder for Milton by the fact that there is potential for contradiction about God's nature on two counts. Firstly, the Book of Genesis presented a structural dichotomy because there were two authors of the creation story, each with a distinctive characterisation of the creator. How could Milton choose between them? Secondly, how could Milton allow God to explain himself without losing some of the awe and mystery? Originally thought to have been by Moses, the Book of Genesis had multiple authors over a long period. Milton's task was to reconcile the disparate images created by additions, revisions, changes of emphasis and stylistic differences which had created more questions than answers concerning the nature of God.

---

134 *The Tyranny of Heaven: Milton's Rejection of God as King*, University of Delaware Press, 2004

The creation account presented in *Genesis 1:1-2:3*[135] differs from the second account in *Genesis 2:4-3:23*[136] in being written in verse rather than prose, utilising a grander style. The first produced a solemnity and precision of language, creating a spare tone to the story. God creates in a regal style, commanding from on high, projecting a stately, ordered process. Order is created out of chaos in a systematic manner, "and it was so" being the repeated and pervading tone. God is shown effortlessly creating many men and women at the same time. He is a distant creator, possessing an abstract authority as he issues commands which are instantly executed. He seems to be pure spirit as he "moved upon the face of the waters"[137]and is referred to as Elohim, indicating a text written in the northern part of the kingdom of Israel.

The second version contains both the creation and the Fall but the creation is a simpler almost domestic process, where we are placed in a garden with dirt and animals and even given the names of rivers and the whereabouts of gold. God is said to have "planted" the garden, while man is made from dust as God works like a potter to mould him into shape and woman comes later, formed from Adam's rib. God seems more present, active and involved in the creative process. He requires the help of mankind in the garden and is shown to sympathise with Adam's feelings of loneliness. He is present in the garden and after the Fall searches for Adam and Eve as if he lacks omniscience.[138] The reader feels closer to this God, as we are told why weeds and clothing exist, why childbirth is painful and work is hard, why there is discord between people, and why men are supposed to rule over women. Here God is Yahweh or Yahweh Elohim, deriving from a more southerly area of Israel.

These linguistic differences point to the existence of two dates and at least two authors, whose works were edited and

135 Referred to as the E text because of the references to God as Elohim

136 The J text from the references to God as Yahweh but referred to as J from the German version of the Hebrew

137 Genesis 1:2

138 Genesis 3:9

joined by a later hand. The detail has long been a source of controversy for biblical scholars but the most recent conclusion suggests that the E text from Genesis 2:4-3:3 is the older text, while the J text is later. Subsequently scholarly priests incorporated the E text into the J text[139] thus creating the latest additions to the Genesis narrative.[140]

Milton faced two representations of God and used both. His God is distant and powerful, yet speaks with Adam about loneliness; he creates man from dust yet complains about his behaviour; he seems obsessed by the concept of obedience and punishment yet allows his own son to become the scapegoat for man's transgression. Did Milton fail to control his material by not choosing carefully how to present God or did he decide to make God an ambivalent figure? It would be easy to understand why the latter might be the case but if so, it came at the price of losing the warmth or closeness a reader might feel towards him. Milton's efforts to be faithful to the duality of the biblical presentation of God and allowing him to speak as a human led to some basic confusion about him.

Why is Milton's God so unsympathetic?

Whilst there are problems associated with the multiple authorship of Genesis, it is fair to ask why God sounds so complaining, obsessed with obedience, contradictory (regarding the issues of free will, foreknowledge and predestination) and lacking in that spirit of compassion which was at the heart of the mystics' experience of him. Why did Milton not control his material more effectively? The God of *Paradise Lost* shares the characteristics of the Old Testament God rather than the more compassionate God (as experienced through the life of Christ) of the New Testament, which even the inclusion of the Son in *Paradise Lost* does little to counterbalance. Was Milton aware of

139 The new version, known as the P or Priestly text

140 See *The Bible as Literature: An Introduction,* by JB Gabel and CB Wheeler, Oxford, 1986 and *The Oxford Companion to the Bible edited* by BM Metzger and MD Coogan, 1993

this defect, and wrote *Paradise Regained* as a necessary antidote to the earlier God? *Paradise Regained* is believed to have been written at the instigation of Thomas Ellwood, who purports to have said to him that Milton had presented Paradise lost: "but what hast thou to say of Paradise found?"[141]

Milton seemed ambivalent about his presentation of God and did not resolve the extremes of an unknowable, distant deity and a human-sounding, closer figure. Milton's need to include reasoned statements from God about his actions added to a confused picture, which raised more questions than it answered and failed to capture the transcendent relationship between man and God which utilises no known human mechanism.

In *Paradise Lost* it is the Old Testament insistence upon laws and obedience which is the predominant influence. The concept of the test of obedience (for men and angels) stands in the way of a fuller understanding of God because it appears to be God's sole preoccupation. Milton may or may not have intended to portray God as a despot or an earthly monarch but could not extricate himself from his biblical source. In so doing he risked reducing God to the level of an insecure creator, constantly testing his creatures to ensure their fealty. In seeking to understand God and prove the justice of his ways Milton shrinks God to a one-dimensional being who fails to win either our love or wholehearted approval.

Milton had his own difficulties in accepting God's occasionally inscrutable law. The sonnet *On his Blindness* famously seeks solace from blindness in the spirit of sighing acceptance, for "They also serve who only stand and wait." However, in *Paradise Lost* Milton tried to make God's position unassailable. Whether or not he succeeded depends on how far we are influenced by the human expression of God's explanations.

Among the options available to Milton in his dramatisation of God was to present him as a gentler father figure, a distant ethereal voice or perhaps an emotionless automaton. Determined to bring all his protagonists to life in a way with

---

141 Quoted in the introduction to *Paradise Regained* in *Milton's Shorter Poems,* edited by John Carey, Longman, 1968

which the reader could identify, Milton gave God a human voice. Everything therefore depends upon his tone, language and how he manages his authority. It is here that God's insistence on the submission of creation to his will obscures other possible characteristics which may have softened him to human eyes, a God whose tone and manner we might love rather than fear. Milton's talent for characterisation did not work for God.

There are difficulties about God's conduct which have to be faced. Foremost among the problems raised by God's participation as a character is his attempted clarification of his position regarding foreknowledge of rather than his predestination of events, and the free will, which he says he has given to creation and repeatedly uses in his defence. The place of human love and ambition in the scheme of things, the usefulness of man's powers of reasoning in a world governed only by submission to God and God's monarchical preoccupation with the succession of the Son raise further questions.

God appears as light and fragrance but we hear a human sounding voice. Describing a protagonist who possessed a voice but no body was the ultimate challenge. "God is light," (III 3), and is "Bright effluence of bright essence increate" (III 6). This is as close as we shall get to a description, though confusingly he bends "down his eye," (III 58), so if man is made in his image we have one clue about his appearance. After the Fall he appears in Eden as a voice but no body:

> *the voice of God they heard*
> *Now walking in the garden, by soft winds*
> *Brought to their ears,*
>
> (X 97-99)

confirming God's own pronouncement:

> *I am who fill*
> *Infinitude, nor vacuous the space.*
>
> (VII 168-9)

When he speaks "ambrosial fragrance filled/All heaven," (III 135-6). As for his appearance: "the almighty Father shines, / Whom else no creature can behold;" (III 386-7), begging the question how anyone can know that man is made in God's image, though Milton emphasises Adam and Eve's 'divine resemblance': "for in their looks divine/The image of their glorious maker shone" (IV 291- 2) and:

> *so lively shines*
> *In them divine resemblance, and such grace*
> *The hand that formed them on their shape hath poured.*
>
> (IV 363-365)

It is more through his actions that we are led to understand God better. God is not just all talk, for his words always lead to action: "Immediate are the acts of God, more swift/Than time or motion," (VII 176). The angels' reactions to his pronouncements also provide a lead, which is one of their few functions. They shout in acclaim at his magnanimity: "Loud as from numbers without number," (III 346), but the Heavenly chorus is struck dumb following God's request for a volunteer to redeem man:

> *He asked, but all the heavenly choir stood mute,*
> *And silence was in heaven:*
>
> (III 217-8)

However, his reflected glory is helpfully seen in the Son:

> *in him all his Father shone*
> *Substantially expressed, and in his face*
> *Divine compassion visibly appeared,*
>
> (III 139-141)

As God says: "Son in whose face invisible is beheld/Visibly, what by deity I am," (VI 681-2) where unusually in the poem we have a cleverly expressed oxymoron in an attempt to describe the indescribable.

In his characterisation of God Milton openly committed the heresy of subordinationism. The Son is separate to God, genuinely his son; it is not God himself as 'Father in the Son' who redeems mankind but the Son as a separate being, although God takes the credit for it. Milton created a family of sorts but the worst aspect of this is that God is concerned to promote his son in the heavenly hierarchy whilst being prepared to sacrifice him in the cause of his master plan. The anthropomorphic presentation of God finds itself in difficulties when he agrees to his son's self-sacrifice; indeed God had planned that this should be so. This objection to God is one of William Empson's most convincing.[142]

The consequences of Milton's approach

Allowing God to speak as a human means that at times he can sound silly. Lamenting the goings-on in Hell and what will happen to man, the reader is tempted to tell God to do something about it:

> *so bent he seems*
> *On desperate revenge, that shall redound*
> *Upon his own rebellious head. And now*
> *Through all restraint broke loose he wings his way*
> *Not far off heaven, in the precincts of light,*
> *Directly towards the new created world,*
> *And man there placed, with purpose to assay*
> *If him by force he can destroy, or worse,*
> *By some false guile pervert; and shall pervert*
>
> (III 84-92)

God's expression of outrage is more for effect, given that he knows the outcome, but he has to appear sufficiently worried so that the Son will have no choice but to volunteer to save man. God builds a picture of a powerful Satan and when he asks for volunteers to be sacrificed for man, (III 209-12), it is little

142 *Milton's God* 1961, Revised 1965

wonder that no angel wishes to die for a race that cannot obey a simple rule:

> *He with his whole posterity must die,*
> *Die he or justice must; unless for him*
> *Some other able, and as willing, pay*
> *The rigid satisfaction, death for death.*
>
> (III 209-12)

God is delighted when the Son steps forward, gaining the admiration of all Heaven.[143] This is the theological turning point of the poem. It marks the birth of the Christian religion, yet we may be tempted to imagine God's chest swelling like a proud father at the prospect of victory.

Irritatingly God does needless things, such as sending Raphael to check on something God must surely have known:

> *For I that day was absent, as befell,*
> *Bound on a voyage uncouth and obscure,*
> *Far on excursion toward the gates of hell;*
> *Squared in full legion (such command we had)*
> *To see that none thence issued forth a spy,*
> *Or enemy, while God was in his work,*
>
> (VIII 229-234)

Similarly Michael is sent to check that Satan is not up to more mischief:

> *lest the fiend*
> *Or in behalf of man, or to invade*
> *Vacant possession some new trouble raise:*
>
> (XI 101-103)

God must have known whether or not this was to happen

143 "For as by one man's disobedience many were made sinners, so by the obedience of one shall many be made righteous." *Romans V 12*

and the unnecessary nature of the trip results more from Milton's need to make him sound busy than a theological necessity.

By possessing human characteristics God speaks in a manner that is in danger of reducing his authority. His moment of self pity, claiming loneliness in the face of Adam's request for a mate, is demeaning since God could presumably create a mate for himself. He regards conversation with the creatures he has made as second best:

> *Who am alone*
> *From all eternity, for none I know*
> *Second to me or like, equal much less.*
>
> (VIII 406-407)

That this may be a ruse, encouraging Adam into asking for a mate, thus precipitating the Fall, makes God even less likeable.[144] As a God of Puritan Reason he explains, reminds, exhorts and then punishes in a flow of self-justification. Immediately after the Fall he appears unmoved by the frailty of Adam and Eve, expressing no compassion for those in unimaginably difficult predicaments such as choosing between love for a mate and love for God. He will not tolerate any failure to use the faculty of reason. He appears too satisfied to see that man assumes there is to be no harsh punishment for his sin because it has not yet happened: "but soon shall find/Forbearance no acquittance ere day end."[145] Similarly the Fallen Angels hope to feast on "fruitage fair to sight" but God ensures they: "Chewed bitter ashes" in cruel recognition of the "the bait of Eve/Used by the tempter."[146]

When issuing man's punishment in Book XI God's voice sounds querulous as he lists what he has done for them: "I at first with two fair gifts/Created him endowed, with happiness/And

144 See Fowler's note to VIII 416-9

145 See X 47-54

146 X 547-572

immortality:" (XI 57-60), which is not his only self-righteous speech. God may have every right to sound self-righteous but it detracts from his gravitas and warmth and reduces him to the level of special pleading. There is a gentler feel by the end of the poem, when God accedes to the Son's supplication on man's behalf and gives instructions to Michael:

> *Yet lest they faint*
> *At the sad sentence rigorously urged*
> *For I behold them softened and with tears*
> *Bewailing their excess, all terror hide.*
> *If patiently thy bidding they obey,*
> *Dismiss them not disconsolate: reveal*
> *To Adam what shall come in future days,*
> *As I shall thee enlighten, intermix*
> *My Covenant in the woman's seed renewed;*
> *So send them forth, though sorrowing, yet in peace:*
> (XI 108-117)

However, God cannot stop himself reminding the Son: "All thy request for man, accepted Son, /Obtain, all thy request was my decree:" (XI 46-7). Original ideas are not allowed. Nor may any creature have ambition to know more: the pace of God's scheme must be obeyed: "O sons, like one of us man is become/ To know both good and evil," "but let him boast/His knowledge of good lost, and evil got,/Happier, had it sufficed him to have known/Good by itself, and evil not at all."[147]

The egocentric nature of Milton's God is unappealing. In his speech describing Milton's Arminian view concerning the salvation of the good God uses 'me' or 'my' six times in the first twelve lines.[148] The many warnings[149] given to Adam about the rule forbidding them to eat fruit from the Tree of Knowledge and his consequent duty of authority over Eve are designed to

147 XI 84-89

148 III 173-184

149 For example VII 542; VIII 321; VIII 634

absolve God from personal blame for the Fall.[150] God complains, almost whining with indignation, that man will fall despite the advantages given to him:

> *whose fault?*
> *Whose but his own? Ingrate, he had of me*
> *All he could have; I made him just and right,*
> *Sufficient to have stood, though free to fall*
>
> (III 96-99)

The number of references to divine decrees preparing for the Fall suggest otherwise, not least at XI 46-7 mentioned above. God's comment on the Fall demonstrates his petulance but also his plans, for he 'suffers' evil to enter the world when he could have stopped it; it was a conscious decision not to act against Satan at this point:

> *See with what heat these dogs of hell advance*
> *To waste and havoc yonder world, which I*
> *So fair and good created, and had still*
> *Kept in that state, had not the folly of man*
> *Let in these wasteful furies, who impute*
> *Folly to me, so doth the prince of hell*
> *And his adherents, that with so much ease*
> *I suffer them to enter and possess*
> *A place so heavenly,*
>
> (X 616-624)

Allied to the monarchical tone of God's pronouncements are the trappings of an hereditary monarchy. Heaven is decked out in opulent fashion. Satan sees the gates:

> *The work as of a kingly palace gate*
> *With frontispiece of diamond and gold*

---

150 On God's grace see 'Covenant and the Crowne of Life – A figural Tapestry in *Paradise Lost*' by Patricia Elizabeth Davis in *Milton Studies* 1986

> *Embellished, thick with sparkling orient gems*
> *The portal shone*
>
> (III 505-8)

with "a sea of jasper or of liquid pearl"[151] and "steps of gold."[152] As heir apparent the Son is to be "Anointed universal King" to "reign for ever"[153] while God sits "High throned above all highth".[154]

Milton seeks to make God appear less of a tyrant by the love he shows for his son and in the way the Son will help to save man:

> *O Son, in whom my soul hath chief delight,*
> *Son of my bosom, Son who art alone*
> *My word, my wisdom, and effectual might,*
> *All thou hast spoken as my thoughts are, all*
> *As my eternal purpose hath decreed:*
> *Man shall not quite be lost, but saved who will,*
> *Yet not of will in him, but grace in me*
> *Freely vouchsafed;*
>
> (III 168-175)

All will be well, but the final words are unfortunate in their egoism, and the repeated use of personal pronouns does nothing to soften that impression:

> *Once more I will renew*
> *His lapsed powers, though forfeit and enthralled*
> *By sin to foul exorbitant desires;*
> *Upheld by me, yet once more he shall stand*
> *On even ground against his mortal foe,*
> *By me upheld, that he may know how frail*

151 III 519

152 III 541

153 III 317-8

154 III 58

His fallen condition is, and to me owe
All his deliverance, and to none but me.
Some I have chosen of peculiar grace
Elect above the rest; so is my will:

(III 175-184)

God's punishment of the serpent is, however, an example of how readers should not misread God's actions and words. The serpent, for example, is presented as the unwitting vehicle for Satan's scheme whose punishment may seem simply vindictive. However, there were theological arguments that God condemned the instrument as well as the source of evil[155] and that Satan was from the first identified as the Serpent.[156] In addition the future destruction of the devil is foretold.[157] Milton would have assumed his readers' familiarity with this material.

On the other hand, and not unreasonably we might say, Adam questions the justice of God's extending his punishment to all mankind:

first and last
On me, me only, as the source and spring
Of all corruption, all the blame lights due;
So might the wrath.

(X 831-34)

By punishing succeeding generations they are doomed to inherit sinful ways, making the exercise of their free will even harder. We might also wonder why God did not suppress the rebellion in heaven more easily than he did: as it is he appears merely to meddle.

155 *Leviticus 20: 15-16* shows that even when an animal is an instrument of sin it is to be killed as well as the sinner and St Chrysostom had written: "Just as a loving father when punishing the murder of his son might snap in two the sword or dagger with which the murder had been committed."

156 Directly for example in *Revelation 12:9* and *20:2* and indirectly in *2 Corinthians 11:3*

157 *Genesis 3:15*

By allowing Satan to act as he does Milton does of course add to God's defence against the possible charge that he created evil.

Worship of God by man, as explained by Raphael in Book VII does not sound like a contentious doctrine until we sense the egoism in the human voice of God making creatures in his image "there to dwell/And worship him," (VII 627-8), and ordaining the Sabbath for his own worship. Adam's God-given instinct is to worship God: "Tell me, how may I know him, how adore, /From whom I have that thus I move and live" (VIII 280-282).

It is God's control of events which raises questions regarding the reality of free will, and there is great difficulty in distinguishing between God's foreknowledge and the apparently predestined acts which bear the hallmarks of his decrees.[158] In his exposition of the future to the Son, (III 56-134), God explains that all this might look: "As if predestination overruled/Their will," (III 114-5), but hastens to add:

> *they themselves decreed*
> *Their own revolt, not I: if I foreknew,*
> *Foreknowledge had no influence on their fault*
> (III 116-118)[159]

He has already maintained quite logically:

> *Freely they stood who stood, and fell who fell.*
> *Not free, what proof could they have given sincere*
> *Of true allegiance, constant faith or love,"*
> (III 102-104)

We may accept that temptation is essential to God's testing regime, the instruction not to eat the fruit being the only way man could demonstrate loyalty to God to avoid the charge of

---

158 Further analysis of God's decrees affecting the outcome of events may be found in Chapter 28

159 For an interesting discussion of this see Paul R Sellin in *Milton Studies* 1986

being merely God's puppet. However, there is special pleading in God's voice as he defends the need for free will, making him sound as though it is for his own gratification that this is so:

> *What pleasure I from such obedience paid,*
> *When will and reason (reason also is choice)*
> *Useless and vain, of freedom both despoiled,*
> *Made passive both, had served necessity,*
> *Not me.*
>
> (III 107-111)

The sense that man would 'serve' God in order to provide him "pleasure" and the two words "Not me" sit uncomfortably in the mouth of God.

Milton's difficulties in representing the Deity were enormous, especially given the complexities involved in portraying the nature of the Trinity. God is also immutable, a human voice which must remain static. Milton's temperament meant that he allowed God to reason things out in public; he would not have followed CS Lewis' advice to keep the portrayal more mysterious.[160] The consequence was summarised by Alexander Pope: "And God the Father turns a School-Divine".[161] God's emphasis on testing, not only regarding the Tree but also the plan for man to know his place and rise by degrees to spirit, makes him seem obsessively controlling: "time may come when men/With angels may participate, and find/No inconvenient diet, nor too light fare:" (V 493-495), "till by degrees of merit raised/They open to themselves at length the way/Up thither, under long obedience tried," (VII 157-159).

Likewise the limits put on man's knowledge are easily used by Satan in his temptation to paint God as a jealous Creator. Raphael seeks to defend God's position on this principle of "knowledge within bounds" (VII 120):

---

160 CS Lewis *A Preface to Paradise Lost* Oxford 1942 Chap XIX

161 Alexander Pope *First Epistle of the Second Book of Horace Imitated* Line 102

Beyond abstain
To ask, nor let thine own invention hope
Things not revealed, which the invisible king,
Only omniscient, hath suppressed in night,
To none communicable in earth or heaven:
Enough is left besides to search and know.
But knowledge is as food, and needs no less
Her temperance over appetite, to know
In measure what the mind may well contain,
Oppress else with surfeit,

(VII 120-129)

And later:

the rest
From man or angel the great architect
Did wisely to conceal, and not divulge
His secrets to be scanned by them who ought
Rather admire;

(VIII 71-75)

Repeatedly this theme is rehearsed:

God to remove his ways from human sense,
Placed heaven from earth so far, that earthly sight,
If it presume, might err in things too high,
And no advantage gain.

(VIII 119-122)

Solicit not thy thoughts with manner hid,
Leave them to God above, him serve and fear;

(VIII 167-168).

Milton's theological and artistic problem is clear in Raphael's description of God as "the invisible king" (VII 127). Milton attempted to represent a God we might have begun to understand but the picture which emerges is of a distant autocrat, whose commands are difficult, if not impossible for man to fathom.

By dramatising the story and giving God a role complete with human voice, Milton attempted to bring him closer to the reader. However, the more human God is made to sound and act, the more incomprehensible and unlikeable he appears. There can be no easy human understanding of God's insistence upon living earthly lives where ambition and human love count for nothing against obedience to God, and where movement through the states of being from earth to heaven seems to serve no purpose other than to please God. Broadbent[162] rightly highlights the similarities between God's language and that of Puritan sermons which "had affinities with the rationalist discourse and the academic exercise," concluding: "By the time *Paradise Lost* was published, the Father's speech was antiquated. That Milton should have made him speak so skeletally implies anxiety, as if he were trying to authorize the dogma by solidification." Unless Milton presented God as a distant authority figure he had a problem about what linguistic register to give him. Poetry that was 'simple, sensuous and passionate' would have been lightweight, though God is given brief moments of compassion. Although the mystical description of God at III 372ff is effective, only by the emotional experiences of the mystic will this draw man closer to him, so Milton's God must participate in rational discourse and make statements comprehensible to man. However, they run the risk of making God sound irascible.

Without any convincing clarification we are told to trust in God's law despite appearances to the contrary, abandoning ambition and love in favour of obedience. God's ways remain baffling: this is the glum conclusion of the poem. Though we might not like the sound of God, there is consolation in that the wicked are punished, whilst Adam learns his sober lesson: "Henceforth I learn, that to obey is best" (XII 561). It appears, however, a self-limiting, frequently negative state of being.

In the context of a verse drama where each protagonist is given a voice, Milton faced a tough challenge to present the

162 Op cit

perfect image of God, whatever that may be. The inconsistencies and muddles (particularly regarding decrees and free will) could have been avoided, and God's manner could have been softer, his egotistical tone and frequent complaints about man's ingratitude being his least endearing characteristics. Within the framework of a testing regime the relentless force of obedience to God would be hard to avoid, though might have been tempered. God's often repeated tone of disappointment over man's disloyalty and Adam's failure to control Eve do little to endear him to the reader; neither does the tone he adopts in the 'promotion' of the Son, which creates an unintended aura of nepotism and plays into Satan's hands.

The whole enterprise ran the risk of not helping God's cause, since presenting God must inevitably be a feat of the imagination. Making him a misty entity lacking substance would have been out of place in a poem laden with dialogue and following a disputatious format. Readers throughout the centuries have felt uneasy about God's demand for total obedience and the egotistical impression he presents by speaking in a human voice. From the beginning the words "Of man's first disobedience" alert us to the unbending theology of the poem. By allowing God to speak as a man and a father, Milton sought to make him comprehensible to us but he reduced God's standing. As chief spokesman for himself God fails to endear: his apparent lack of warmth and insistence on subservience ruin his cause. And this is not simply because we are fallen beings who are misinterpreting God's ways. The complexities of human life appear to be ignored in God's self-justification. He will not tolerate the wrong aspirations and places mankind in a position where to follow God involves turning aside from love for a fellow human being.

Giving Milton the benefit of the doubt we could say that readers run the risk of succumbing to theological traps laid by Milton in the questions about God's motives raised by Satan and Eve. Victoria Silver, for example, excuses Milton in an ingenious defence of Milton's God as the father who knows best by arguing that in the style of a New Testament parable God is only cruel to be kind and appearances are deceptive: though we cannot understand his ways we must believe that he knows best.[163] However, elaborate literary tricks do not sit comfortably with Milton's epic ambitions. God is left with too many unlikeable characteristics. The result is that Milton did not make it easy for the reader to warm to him or his pronouncements: God himself becomes the weakest link in Milton's justification of his ways.

The Son

The Son is an intruder in the Genesis account of the Fall, though his coming is prefigured in the Old Testament.[164] In the context of an epic poem, however, as with the angels it is useful for Milton to have such a figure. The Son's promotion provides a credible device for the origin of Satan's envy and the subsequent rebellion, and serves as a stark contrast to Satan's own child, Sin. In addition the Son provides balance by allowing the presentation of a gentler aspect of God's nature, prefiguring the message of the New Testament. However, the outcome is not straightforward.

As with God Milton's picture of the Son represents a mixed and ambivalent image of godhead which again derives from the fact that we hear him speak. On the surface he represents everything we might expect:

> *In him all his Father shone*
> *Substantially expressed, and in his face*
> *Divine compassion visibly appeared,*
> *Love without end, and without measure grace,*
>
> (III 139-142)

163 'The Problem of God' in *The Cambridge Companion to Paradise Lost*, 2014

164 For example in Isaiah 7:14

Indeed he proceeds to sound solicitous for God's reputation, trying as tactfully as possible to warn that should man "thy youngest son" (III 151) be allowed to sin and fall, causing God to destroy his own creation, then: "So should thy goodness and thy greatness both/Be questioned and blasphemed without defence" (III 165-166). However, it is not long before the reader suspects that many of the words ascribed to the Son are placed there by God in order for him to make pronouncements about his plans for mankind: "Man shall not quite be lost, but saved who will," (III 173). However, the Son as a vehicle for God's plans begins to take on a new meaning when it is appreciated just how manipulative Milton's God is in his use of the Son.

The Son's offer to redeem mankind has an ambivalent tone. On the one hand when no other volunteer steps forward he sounds like the ambitious employee who is forever volunteering, attentive to God's every need, or a child eager to please his father by offering to do a chore:

> *I for his sake will leave*
> *Thy bosom, and this glory next to thee*
> *Freely put off, and for him lastly die*
>
> (III 238-240)

Yet his apparently generous offer to die is blunted when it is revealed that he knows he cannot die:

> *I shall not long*
> *Lie vanquished; thou hast given me to possess*
> *Life in myself for ever,*
>
> (III 242-244)

The Son is granted riches and power everlasting as his reward: "all power/I give thee, reign for ever," (III 317-318). The ambitious Son has been promised chairmanship of the Board in the family business, confirmed a little later when God calls him: "heir of all my might," (V 720), But the scheming father had planned it all. The angels sing praises to the Father and the Son,[165] just as in Book II the Fallen Angels through sheer relief had praised the courage of Satan's offer to travel to earth.

The Son's role as heir apparent is also shown in the major role he plays in the creation of the earth. God is clearly the force behind the creation but the Son is the instrument, in charge of operations:

> *The Son*
> *On his great expedition now appeared,*
> *Girt with omnipotence, with radiance crowned*
> *Of majesty divine, sapience and love*
> *Immense and all his father in him shone.*
>
> (VII 192-196)

There is an uncomfortable sense of self-satisfaction in the Son's comments regarding the inevitable outcome of his tussle with Satan's forces:

> *Mighty Father, thou thy foes*
> *Justly hast in derision, and secure*
> *Laugh'st at their vain designs and tumults vain,*
> *Matter to me of glory, whom their hate*
> *Illustrates, when they see all regal power*
> *Given to me to quell their pride, and in event*
> *Know whether I be dextrous to subdue*
> *Thy rebels, or be found the worst in heaven.*
>
> (V 735-42)

In the heavenly rebellion God provides the Son with another opportunity to shine. As Milton tells us in the Argument to Book VI, though Michael and his force counter the devils' 'engines': "God on the third day sends Messiah his Son, for whom he had reserved the glory of that victory", and the Son chases the devils over the edge of Heaven "into the place of

165 III 372-415

punishment." However, he does not strike the tone that might be expected. He sounds too gushing, too eager and too relieved at last to be given a task:

> *this I my glory account,*
> *My exaltation, and my whole delight,*
> *That thou in me well pleased, declar'st thy will*
> *Fulfilled, which to fulfil is all my bliss.*
> *Sceptre and power, thy giving, I assume,*
> *And gladlier shall resign, when in the end*
> *Thou shalt be all in all, and I in thee*
> *For ever, and in me all whom thou lovest:*
> *But whom thou hatest, I hate, and can put on*
> *Thy terrors, as I put thy mildness on,*
> *Image of thee in all things;*
>
> (VI 726-736)

Though it has precedents in scripture[166] hearing the Son say that he can assume a guise of hatred or mildness strikes a harsh chord, and he certainly appears to relish his part in the rout of Satan, though in keeping with biblical evidence regarding the proper judgement and punishment of sinners. Here is an Old Testament warrior, eager for the fray.

The Son's manner is ironically better when in Book X he is sent to be the judge of Adam and Eve and to issue their punishments. The just but merciful figure of the New Testament finally appears when after the Fall he intercedes on behalf on man:

> *let me*
> *Interpret for him, me his advocate*
> *And propitiation, all his works on me*
> *Good or not good ingraft, my merit those*
> *Shall perfect, and for these my death shall pay.*
>
> (XI 32-36)

166 See John 17: 1-23

However, no sooner has this long-awaited moment arrived than Milton snatches it away from us, as God accepts the proposal, adding: "all thy request was my decree:" (XI 47). The Son is once more left stranded in an avalanche of ambivalence. The Son is nevertheless sent: "the mild judge and intercessor both/To sentence man:" (X 96-7), and again "both judge and saviour sent," (X 209). Milton adds to this by reminding the reader that Mary, the second Eve, will give birth to Jesus (the New Testament name being used here) and foretells the resurrection and the victory over Satan (X 182-192). Having issued their punishments to Adam and Eve the Son shows pity for them, and just as he will later wash the servants' feet he here acts like a father and covers their nakedness: "And thought not much to clothe his enemies" (X 219). The Son's success in assuaging the pain of Adam and Eve is seen prominently in the way that Adam feels sufficiently strong that he can offer consolation to Eve, believing that in the end God: "will relent and turn/From his displeasure;" (X 1093-4).

The Son is placed in a potentially difficult position but in the denouement he handles his role adroitly, successfully managing two contrasting moods. Unfortunately he is never quite able to fulfil his role as a willing and independent supplicant for man since there are too many problems associated with Milton's presentation of his personality and function as a player in the drama that God is writing, producing and directing. It is significant that the poem closes with Michael's description of the crucifixion. Confusingly this leaves the poem in its final moments lacking any real warmth, compassion or love. The image is of pure violence:

For this he shall live hated, be blasphemed,
Seized on by force, judged, and to death condemned
A shameful and accurst, nailed to the cross
By his own nation, slain for bringing life;

(XII 411-414)

The images are financial and legal: "Thy ransom paid," (XII 424), "this Godlike act/Annuls thy doom" (427-8) followed by a scene of victory but also of violence:

> *this act*
> *Shall bruise the head of Satan, crush his strength*
> *Defeating Sin and Death, his two main arms,*
> *And fix far deeper in his head their stings*
> *Than temporal death shall bruise the victor's heel,*
> (XII 429-433)

Even the Son's remaining time on earth will be brief.[167]

The facts of the Bible are of course correctly stated but the mixed messages contribute to a stark atmosphere at the poem's close. *Paradise Lost* is a verse drama, tragic in tone and outcome, but Milton's aim to defend God's ways is not helped when God and the Son both appear to have character defects and God seems not merely to have foreseen but to have contrived events. The Son's nature is overshadowed by Milton's portrayal of God's handling of the Son's rise to authority and God's manipulation of events. The result is that the Son is unable to establish his own unambiguous identity. We see a manipulative God who enjoys testing his subjects and punishing them severely when they fail. Milton's assertion that God must be right despite appearances to the contrary turns his desire for mankind's unquestioning obedience into trust without evidence. Adam and Eve may have learned from their mistakes but it is submission to rather than love of God that is the overriding impression at the end of the poem.

Milton's was a harsh religion but his decision to control our perceptions of God and the Son in this manner does not leave the reader with a calm or wholly optimistic view of the future, which will be beset by pain and hardship. Indeed, it may not be unreasonable to ask why the sins of the father have been visited on the children. In seeking to find hope in the poem Russell M

167 XII 436-445

Hillier wrote: "The great argument to Milton's *Paradise Lost* is a stirring reminder of the Christian example of humiliation before exaltation, descent before ascension, and *kemosis* as requisite to *theosis*, all of which the poem enacts and memorializes in its justification by faith in God's ways through his redeemer."[168] This misses the point that Milton did not write a devotional work, the poem is not a spiritual exercise opening a gateway to the truth. It is a defence of God's plan for mankind in the form of a drama. It is the characters, therefore, who must carry the weight of the argument. Should there be any doubt about the nature of any protagonist then that defence is in danger of faltering.

Neither Milton's portrait of God enhances our view of his ways, nor does the use made by him of the Son encourage us to warm to him completely. Milton's decision to show them as Chairman and Chief Executive does little to raise the reader's esteem for and love of God, nor at times even of his Son.

---

168 *Milton's Messiah: The Son of God in the Writing of John Milton*, Oxford 2011

21

Satan

The surprisingly complex Satan

Conversely by enlarging Satan's character Milton provided a more balanced appraisal, avoiding one-dimensional wickedness. In his portrayal of Adam and Eve Milton created complex and compelling characters who face dramatic moral decisions. Milton plumbed the depths of human emotion, with the effect that they evolve from being the thinly drawn figures of Genesis into credible personalities, while (as would be expected of an angel) Satan is shown to retain some admirable qualities befitting a former Archangel. By being unexpectedly sympathetic characters they subvert much of the poem's argument and from our fallen state we can identify with their dilemmas and emotions.

Milton famously made Satan so convincing that some readers have favoured him, including those who agree with Blake that "Milton was of the devil's party without knowing it."[169] It is clear, however, that Milton takes pains to show Satan's weaknesses and wickedness. To say Milton was on Satan's side involves accepting that Milton could have wished for the triumph of evil over good. He may have believed that the Parliamentary cause was a justifiable cause on earth, enabling him to identify with Satan's rebellious energy and inventiveness, but there is no evidence to suggest that he withdrew from his Christian faith in favour of devil worship. His ambition was to write a Christian epic and to remind his readers that, possibly at times despite appearances to the contrary, God's ways are just.

---

169 William Blake *Marriage of Heaven and Hell*

In Milton's mind was the belief that we should keep faith and continue to obey in order to find that following God's ways is in our best interests.

The way of Milton is hard; a road which encounters setbacks and unfathomable dilemmas which we must confront, but which with continuing obedience to God will be for the best. However, the presentation of God almost encourages the reader to sympathise with Satan, just as we might empathise with the decisions made by Adam and Eve. In *Paradise Lost* Satan's stature gains, just as God's shrinks, partly because as 'fallen' readers we are more able to penetrate Satan's character. Many of the points made by Satan to Eve as he questions God's motives for forbidding Adam and Eve to eat the fruit of the Tree of Knowledge are entirely comprehensible lines of enquiry concerning God's ways. Herein is the heart of the dilemma.

Possible Hebraic influences on the character of Satan

Milton could have constructed one-dimensional characters which, like pieces on a chess board, would have been moved in a masterly game of 'justify God's ways,' culminating in victory for God. It was, however, the power of Milton's humanism which drove him to create something different from the thinly drawn biblical characters, whose very simplicity could have helped the cause of justifying God by not raising difficult questions. He appears to have seen a need to balance what may have been an impression of legalism, a monotonous diet of rules and obedience, with the face of humanity. It was here that Milton's knowledge of earlier models for Satan, including possibly *Midrash,* came to his aid. The result is that Satan does not neatly fulfil his role, reading faultlessly from his script.

Milton's determination to develop the character of Satan is seen in his presentation of Eve's temptation by Satan which went beyond even what the Rabbis wrote, though as Werman points out there are structural similarities between Chapter 13 of *Pirkei de-Rabbi Eliezer* and Book IX of *Paradise Lost*.[170] Once again it is Milton's artistic choices which shaped his presentation of Satan. His choice of Eve as the easier target, and the addition of a command not to touch the tree in addition to not eating the fruit are among the most important of Milton's additions, possibly deriving from *midrashic* borrowings.

Milton's boldest borrowing from the past was the idea of Satan entering the body of the serpent.[171] There is no mention in the Bible of Satan searching for a suitable vehicle through which to tempt Eve, merely: "Now the serpent was more subtil than any beast of the field which the Lord God made".[172] But the Rabbi writes that Satan : "descended and saw all the creatures which the Holy One, blessed be He, had created in His world and he found among them none so skilled to do evil as the serpent." Milton too has Satan roaming in search of the most suitable animal.[173] He describes the serpent's characteristics in detail as the:

> *Fit vessel, fittest imp of fraud, in whom*
> *To enter, and his dark suggestions hide*
> *From sharpest sight*

and thus not arouse suspicion "which in other beasts observed/ Doubt might beget of diabolic power."[174]

Pirkei de-Rabbi Eliezer wrote a parable to illustrate that the serpent was simply the vessel of Satan's evil. Milton took this one step further and has Satan enter the serpent through its mouth while asleep, whereas Eliezer describes the serpent having the appearance of a camel which Satan rides. Milton's development of the idea demonstrates his own skill as a storyteller, and has the advantage of displaying Satan's powers and astuteness.

170 Op cit Chapter 3

171 Werman op cit page 61-2

172 Genesis 3.1

173 IX 82-86

174 IX 89-95

Milton may also have derived the concept of God's envy of mankind from *Midrash*.[175] Eliezer's Satan mentions God's plan to withhold knowledge from mankind lest he should become like God, which Milton's Satan echoes in: "that ye should be as gods."[176] Satan uses the word envy to describe God's denying them the fruit but like Iago, having planted the seed of doubt in Eve, he quickly asserts that this is impossible: "can envy dwell/ In heavenly breasts?"[177] This leaves the impression of innocently thinking aloud only to dismiss the idea.

Milton's particular view of Satan

Milton did not mindlessly plagiarise other versions of the Fall of man; it is the choice of source and his novelty of presentation which defined the writer. Milton brought to bear his understanding of persuasive oratory on Satan's speeches to the Fallen Angels; his courage, inner torment and the mystery of his motivation all derive from Milton's imagination. The parallel with Iago becomes clear. Coleridge, finding it impossible to discover a key to understanding Iago's personality described his soliloquy: "The last speech, the motive-hunting of a motiveless malignity".[178] In the case of Satan it is the sin of envy which is the catalyst for all his other defects, including a psychotic sense of self-loathing, which ironically generates a pride, an 'hauteur,' leading to the delusion that he can defeat God.

Satan's envy and need for recognition

By interweaving a range of literary and theological influences within the Genesis account Milton created one of the most

175 Werman page 62

176 IX 708

177 IX 729-30

178 *Notes on the Tragedies of Shakespeare, Othello*

dangerously charismatic characters in literature. He could not penetrate the mind of God but he could delve into the head of Satan. Milton had to make Satan a worthy opponent of God and a threat to mankind but by asking Eve such searching questions about God's motives for his treatment of mankind Milton unleashed the prospect of radical questions and ideas undermining his defence of God. There is no human answer to Satan's questions: they hang in the air of Eden, endlessly and tantalisingly unanswerable. It is all too easy for Eve and the reader to be persuaded by them.

Even before the Infernal debate begins Milton alerts us to Satan's rebelliousness, guile, envy, pride and ambition, all of which are emphasised through the poem:

> *he it was, whose guile*
> *Stirred up with envy and revenge, deceived*
> *The mother of mankind, what time his pride*
> *Had him cast out from heaven, with all his host*
> *Of rebel angels, by whose aid aspiring*
> *To set himself in glory above his peers,*
> *He trusted to have equalled the most high,*
> *If he opposed; and with ambitious aim*
> *Against the throne and monarchy of God*
> *Raised impious war in heaven and battle proud*
> *With vain attempt.*
>
> (I 34-44)

This is not a strong character reference. Crucially he is "racked with deep despair", (I 126), and commits himself to evil: "To do aught good never will be our task, /But ever to do ill our sole delight," (I 159-600); indeed, he aims to "pervert" God's will, (I 164). Thwarted ambition, envy and a need to be esteemed by his peers combine to distort any qualities Satan might display, and his positive energy becomes misdirected. He is so proud that he claims it is: "Better to reign in hell, than serve in heaven"(I 263). Later Satan accuses Abdiel of leading a slothful, servile existence in Heaven (VI 164-170): he will never accept second place.

It is clear that, despite the unselfish impression he wishes to give in the debate when offering to travel to earth to ruin God's new creation, everything is for the greater glory of Satan. The debate is carefully stage-managed so that Satan's offer, coming at the end of a series of alternative suggestions, provides hope for the Fallen Angels and a comforting feeling that something is being done but at no cost to themselves. Their idolatory should alert us to the point:

> *Towards him they bend*
> *With awful reverence prone; and as a god*
> *Extol him equal to the highest in heaven:*
>
> (II 477-479)

The horror of Sin's birth and the fathering of Death – both son and grandson – are unambiguous commentaries on Satan's place in the moral scheme. The "hell within him," (IV 20), consists of envy and rage as he approaches earth. He admits that "pride and worse ambition threw me down," (IV 40), and shows that it is loss of face with the Fallen Angels which is part of his problem:

> *my dread of shame*
> *Among the spirits beneath, whom I seduced*
> *With other promises and other vaunts*
> *Than to submit, boasting I could subdue*
> *The omnipotent."*
>
> (IV 82-86)

His speech on returning to Hell reeks of self-congratulation:

> *What I have done, what suffered, with what pain*
> *Voyaged the unreal, vast, unbounded deep*
> *Of horrible confusion, over which*

By Sin and Death a broad way now is paved
To expedite your glorious march; but I
Toiled out my uncouth passage, forced to ride
The untractable abyss, plunged in the womb
Of unoriginal Night and Chaos wild,
That jealous of their secrets fiercely opposed
My journey strange, with clamorous uproar
Protesting fate supreme;

(X 470-480)

It is fear of failure before his fellow rebels, envy and ambition which provide the courage, energy and drive for his perilous journey. Echoing Iago's words, Satan's chilling line: "evil be thou my good," (IV 110), represents a deranged reversal of the heavenly code as he begins his evil quest.

Satan lies: he was "the first/That practised falsehood under saintly show," (IV 121-2), and twice tries to tempt Eve. The dream is a failure, but illustrates Eve's vulnerability when the prospect of god-like knowledge is held before her. Fortunately Adam reassures her next morning, but his second attempt is successful. Animal images are frequently used to describe Satan – a prowling wolf, (IV 183ff), a cormorant, (IV 196) and a toad (IV 800). His lies are exposed by the angel who sees through Satan's false explanations as to why he has come to Eden: "Argues no leader but a liar traced," (IV 949). Eve's description of her tempter in the dream is full of significance: "his dewy locks distilled/Ambrosia," hinting at an alluring but fake perfume, while Satan's emphasis on the fruit's sweetness and Eve's likeness to a goddess are all part of the Satanic flattery. However, Eve's memory of his alluring description of the Tree of Knowledge contains the entirely sensible question "is knowledge so despised?" (V 60), which is never fully answered. Amidst Satan's deceit lurk many unanswered questions concerning God's motives in creation.

The hurt of a thwarted ambition resounds:

For only in destroying I find ease
To my relentless thoughts

(IX 129-130)

and "all good to me becomes bane," (IX 122-3). Satan's goal is to destroy in one day what it took God six to create:

To me shall be the glory sole among
The infernal powers, in one day to have marred
What he almighty styled, six nights and days
Continued making,

(IX 135-138)

In a breathtaking act of defiance he had previously committed the sin of denying that God had created the angels at all: "We know no time when we were not as now; /Know none before us, self-begot, self-raised" (V 859-60). At his worst Satan spits: "spite then with spite is best repaid" (IX 178). His ploy moves in subtle stages, from extolling the physical attributes of the fruit through to the most sophisticated of lies. He lies about the effect of the fruit on the serpent. He flatters Eve that she will be hailed as a goddess. He questions God's law, but logically argues that God would never destroy his creation, therefore there is nothing to worry about: "God therefore cannot hurt ye, and be just;" (IX 700). Finally, he even suggests that God is withholding knowledge out of envy, which raises a good question about God's plan.

The punishment Satan receives from God is his final humiliation, confirming his wickedness and the triumph of God's grace with regard to Adam and Eve. "From hero to general, from general to politician, from politician to secret agent, from secret agent to Peeping Tom is the progress of Satan's character."[179]

CS Lewis's description of Satan's decline may be accurate on a narrative level, but does not do justice to the complexity of Milton's portrait of evil and Satan's continuing ingenuity and

179 CS Lewis. op cit

strength of will. Satan's envy of Adam and Eve's relationship tells much about his own empty and passionless life. Satan does not appear to have enjoyed a relationship with another angel. His daughter Sin springs from within his own mind and he fathers Death with his self-begotten daughter. He has known no meaningful relationship with a being outside himself. It would not have been sensible to leave Satan as a melodramatic villain (there are already some parallels with Elizabethan stage villains),[180] because he would not have been a convincing vanquisher of Eve, or a worthy opponent of God. There were, therefore, strong theological reasons why the portrait of Satan had to be fuller than that. Significantly, it is not only Milton's inclination to allow both sides of an argument to be heard, but also the artist's desire to present fully worked figures that caused Milton to infiltrate the persona of his creation, just as Satan climbed inside the body of the serpent, giving voice to the many facets of the character.

Fallen heroism

Satan is not the hero of the poem, theologically only the Son is that,[181] though Adam has a strong claim to the title. But Satan retains some heroic qualities, as befits a Fallen Angel. We must not forget that he is successful in his mission: "him by fraud I have seduced/From his creator, and the more to increase/ Your wonder, with an apple;" (X 485-7). Courage, energy, perseverance, eloquence – Satan has them all. Milton knew about energetic revolutionaries, (he had, after all, been one), and understood this side of Satan's character. Not only is he a strategist, but he can improvise, as when he meets Uriel, (III 654), and when he arrives in Paradise, he can attune his approach to the character of Eve.

Satan is an adept debater but it is his spirit that so captivates:

180 See Barbara K Lewalski 'The Genres of *Paradise Lost*: Literary genre as a means of Accommodation' in *Milton Studies 1987*

181 See 'Heroic Virtue and the Divine Image in *Paradise Lost*,' by JM Steadman in *Journal of the Warburg Institute 22 1959*

What though the field be lost?
All is not lost; the unconquerable will,
And study of revenge, immortal hate,
And courage never to submit or yield:

(I 105-108)

"To be weak is miserable," strikes the right note with the Fallen Angels, and the psychological boost they need is delivered: "The mind is its own place, and in itself/Can make a heaven of hell, a hell of heaven" (I 254-5). He makes a virtue out of the fact that at least they are free from God's dominance: "Better to reign in hell, than serve in heaven"(I 263). Who could resist the call: "Awake, arise, or be for ever fallen"?

Satan appears the epitome of heroic leadership:

he above the rest
In shape and gesture proudly eminent
Stood like a tower; his form had yet not lost
All her original brightness, nor appeared
Less than archangel ruined,

(I 589-593)

Clearly he had charisma, because in spite of Abdiel's subsequent rejection of him, Satan persuaded the angels to join in rebellion, pointing to their current state of servitude, the Son's inferior powers, and the lack of need for a superior to govern them. Adopting the ploy of turning the attention of the people from domestic problems to external threats (ie the Son) Satan strikes a chord with his audience:

Thrones, dominations, princedoms, virtues, powers,
If these magnific titles yet remain
Not merely titular, since by degree
Another now hath to himself engrossed
All power, and us eclipsed under the name
Of king anointed, for whom all this haste

Of midnight march, and hurried meeting here,
This only to consult how we may best
With what may be devised of honours new
Receive him coming to receive from us
Knee-tribute yet unpaid, prostration vile,
Too much to one, but double how endured,
To one and to his image now proclaimed?
But what if better counsels might erect
Our minds and teach us to cast off this yoke?

(V 772- 786)

The language is obsessed with the behaviour of court life which means much to Satan and his ambitions. He attempts to persuade the Fallen Angels they have been deposed, the talk is of an anointed king and of prostration before the monarch.

"Majestic though in ruin," Satan flatters the devils, makes them believe in themselves, encourages them to believe that nobody could have foreseen their defeat (a piece of special pleading on his own behalf here), and when the alternative ways forward have been put (which all have their own drawbacks) gives the ideal solution: they cannot be weak and do nothing, but he will go on the dangerous journey alone, to attempt something that is possible rather than impossible, leaving the rest to remain behind secure, constructively employed. The emotional response of the Fallen Angels means they fail to realise that this act of vandalism is not so great after all. Like the consummate politician that he is, in absolving the rest from action, Satan receives their grateful thanks and admiration.

The inner workings of Satan's mind

Milton provided detailed insight into Satan's psyche by including five soliloquies, all found in the key Books IV and IX, which betray his inner doubt and turmoil.[182] On his arrival

182 IV 32-113; IV 358-92; IV 505-35; IX 99-178; IX 473-93

at Eden in Book IV he admits to "pride and worse ambition", and that God did not deserve such treatment from him, nor was God's "service hard" (II 45). It is as if Satan attempts his own psychoanalysis, searching for the cause of his malignity, given that it would have been easy to render God praise and thanks:

> *Yet all his good proved ill in me,*
> *And wrought but malice*
>
> (IV 48-9)

He even wishes he had been created a lesser angel, and thus have resisted ambition. In an extraordinarily ironic analysis of his motives Satan's conclusion is that God was too loving in allowing the angels freedom to stray from goodness: "Be then his love accursed, since love or hate, /To me alike, it deals eternal woe" (IV 69-70). The pain he feels in his humiliation is palpable. He might be leader of the Fallen Angels but he is "only supreme/In misery;" (IV 91-2). He even wonders if penitence would be an option: "is there no place/Left for repentance, none for pardon left?" (IV 79-80) but he is sufficiently self-aware to know he is incapable of paying the price for that, which could only be "by submission; and that word/Disdain forbids me," (IV 81-82). What is more, he admits that fear of failure drives him to fulfil some triumph that he can report back to the Fallen Angels to gain their approval (IV 82-6).

Satan craves attention and praise; he cannot come to terms with the punishment he has received for letting his pride and ambition get the better of him. His inner despair is graphically conveyed as he interprets Hell as a state of mind:

> *Me miserable! Which way shall I fly*
> *Infinite wrath, and infinite despair?*
> *Which way I fly is hell: my self am hell;*
>
> (IV 73-75)

Repeatedly we find Satan is acutely self-aware, and as an angel, albeit fallen, he retains a residual awareness of God's love, as when he first spies Adam and Eve in Eden:

> *Not spirits, yet to heavenly spirits bright*
> *Little inferior; whom my thoughts pursue*
> *With wonder, and could love, so lively shines*
> *In them divine resemblance, and such grace*
> *The hand that formed them on their shape hath poured.*
> (IV 361-365)

Similarly he senses the heavenly goodness of the angelic guard, sent by God to patrol Eden: "And felt how awful goodness is, and saw/Virtue in her shape how lovely, saw, and pined/His loss;" (IV 847-849).

He even contemplates a pact with humans: "league with you I seek," (IV 375). Milton momentarily shifts to painting the devil of the Mystery play, as he rubs his hands and turning to the audience gloats on what is to befall the unknowing happy couple:

> *Ah gentle pair, ye little think how nigh*
> *Your change approaches, when all these delight*
> *Will vanish and deliver ye to woe,*
> (IV 366-368)

However, Milton pulls back and returns to psychology, as Satan's manic drive to destroy resurfaces:

> *By conquering this new world, compels me now*
> *To do what else though damned I should abhor.*
> (IV 391-2)

Milton's engagement with Satan's thought processes extends to a description of how Satan arrives at the idea of using the fruit of the forbidden tree in order to corrupt mankind. Upon seeing

Adam and Eve together his thinking is more complex than CS Lewis' "peeping Tom" suggests. True, Adam and Eve remind Satan of what he has lost: "Sight hateful, sight tormenting! Thus these two/Imparadised in one another's arms/The happier Eden, shall enjoy their fill/Of bliss on bliss, while I to hell am thrust," (IV 505-508). But he quickly moves on to calculate how he can use the happy couple in his plan. Aware that the Tree of Knowledge is out of bounds he deftly thinks that this seems "suspicious, reasonless" (IV 516) but he does not know the whole point of the exercise.

Satan goes on to ask the questions that anyone might ask; just as in an academic dispute the contrary case was put:

> *Why should their Lord*
> *Envy them that? Can it be sin to know,*
> *Can it be death? And do they only stand*
> *By ignorance, is that their happy state,*
> *The proof of their obedience and their faith?*
>
> (V 516-520)

But Satan is more devious than this; he does more than ask the questions. He uses these questions as the foundation on which to build the destruction of the couple whom he simultaneously admires, envies and hates. It is in Satan's most wicked moment that Milton portrays him at his most inventive. It is in this psychological understanding that Milton the dramatist excelled.

In the temptation itself Satan's awareness of the conflicting emotions within him becomes even greater. Continuing to admire the beauty of Eden he believes Earth is more beautiful than Heaven: "seat worthier of gods, as built/With second thoughts, reforming what was old!" (IX 100-101). This is of course heretical, for it implies that God is capable of creating the imperfect; nevertheless, Satan does not pursue this line of thought. Instead he reverts to jealous thoughts, and his desire to lash out in spiteful revenge. When he sees beauty and virtue he realises what he has lost: "all good to me becomes/Bane,"

(IX 122-3). But tortured inwardly, he cannot rest: "For only in destroying I find ease/To my relentless thoughts" (IX 129-30) which is coupled with the approval of others which he continually seeks:

> *To me shall be the glory sole among*
> *The infernal powers, in one day to have marred*
> *What he almighty styled, six nights and days*
> *Continued making,*
>
> (IX 135-138)

He does, however, retain an appreciation of beauty, responding to Eve's appearance by comparison with heaven: "her heavenly form/Angelic, but more soft, and feminine," (IX 457-8). Truthfully he can impress Eve with words of praise: "Empress of this fair world, resplendent Eve," (IX 568).

Shame and hurt pride are Satan's underlying feelings as he contemplates how man will evolve to the stature of angels and assume the space vacated by the Fallen Angels. He hates the thought of having to skulk around Eden in order to avoid the angelic police force God put there to protect mankind. Worst of all he has to squeeze into the body of an animal as a disguise:

> *I who erst contended*
> *With gods to sit the highest, am now constrained*
> *Into a beast, and mixed with bestial slime,*
> *This essence to incarnate and imbrute,*
>
> (IX 163-166)

Despite all his courage and intelligence Satan tellingly betrays a blind recklessness as he begins the temptation of Eve. Past caring, he needs to feel the heady gratification of the drug called 'revenge':

> *Revenge, at first though sweet,*
> *Bitter ere long back on itself recoils;*

Let it; I reck not, so it light well aimed,
Since higher I fall short, on him who next
Provokes my envy, this new favourite
Of heaven, this man of clay, son of despite,
Whom us the more to spite his maker raised
From dust; spite then with spite is best repaid.

(IX 171-178)

As Satan prepares himself for the temptation it is as if he cannot let go of the notion that his one solace now is destruction:

Thoughts, whither have ye led me, with what sweet
Compulsion thus transported to forget
What hither brought us, hate, not love, nor hope
Of Paradise for hell, hope here to taste
Of pleasure, but all pleasure to destroy,
Save what is in destroying, other joy
To me is lost

(IX 473-479)

Pausing for a while as he spies Eve and concluding that the time is ripe for her temptation, there is a sense that Satan stands outside himself, looking in disbelief at his now enfeebled state. As if he cannot believe how far he has fallen, that to destroy what he cannot have for himself is all that is left to him, he prepares for action. He has worked out that Adam is intellectually stronger than Eve, regretting that his own weakened situation means he must strike at the weaker enemy: "so much hath hell debased, and pain/Enfeebled me, to what I was in heaven" (IX 487-488). It is then, just before the decisive action of the drama, that Milton paints for us a portrait of Satan who is all show, not only in his lies to Eve "under show of love well feigned," (IX 492), but in the show of bravado he put on for the other Fallen Angels.

Certainly there are times when Satan demonstrates guts, endeavour, the rhetorical capabilities of a charismatic leader, powers of invention, strategy and tactical know-how, together with the ability to improvise; yet we now see how fragile he is. The reader may be beguiled by the character who is eye-catchingly the man of action; imaginative, flamboyant and adventurous, who leads an apparently much more exciting life than Adam and Eve. However, when we listen to Satan's soliloquies it should not take long for us to see the skull beneath the skin, the tortured soul of the father of evil.

The truth behind Satan's questioning of God's ways

Milton might have been pleased so far with this reading of Satan's characterisation. There is, however, one aspect of this portrayal that should cause us to reconsider Milton's success. By asking questions about the nature of God, the authority for his power and the execution of that authority Satan steals the show. Indeed, Satan produces another show entirely.

Chief among the questions he raises regarding godhead is the notion of servitude, of unquestioning obedience and submission to God. Second is the issue about what is wrong in trying to better oneself, of possessing the sin of ambition. Why is it that God wants to keep mankind down? By refusing him lawful access to the Tree of Knowledge of Good and Evil we may deduce that God wilfully stifles man (and to a lesser extent the angels themselves) through a hierarchical and secretive dictatorship. Theologically any object could have been used as a test of obedience but God chose the Tree of Knowledge. The entire creation depends upon hierarchy and progression at a pace set by God and Satan asks why this should be. Without any answers Milton's justification founders.

The corner into which Milton writes himself resulted from his dramatic skill in presenting convincing characters and his intellectual honesty in representing all viewpoints. Satan's ambition is based on envy. This is quite different from Adam's genuine desire to know more about creation and Eve's desire to improve efficiency in the garden and make herself more useful and therefore more valued. Although we must not be seduced by Satan's views on God, because his ambition is founded on self-loathing and a need for popularity, his questioning of God's plan based on a universe moving at a pace set by God is understandable. This explodes Milton's plan to justify God's ways, since in this case there can be no response from God because Milton did not know the answer. The portrayal of Satan is so full, subtle and convincing that Satan's 'wrong' ideas about God's relationship with man assume an unexpected reasonableness. So caught up are we in Milton's delineation of Satan's character that it is too easy for us to agree with the matters he raises. By any definition of reason Satan's questions are reasonable. Milton clearly cannot know God's mind and motives so we must be content either to suppress these reasonable queries or simply obey and submit. Similarly in Eve's questions to Adam about her role in Eden and their relationship with God, and in Adam's questions to Raphael about God and the universe, it is reasonable for them to want some answers. Indeed there is something to admire in them for using their minds in this manner.

Satan emerges as a figure tortured by thwarted ambition and twisted by self-obsession, who craves the drug of popularity and feels loss and regret, which fatally leads to envy, face-saving self-aggrandisement and pointless destruction. He is self-aware, particularly regarding his destructive tendencies, yet he is incapable of stopping. We are taken on a journey to the centre of Satan's mind. As with Iago we admire the cunning and finesse of his deception, but whereas the motivation for Iago's actions are more confused there lies behind Satan's thoughts and actions a more fully worked out psychological profile. As a tragic figure with talent but fatal flaws (not knowing when to quit in the face of stronger opposition being foremost among them) Milton's picture of Satan can easily persuade the reader into reading the 'wrong' poem. It should not but it does because Satan's questions are reasonable and receive no answer.

Blake was wrong about where Milton's loyalties lay but correct in one particular. Milton's energetic and clever portrait of the arch devil, second to his portrait of God, can subvert the poem's aim through the questions Satan asks. It is clear, however, that though Milton described him brilliantly, he was not on Satan's side. The issue we face is whether Milton's insistence on mankind's submission to God is sufficiently convincing to rebuff the questions about God raised by Satan and Eve.

Did Milton hope that readers would set aside these questions about God's purposes raised by his characters? Content to subscribe to the notion of obedience in the belief that there are limits to what we may know, did he think we would be satisfied that freedom is gained by submission to God in spite of intellectual difficulties which it is not our place to understand? Paradoxically, in a poem which advocates reason, it is the powerfully logical questions raised by Satan which, while it was intended to be blasphemy, force us to consider them. Satan's questions are entirely relevant to a justification of God's ways. Why would a God create such a universe with such inhabitants? If Milton's answer is that we cannot know and must obey, then reason is of limited use. Added to this is Milton's presentation of God, who provides little comfort, no warm reassurances that might satisfy us. Set against the unprepossessing figure of God, the thin, somewhat ambiguous picture of the Son, and combined with some equally searching questions about God's ways put by Eve, we are led to a very different place from the destination Milton intended.

There are times when Adam, Eve and even Satan sound like people we might know, or give voice to thoughts which we might have: that is their power. Perhaps nothing Milton could write about God's ways would convince the unconvinced, for it is the complexities of religious faith that Milton exposed in *Paradise Lost*.

22

Adam and Eve

Adam and Eve's prelapsarian state may appear uneventful compared with Satan's exploits but we should not be misled. Their relationship with each other and with God is complex and intense, for even in the prelapsarian state they experience intense moral pressure regarding the parameters within which they must live. We discover complex aspects relating to the relationship between husband and wife, but the most serious matter concerns their place in the scheme of things. Adam has the sterner task of having control over Eve, "He for God only, she for God in him," (IV 299), but this is not to say that Eve is without brains, or that Adam lacks courage. In the crucible of the garden the nature of creation and mankind's purpose is analysed and our future state set in motion.

Both Adam and Eve must confront seminal issues, and Milton endows them with distinct personalities which differ from the bare Genesis account of the Fall. Eve's character gains in stature as she grapples with the tension between obeying Adam (and therefore God) and asking searching questions about the boundaries within which they must live. His initially suffers through appearing to be a weak husband but also because of the function he must play, particularly as an acquiescent inquisitor of Raphael, whose responses are central to Milton's narrative requirements while helping to build a case in support of God. Following Raphael's warning to Adam that there are limits set on man's knowledge of the universe Adam is given a long piece of narrative concerning amongst other things his ability to speak, the naming of animals, his desire for a companion and crucially the rule that he should not eat the fruit from the Tree of Knowledge of Good and Evil.[183] His two functions here are to complete the story of creation but also to demonstrate that from the outset he was made aware of the rule not to eat the forbidden fruit, which is crucial to God's subsequent case against him. However, finally Adam is seen to possess immense courage and devotion when his love for Eve persuades him to disobey God.

The rules of the Garden and Adam's role

It was important that Milton's description of Adam and Eve's life in Eden should hit the correct note, given that the setting of Eden would be a reflection of God's intentions in his creation. Genesis provided the sparsest possible information. According to the P text the earth has grass, "herb yielding seed" and fruit trees[184] while the J text refers to plants and trees,[185] specifically trees which are attractive and provide food, as well as the trees of Knowledge and Life.[186] Details of the rivers are followed by two instructions; that Adam is placed there "to dress it and to keep it"[187] and that he should not eat fruit from the Tree of Knowledge.[188] Adam names the animals and the narrative moves swiftly to the creation of Eve and her temptation. Milton's imagination, enhanced by other possible influences including *midrashic* material, would therefore be necessary to enrich the scene.

There is little complicated gardening to do. The chief task consists of controlling the extravagant plant growth, since Eden already possesses ideal growing conditions. In suggesting that

---

183 VIII 250-560

184 1:11-12

185 2: 5

186 2:9

187 2:15

188 2:17

they divide their labours in order to improve efficiency Eve produces the only possible new idea in Eden. The implication of "to dress it and to keep it" is that this is a duty, an obligation placed on them: it is another aspect of obedience. The notion that work is a duty raises several questions. Can Adam and Eve suffer from overwork? What is the nature of tiredness in Eden? Is there pruning that is too hard for them to manage? It seems, however, that it is not the technique of gardening but the obedience that matters.

Milton's emphasis on obedience derived from Genesis but possibly also the *midrashists* who developed the notion of work as a metaphor, though Milton's debt to Midrash here is not necessarily as far reaching as Werman argues. Milton's treatment of work in the garden is, for example, more complicated than this implies, as shown in Eve's argument that they could improve their work rate by dividing their labours, an idea which has considerable merit. According to Werman[189] in *Pirkei de-Rabbi Eliezer* Milton would have been aware of the idea that working in the garden should be seen as: "being occupied with the words of the Torah and keeping all its commandments."[190] This argues Werman, demonstrates that: "work is the allegorical representation of devotion to study and the moral life." Furthermore, in order to avoid work being seen as "an empty pursuit," "Adam and Eve's effort to control the Garden can be related to their struggle in controlling their own temptation," and it is only when they separate that Eve demonstrates she does not understand the true meaning of their work. Here Werman pushes the metaphor too far. The theory that work in Eden is intended to be an allegorical representation of devotion to study and the moral life is only partially correct, not least because we know that Milton's God frequently gives his angels pointless tasks; their obedience is more important than the precise duty. In fact Milton elaborates on the practical

189 Op cit pages 58-61

190 Repeated in *Targum Yerushalmi* and *Avot de-Rabbi Nathan*. See Werman page 80 and 89-90

realities of life in Eden and how Adam and Eve responded to their duty to manage the garden, which is Eve's concern. Milton develops this to examine the nature of their relationship with each other and with God, when Eve suggests a novel way of improving their efficiency.

The nature of Adam and Eve's relationship has frequently been regarded as seminal in the development of new ways of looking at marriage and relationships by Protestant writers.[191] One of the central issues concerns the desirability of compatibility in marriage, which is to say the pairing of equals in order that conversation may be had on a satisfying level. Halkett[192] put the case simply: the new Protestant concept of companionate marriage was based on the classical ideal of male friendship transferred to a heterosexual relationship between partners of equal mental capacity. Certainly this is seen in Milton's Divorce Tracts, *Colasterion* making the point clearly. Grantham Turner[193] develops this and examines the status of sexual relations in Eden; do they represent "Paradise" or "Serpent"? He concludes that Milton was torn between a radical, erotic, egalitarian view of marriage and a conservative, patriarchal view which disdains the 'flesh': in short, does Milton favour a prelapsarian marital equality and innocence or a subordinate role for Eve before, as well as after the Fall? It becomes apparent that Milton supported the latter and makes this clear in his description of prelapsarian Eden. Luxon[194] develops the topic arguing that what distinguished man from God was the ability to withstand loneliness, man requiring company (though Luxon neglects that God does admit to being lonely but does nothing to rectify

191 See for example: *Milton and the Idea of Matrimony: A Study of Divorce Tracts and Paradise Lost* by John Halkett, Yale University Pres 1970; *One Flesh: Paradisal Marriage and Sexual Relations in the Age of Milton* by James Grantham Turner, Clarendon Press, Oxford, 1987 and *Single Imperfection: Milton, Marriage and Friendship* by Thomas Luxon, Duquesne University Press Pittsburgh, 2005

192 Op cit

193 Op cit

194 Op cit

this) and that while Milton followed Protestant thinking about friendship and compatibility in marriage he did not accept the notion of equality between partners. This is certainly accurate.

Eve regards Adam as her "author and disposer," (IV 635), her hair suggesting her subjection to him:

> *She as a veil down to the slender waist*
> *Her unadorned golden tresses wore*
> *Dishevelled, but in wanton ringlets waved*
> *As the vine curls her tendrils, which implied*
> *Subjection,*
>
> (IV 304-308)

Eve is always willing to play a subservient role and even when Adam is engaged in hearing more about the creation from Raphael she hangs back, openly preferring to have information relayed to her by Adam.[195] No doubt at this point Eve lives her life through Adam, and it is not until Satan as the serpent raises questions concerning God's ways that she shows a more inventive mind and a confidence to articulate ideas to improve their work rate in the garden.

Adam does, however, admit that he takes inspiration from Eve:

> *I from the influence of thy looks receive*
> *Access in every virtue, in the sight*
> *More wise, more watchful, stronger,*
>
> (IX 309-311)

Somehow he feels wiser and empowered by the way Eve looks at him. This power which Eve holds derives from the fact that she adores him and crucially looks up to him, since she regards herself as his inferior, thus enabling him to feel the stronger partner. This special but unexplained relationship leads to his confusion over whether to accept blame for their sin: "either

195 VIII 48-57

to undergo/My self the total crime, or to accuse/My other self, the partner of my life;" (X 126-128). Eve is a part of him, made from him and the source of his self-confidence but crucially he has responsibility for their combined obedience to God in Eden. Adam's role as a quasi-representative of God on earth can make him sound priggish, but when he reminds Eve about how easy their task in the garden is, a role bestowed on them by a munificent deity, his confidence derives from the empowerment he receives from his partnership with Eve:

> *needs must the power*
> *That made us, and for this ample world*
> *Be infinitely good, and of his good*
> *As liberal and free as infinite,*
> *That raised us from the dust and placed us here*
> *In all this happiness, who at his hand*
> *Have nothing merited, nor can perform*
> *Aught whereof he hath need, he who requires*
> *From us no other service than to keep*
> *This one, this easy charge, of all the trees*
> *In Paradise that bear delicious fruit*
> *So various, not to taste that only tree*
> *Of knowledge, planted by the tree of life,*
>
> (IV 412-424)

His language here contains fulsome thanks and praise; however, words such as ample, infinitely good, liberal, free, happiness and delicious fruit subsequently become their ironic opposites. Adam enjoys acting as God's ambassador in Eden but this again derives from hierarchy and is seen in his dominion over the animals: "Hast thou not made me here thy substitute, /And these inferior far beneath me set?" (VIII 381-2). Unfortunately for our perception of Adam's nature, Milton uses him for narrative purposes as well to remind the reader about the rules of Paradise in order to enhance God's defence, but such comments may grate with the reader. Adam appears superficial and naïve when he plays down the difficulty of fulfilling God's task for them in the garden, suffering also from Milton's desire to achieve dramatic irony within the narrative.

In an effort to create a strong case for Adam's failings Milton sounds early warning signals concerning the "uxorious King" Solomon (I 444), later enlisting Michael's prosecution witness statement: "From man's effeminate slackness it begins," (XI 634) and gives Adam words suggesting his weakness in the face of Eve's beauty: "here only weak/ Against the charm of beauty's powerful glance" (VIII 532-3), whilst painting Eve "in outward show/Elaborate, of inward less exact" (VIII 538-9). This amassing of evidence highlights the clash between the love between man and woman and obedience to and love of God, as Milton becomes engaged in an increasingly empathetic presentation of the pair by highlighting the choices they face concerning choosing between God and his or her beloved. Milton is steadfast, however, in his insistence on the way Adam allowed the God-given order, man over woman, to be subverted.

Adam receives information and messages direct from God, though we do not hear how he knows Eve's name, or how he knows that evil thoughts do not necessarily influence the mind of the thinker. To his credit he wishes to understand more about their position and the difference between earth and heaven. Luxon[196] argues that Adam's relationship with Raphael is more of an egalitarian friendship than his relationship with Eve. This is correct in the sense that they seem to relate easily with each other, naturally discussing aspects of creation and history which are unknown to Eve and which therefore she could not discuss with Adam. He is not, however, an equal partner in his relationship with Raphael, though he tries to ask searching questions. Adam cannot contribute much to the dialogue other than questions (except when he tells Raphael about his and Eve's creation) and importantly there are limits to what Raphael is allowed to tell him. Unlike Eve

196 Op cit

in her conversation with the serpent Adam is acquiescent when presented with the permitted information, letting Raphael off the hook too easily. In Book V he entertains Raphael to a meal, which precipitates his question about the difference between earthly and heavenly food. His question is "wary" (V 459) and without demur he accepts Raphael's explanation about degrees of being, a direct contrast with Satan's desire to overthrow the accepted order. Adam is all acceptance:

> *O favourable spirit, propitious guest,*
> *Well hast thou taught the way that might direct*
> *Our knowledge, and the scale of nature set*
> *From centre to circumference, whereon*
> *In contemplation of created things*
> *By steps we may ascend to God.*
>
> (V 507-512)

Nothing in his experience so far has caused Adam to question this gradual movement towards the ethereal.

He seems incredulous when Raphael reminds him about obedience to God's law, finding it inconceivable that they would ever disobey their maker:

> *What meant that caution joined, If ye be found*
> *Obedient? Can we want obedience then*
> *To him, or possibly his love desert*
> *Who formed us from the dust, and placed us here*
> *Full to the utmost measure of what bliss*
> *Human desires can seek or apprehend.*
>
> (V 513-518)

This has the unfortunate result that Adam's apparent naivety makes him appear overconfident and lightweight. When he asks Raphael to relate the events in heaven it is out of disbelief at the Fallen Angels' rebellion rather than a desire to learn how to be a radical:

> *though what thou tell'st*
> *Hath passed in Heaven, some doubt within me move,*
> *But more desire to hear, if thou consent,*
> *The full relation, which must needs be strange,*
> *Worthy of sacred silence to be heard.*
>
> (V 553-557)

By the end of Book VII it is as if Adam's jaw has dropped at the story of Satan's rebellion, and not wishing to be thought impressed by Satan and his followers, Adam is keen to establish his obedience, indeed subservience to God and thanks for being given early warning of danger:

> *Great things, and full of wonder in our ears,*
> *Far differing from this world, thou hast revealed*
> *Divine interpreter, by favour sent*
> *Down from the empyrean to forewarn*
> *Us timely of what might else have been our loss,*
> *Unknown, which human knowledge could not reach:*
> *For which to the infinitely good we owe*
> *Immortal thanks, and his admonishment*
> *Receive with solemn purpose to observe*
> *Immutably his sovereign will, the end*
> *Of what we are.*
>
> (VII 70-80)

Milton's accumulation of dramatic ironies depends upon using Adam as a mouthpiece in this manner. However, despite the almost unctuous tone here Adam asks for more information about the reasons for the creation of heaven and makes the good point that this information may help them: "What may no less perhaps avail us known," (VII 85). Polite questioning is the hallmark of Adam's long meeting with Raphael, who makes clear that the knowledge he imparts has strict limitations:

Yet what thou canst attain, which best may serve
To glorify the maker, and infer
Thee also happier, shall not be withheld
Thy hearing, such commission from above
I have received, to answer thy desire
Of knowledge within bounds; beyond abstain
To ask, nor let thine own inventions hope
Things not revealed, which the invisible king,
Only omniscient, hath suppressed in night,
To none communicable in earth or heaven:
Enough is left besides to search and know.
But knowledge is as food, and needs no less
Her temperance over appetite, to know
In measure what the mind may well contain,
Oppresses else with surfeit, and soon turns
Wisdom to folly, as nourishment to wind.

(VII 115-130)

Adam's words suggest the boundaries within which they operate in Eden; the earlier words describing freedom and bounty replaced here by service, constraint, abstinence, suppressed and temperance in the service of an invisible king. Here we have a clear sense of the immense moral pressure under which Adam and Eve live in Paradise. This is the message of dictators throughout the ages: 'you only need to know what I decree is sufficient for you to know.' Unlike Satan, however, Adam accepts the boundaries. Having heard about the seven days of creation, by the beginning of Book VIII Adam's curiosity is satisfied: "divine/Historian who thus largely hast allayed/ The thirst I had of knowledge," (VIII 6-8). Yet his final question 'concerning celestial motions' is 'doubtfully answered' (The Argument Book VII). Raphael understands Adam's question "for Heaven/Is as the book of God before thee set," (VIII 66-67) but refuses to divulge what is beyond the limits of man's understanding as laid down by God: "His secrets to be scanned by them who ought/Rather admire;" (VIII 74-5). Indeed, Book VIII is all about God's secrecy:

> *God to remove his ways from human sense,*
> *Placed heaven from earth so far, that earthly sight,*
> *If it presume, might err in things too high,*
>
> (VIII 119-121)

Adam accepts without question Raphael's summation: "Leave them to God above, him serve and fear;" (VIII 168). Adam seems happy with the quiet life:

> *How fully hast thou satisfied me, pure*
> *Intelligence of heaven, angel serene,*
> *And freed from intricacies, taught to live,*
> *The easiest way, nor with perplexing thoughts*
> *To interrupt the sweet of life, from which*
> *God hath bid dwell far off all anxious cares,*
>
> (VIII 180-185)

Even worse, Adam admits that things "obscure and subtle" (VIII 192) are not relevant to their daily lives; more than that he says is "fume,/Or emptiness, or fond impertinence," (VIII 194-5). Eager to please Raphael lest he be thought too forward, Adam relates his own and Eve's creation, facts surely already known to Raphael.

Adam appears alarmingly over-confident about the crucial point:

> *Yet that we never shall forget to love*
> *Our maker, and obey him whose command*
> *Single, is yet so just, my constant thoughts*
> *Assured me, and still assure:*
>
> (V 550-553)

Before the Fall then, Adam's characterisation suffers through his role as God's mouthpiece. However, life in Paradise is not straightforward. Adam and Eve must exercise their brains to deal with the moral pressure of obeying God's command, more particularly in the injunctions regarding the forbidden fruit and suppressing any thirst for knowledge. Adam's conversation with Raphael reinforces the constraints within which they are supposed to live and work. Apart from the temptation to be like Narcissus in Eve's Satan-induced dream, fairly easily negotiated by Eve with Adam's help, superficially life passes uneventfully, Adam and Eve handling their roles and responsibilities for Paradise and the propagation of mankind with equanimity. However, the inner moral alertness they are required to exercise using reason is repeatedly mentioned. Nevertheless, without an obvious challenge prelapsarian life may seem dull, though Milton carefully placed warning signs regarding steadfast obedience. Milton's characterisation may lead us to compare them and their stay-at-home lives in the garden less favourably with the adventurous derring-do of Satan. This was a temptation Milton surely intended.

However, the portrayal of Adam and Eve as fuller human characters created difficulties. In Genesis the simpler, thinly drawn images of Adam and Eve operate on a one-dimensional plane, which does not complicate the idea of obedience in the way that Milton does. Milton's account leaves too many unanswered questions about God's ways, which are glimpsed in the early revelation that there is a limit placed on man's allowed knowledge.

Love and sexual relations

The nature of prelapsarian love and sexual relations had been a matter of contention amongst theologians for centuries before Milton attempted his account. Protestant opinion argued that prelapsarian sex was all controlled by reason and ingenious ways around the issue of physical sex were contrived.[197] Taking the opposite view Milton describes the love between Adam and Eve before the Fall as idyllic, mutually and physically pleasurable

197 See *John Milton' Life, Work and Thought* by Gordon Campbell and Thomas Corns, published Oxford University Press 2008 pp 338-9

and beneficial. Milton has no hesitation in showing that Adam and Eve have a fully physical relationship. Luxon[198] argues that this wedded love is a step on the journey to spiritual love and not a celebration of sexuality *per se*, following Raphael's account of mankind's passage from a bodily to an ethereal form. While this journey is an accepted element of Milton's thinking, and his descriptions of lovemaking do have a spiritual dimension, Milton does not, however, deny the pleasure of a physical union.

In fact Anna Beer[199] contends that prelapsarian sex is "good sex" compared with paid sex offered by the harlot,[200] and that whereas earlier Milton had idolised a classical view of male friendship he celebrated physical heterosexual love in *Paradise Lost.*[201] This view is supported by Campbell and Corns: "The young Milton may have looked with bewildered disdain on the fornications of his student contemporaries, and celebrates, in his masque, the victory of unconquerable chastity, but the thrice-married older man, newly wed to his much younger bride, displays an evident enthusiasm."[202]

Milton's debt to Hebraic sources (and also in how they influenced other Protestant theologians) on this occasion may well have been significant, having profound implications for our attitude towards Adam and Eve's relationship and consequently on the balance of our sympathies in the poem. In Adam's decision to eat the fruit because of his love for Eve, and her fear that Adam will take another woman should he survive her, their position is made increasingly secure as the strength of their love for each other is understood, to the point that it threatens our censure of their disobedience.

Werman traces Adam's desire for company from the Genesis 2:2 comment: "But for Adam there was not found an helpmeet for him," to the *Midrash* of Genesis Rabbah: "He brought forth

---

198 Op cit

199 *Milton,* published Bloomsbury, 2008

200 IV 765-7

201 Op cit p 326

202 Op cit p 339

all living creatures before Adam in pairs. Adam said, 'For each one there is a partner, but there is no partner for me'." The conversation between Adam and God on the matter of their respective solitude represents a key moment in the poem for both, culminating in creation of Eve.[203]

Milton appears to have relied on Rabbinic writings for his defence of divorce in the *Doctrine and Discipline of Divorce,*[204] and for the celebration of married sexual relations. In contrast to Catholic and Protestant teaching Milton did not see marriage as a second-best state, designed for those who could not contain themselves, but celebrated "wedded love". Before the Fall Adam and Eve's lovemaking is open and joyous. True, Adam experiences something akin to lust immediately after the Fall, but this soon returns to the quality of their previous relationship. This is covered extensively in *Ze'enah U-Re'enah.*[205]

Milton was also influenced by the passing of the Adultery Act in 1650. This was a Puritan driven law which sought to replace ineffectual ecclesiastical courts with an enforceable law based on biblical precedents. The act was not a success; it was generally ignored by civil authorities, and by the Restoration had fallen away completely. Milton had been suspicious of the Act's capacity to transfer biblical teaching into law and did not share the squeamish Puritan approach to sex. He preferred the prescripts of the Hebrew Bible and the Rabbis' acceptance of the reality of human sexuality.[206] In Book IV Milton celebrated "wedded love" and criticised chastity.[207] All this is likely to have been Milton's response to the zealous intentions of the Adultery Act; even when Eve suggests they forgo sex after the Fall[208] Adam overrules her. If marriage could be interpreted as a symbol of

203 VIII 510-14. See Werman pages 57-58 for the link to *Pirkei de-Rabbi Eliezer*

204 1643

205 See Werman page 124

206 Werman page 153

207 IV 736-775

208 X 987-8

the "mystical union that is between Christ and his Church"[209] Milton's clear celebration of Adam and Eve's relationship in *Paradise Lost* seems more potent than any expressions of love for man spoken by God. Once again Milton steers the reader towards a human rather than a divine perspective.

Adam needed Eve for company, for "rational delight," (VIII 391), or "Food of the mind," (IX 238), though it is never made clear how 'rational' delight might be achieved either within the limits of allowed knowledge or Eve's supposed inferior mind. Without doubt God implanted the desire for a companion in Adam, which is where Milton is on firm biblical ground with a theme repeated throughout the ages:[210]

> *In solitude*
> *What happiness, who can enjoy alone,*
> *Or all enjoying, what contentment find?*
>
> (VIII 364-366)

God's claim that he too is without a friend may be a trial of Adam's power of reasoning, but it sounds weak, coming from a God who, as Adam correctly replies, does not need to "propagate", and is in himself perfect: "Thou in thy self art perfect, and in thee/Is no deficience found; not so in man," (VIII 415-416). This is important because Adam was created with the instinct for love and companionship, which is likely to put him in a difficult situation should he have to choose between obeying God's law and love of Eve – though both impulses come from God.[211] Milton does not help to make clear his position on prelapsarian sex when he displays knowledge of traditional Protestant teaching in the narrator's comment that: "Wedded love" is "Founded in reason, loyal,

---

209 Solemnization of Matrimony in *The Book of Common Prayer*

210 See *The Time Machine* by HG Wells: "It would be no paradise if it belonged to me alone"

211 For further discussion see Peter Lindenbaum 'Lovemaking in Milton's Paradise', *Milton Studies 1974*

just, and pure" (IV 755), distinguishing man from "the bestial herds". It is, however, clear that he sees physical love as important, even in prelapsarian Eden, though eventually the love for each other of Adam and Eve fatally clashes with love of and obedience to God. Accusations of weakness against Adam for allowing himself to be dominated by his wife, and repeated reminders of Adam's senior role similarly complicate the picture Milton paints. The reader must be aware that love and beauty are so powerful that they can be both positive and negative influences.

There is no doubt that Adam and Eve are deeply in love. Adam loves Eve from the first moment he sees her:

> *a creature grew,*
> *Manlike, but different sex, so lovely fair,*
> *That what seemed fair in all the world, seemed now*
> *Mean, or in her all summed up, in her contained*
> (VIII 470-73)

and:

> *here passion first I felt,*
> *Commotion strange, in all enjoyments else*
> *Superior and unmoved, here only weak*
> *Against the charms of beauty's powerful glance*
> (VIII 530-533)

Milton is careful to remind the reader that love can be dangerous as well as uplifting but he does not relate this to the fact that mankind is unable to detect hypocrisy. Even if beauty should take second place to the quality of the woman's thinking and words Adam would not be in a stronger position.

Adam is captivated by Eve, and in an expression of perfect love he describes the idyllic union of two people until they become as one:

So much delights me as those graceful acts,
Those thousand decencies that daily flow
From all her words and actions mixed with love
And sweet compliance, which declare unfeigned
Union of mind, or in us both one soul;

(VIII 600-4)

Milton combines an acceptance of joyous physical love in Eden with a notion that in their everyday lives they may gain a glimpse of a more spiritual relationship, which Raphael later describes in response to Adam's question concerning the love lives of angels. Milton certainly does not, however, condemn their physical relationship.

Reference to "sweet compliance", does, however, carry overtones of Eve's obedience and the superiority of Adam over her which recur in the poem. Even before the Fall Eve is clearly the subject of Adam's higher status. Adam also admits that Eve has the power to cloud his mind: "what she wills to do or say,/Seems wisest, virtuousest, discreetest, best;/All higher knowledge in her presence falls/Degraded," (VIII 549-552). This is a key admission for the stern critics of his subsequent uxorious behaviour.

In a state of perfect harmony they show mutual respect in their lovemaking: though Eve is 'knowing' she is still in a state of submission as she 'yields':

She as a veil down to the slender waist
Her unadorned golden tresses wore
Dishevelled, but in wanton ringlets waved
As the vine curls her tendrils, which implied
Subjection, but required with gentle sway,
And by her yielded, by him best received,
Yielded with coy submission, modest pride,
And sweet reluctant amorous delay.

(IV 304-311)

She displays due respect, described by Milton as "subjection" to Adam, yet through her well-chosen words of adoration we sense she knows how best to keep her man:

> *thy gentle hand*
> *Seized mine, I yielded, and from that time see*
> *How beauty is excelled by manly grace*
> *And wisdom, which alone is truly fair.*
>
> (IV 488-491)

This is all too much for Satan, to see "these two/Imparadised in one another's arms" (IV 505-6). In the bower Adam did not turn: "from his fair spouse, nor Eve the rites/Mysterious of connubial love refused:" (IV 742-3). The love of Adam and Eve is powerfully all of a piece with nature where:

> *they led the vine*
> *To wed her elm; she spoused about him twines*
> *Her marriageable arms, and with her brings*
> *Her dower the adopted clusters, to adorn*
> *His barren leaves.*
>
> (V 215-219)

This unselfish love contrasts with postlapsarian sex, which is less gentle and more self-centred. Earlier Adam and Eve: "into their inmost bower/Handed they went;" (IV 738-9), whereas after the Fall: "Her hand he seized, and to a shady bank, /Thick overhead with verdant roof embowered/He led her nothing loth;" (IX 1037-1039). He grabs Eve and takes her to the nearest bank, not for pure love, but for personal gratification:

> *For never did thy beauty since the day*
> *I saw thee first and wedded thee, adorned*
> *With all perfections, so inflame my sense*
> *With ardour to enjoy thee,*
>
> (IX 1029-1032)

Eve's earlier modesty – "I led her blushing like the morn:" (VIII 510), contrasts with: "Eve, whose eye darted contagious fire." (IX 1036). Significantly too, prelapsarian love had been uplifting: "With thee conversing I forget all time, /All seasons and their change," (IV 639-40). This piece continues with some sensitive love poetry, where Eve describes how none of the beauties of Paradise would be worthwhile without Adam, what Milton described as: "the cheerful society of wedlock… this pure and more inbred desire of joining to itself in conjugal fellowship a fit conversing soul (which desire is properly called love) which is stronger than death, as the spouse of Christ thought, many waters cannot quench it, neither can the floods drown it."[212] This becomes significant when Adam must choose between Eve and God.

Milton had to be careful in his openly human descriptions of their lovemaking because of the church's negative teaching on sexuality. Milton has Adam warned about this; he is reminded that there is a difference between the passion known to beasts and human love controlled by reason:

love refines
The thoughts, and heart enlarges, hath his seat
In reason and is judicious,

(VIII 589-91)

Adam and Eve also possess a need for human companionship, not just sex. Raphael has some of the most important words in the poem about the power of love:

For love thou say'st
Leads up to heaven, is both the way and guide;

(VIII 612-3)

Love may provide a glimpse of heaven but it has potential dangers, which may deceive and subjugate as well as uplift. It

212 *Doctrine and Discipline of Divorce* III 396-7. See also III 382; 391-2;481;492

transpires that real life is not straightforward, for love does not lead to heaven if it dulls the brain and eventually Adam must choose between love for Eve and obedience to God.

Temptation

Navigating between the Genesis account, Hebraic influences, Protestant attitudes to love and sex, and Milton's own view of a man's superior status, his task of describing the moment of the Fall was not to be straightforward. When, for example, Eve eats the fruit she challenges the hierarchy of Eden by asking the powerful question: "for inferior who is free?" (IX 825). Similarly we must confront the matter of whether, when Adam agrees to eat the fruit, he is behaving in an uxorious fashion, or is it that he loves Eve and cannot bear to be parted from her? The theological question underpinning the entire scenario is that if God needed a test of Adam and Eve's obedience why did he forbid them from eating the fruit of the Tree of Knowledge of Good and Evil, since it complicates the theology and the characters of Adam, Eve and Satan? Milton explores this, but does not resolve it beyond the argument of obedience. Doubts over the nature of God's character are raised when he is so adamant that man should not aspire to the level of godhead, thereby enabling Satan to raise questions about this in Eve's mind. It also provides Satan with an opportunity, as he speaks through the serpent, to give an apparently convincing reason for Eve to believe him about the properties of the fruit, though Milton would argue that her reasoning was defective.

At the outset Adam discharges his duty as senior partner by reminding Eve of the rule concerning the Tree of Knowledge in his first speech, emphasising the dire punishment which could ensue: "what e'er death is,/Some dreadful thing no doubt;"(IV 425-426). Obediently Eve acknowledges her obligations both to God and Adam:

> *My author and disposer, what thou bid'st*
> *Unargued I obey; so God ordains,*

God is thy law, thou mine: to know no more
Is woman's happiest knowledge and her praise.

(IV 635-38)

Were it not that we know what is to follow there could be reasonable confidence in the chances of Eve being successful, given her rectitude in resisting the temptation of her dream. However, the process turns out to be harder once Eve is confronted by Satan's persuasive arguments. In her way Eve is a radical. She may show defective reasoning during the course of Satan's temptation, since she could have asked more searching questions to verify the validity of Satan's statements, but though she should have obeyed Adam her desire to leave, based on the ambition to develop her skills and improve their working practices, mark her out as a woman prepared to take risks, embrace change and extend her knowledge.

Eve's proposal to improve their work rate springs from a desire to be useful and to be more of an equal to Adam. Here Milton's enriched portrait of Eve may render our acceptance of the poem's theological ambitions harder to accept. She has always shown an enquiring mind, and early on asked sensible questions about the night sky: "But wherefore all night long shine these, for whom/This glorious sight, when sleep hath shut all eyes?" (IV 657-8). There is no evidence to suggest that Eve's proposal springs from egoism, and her feelings are all for Adam. Her suggestion to divide their labour is because she appreciates the enormity of their task in Eden:

what we by day
Lop overgrown, or prune, or prop, or bind,
One night or two with wanton growth derides
Tending to wild.

(IX 209-212)

Eve is full of common sense ideas, using her brain to the point of inventing delegation and efficient time management.

Indeed, Adam praises her ideas: "for nothing lovelier can be found/In woman than to study household good," (IX 232-3). Milton immediately moves away from the Genesis account and subsequent church teaching about the perfidy of women and from this point our reactions to Eve's behaviour become more complex.

The turning point in their discussion comes when Eve is shocked by Adam's suggestion that she should not have to face their foe alone. Adam gradually works up to this point. We know from his earlier questioning of Raphael that Adam will be as diplomatic as possible in handling difficult situations. Firstly, he uses the argument that they should not work too hard: "For not to irksome toil, but to delight/He made us, and delight to reason joined" (IX 242-244). He proceeds to make the logical point that in the future they will have children to help them: "younger hands ere long/Assist us" (IX 246-7), which is quickly followed by a diplomat's compromise suggestion that "to short absence I could yield./For solitude sometimes is best society," (IX 248-9). Eve makes no response to these points.

It is different when Adam makes the more subtle point that there is safety in numbers: "But other doubt possesses me, lest harm/Befall thee severed from me:" (IX 251-2), for: "The wife, where danger or dishonour lurks,/Safest and seemliest by her husband stays,/Who guards her, or with her the worst endures" (IX 267-269). Eve's retort that they cannot forever live like frightened rabbits is a fair one, if risky.

Key to Adam's decision to let Eve go is her reaction to his fears for her safety. Parents of teenage children know the difficulty of loosening the reins at the right time. Eve simply says: you clearly don't trust me. Milton's introduction to her words highlights Eve's love and that she feels Adam has been unreasonable:

> *That such an enemy we have, who seeks*
> *Our ruin, both by thee informed I learn,*
> *And from the parting angel overheard*
> *As in a shady nook I stood behind,*

Just then returned at shut of evening flowers.
But that thou shouldst my firmness therefore doubt
To God or thee, because we have a foe
May tempt it, I expected not to hear.

(IX 274-281)

Eve is sufficiently astute to remind Adam that they cannot suffer death or pain, though Adam has already acknowledged that they do not understand what death is. Finally, she utilises her most powerful weapon:

His fraud is then thy fear, which plain infers
Thy equal fear that my firm faith and love
Can by his fraud be shaken or seduced;

(IX 285-287)

Adam's reply is clever, though the force of its logic is questionable. They are safer together he argues, but he avoids calling her weak, claiming an attempted fraud against her is an affront to her dignity: "asperses/The tempted with dishonour foul, supposed/Not incorruptible of faith, not proof/Against temptation:" (IX 296-9). He concludes with the emotional plea that he requires Eve's companionship: "I from the influence of thy looks receive/Access in every virtue, in thy sight/More wise, more watchful, stronger," (IX 309-11), though this might be seen as a weak argument, since it could imply Adam's lack of confidence to stand alone.

Eve's retort is stronger as she demonstrates her creative mind. She wonders how they can ever be happy, never able to be apart in fear of an unknown enemy: "How are we happy, still in fear of harm?" (IX 326), making the appropriate debating point that any dishonour falls on the seducer not the seduced: "his foul esteem/Sticks no dishonour on our front, but turns/ Foul on himself; then wherefore shunned or feared/By us?" (IX 329-332). When Eve uses the argument of *Areopagitica*, a new dimension is opened: "And what is faith, love, virtue unassayed/Alone, without exterior help sustained?" (IX 335-6). This appears to be a fair point, though Milton wishes us to remember that temptation comes to us and does not need to be sought and so Adam mentions this later: "trial will come unsought" (IX 366).

Eve is brimming with reasonable questions about their lives, culminating in the thought that they should move on their lifestyle, otherwise: "Frail is our happiness, if this be so,/And Eden were no Eden thus exposed" (IX 340-1). Had she simply obeyed the rule where would that leave human ambition, creativity and development? Milton has opened Pandora's Box.

Adam's role is to support the law and appropriately he warns Eve she must use reason wisely. Here Milton gives Adam his most subtle statement in the poem, asserting that the greatest danger is not an external enemy but the misuse of reason:

> *within himself*
> *The danger lies, yet lies within his power:*
> *Against his will he can receive no harm.*
> *But God left free the will, for what obeys*
> *Reason, is free, and reason he made right,*
> *But bid her well beware, and still erect,*
> *Lest by some fair appearing good surprised*
> *She dictate false, and misinform the will*
> *To do what God expressly hath forbid.*
>
> (IX 348-356)

This is a forceful defence; Adam must encourage Eve.to use her reasoning with caution lest she be misled. However, the difficulty is that humans are imperfect and cannot detect hypocrisy and Adam does not confront the difficult task of moral philosophy, which is to ask whether or not every aspect of an issue has been fully explored in the reasoning process. Instead he reverts to an emotional statement: "Not then mistrust, but tender love enjoins, /That I should mind thee oft, and mind thou me" (IX 357-8).

Adam's arguments are put to one side. We cannot say whether he does this with reluctance, resignation or discomfort; the fact is he senses Eve has not been convinced. Adam gives way but makes a crucial point: "Go; for thy stay, not free, absents thee more;" (IX 372). He shares a vital characteristic with God, which is that he allows freedom of choice. However, by behaving like God he does not fulfil his role as God's enforcer in Eden. Eve is determined and speaks submissively but has the final say: "Persisted, yet submiss," (IX 377); in a pointedly ambivalent phrase Milton indicates her demeanour but also her determination. She leaves: "With thy permission then, and thus forewarned" (IX 378), clinging to the (incorrect) thought that a foe would not stoop to attack the weaker of the pair. Adam watches Eve leave; significantly "Her long with ardent look his eye pursued/Delighted" (IX 397-8) and all he can think to ask is that she is back home by noon.

Adam is in a unique situation at this stage. Though he disagrees with Eve's decision by allowing Eve free will he loosens her everlasting straitjacket and enables her to grow as a person. His decision has the additional advantage of strengthening the relationship between them, though at considerable risk. In allowing her to fail he displays a similar authority to that exercised by God. Adam could, indeed should have behaved in an authoritarian manner and forbidden Eve to go off alone; instead he gives her the freedom to learn from the experience, whilst demonstrating his trust in her ideas. In fairness Adam does not realise the extent of the possible consequences if Eve fails. God, however, always has foreknowledge, placing him in a superior position. Adam may be guilty of not taking sufficient care of Eve's safety; he should have been 'cruel to be kind' and forbidden her to leave him because she was exposing herself (and consequently Adam) to danger. Obedience should take precedence over love, trust and free will. Obedience is superior to and safer than 'reasoned' choice, lest that reasoning is faulty. Should Adam never allow Eve to go off alone? What is the status of her ambition and her attempts to use her mind by producing new ideas? When in the future might it be possible for Eve to work alone, and how would Adam know? Was there another compromise solution, which might have satisfied both God and Eve? When does free will come second behind obedience and when should individuals be allowed to make mistakes?[213] These are some of the questions Milton's dramatisation raises.

Adam is truly the tragic hero of the poem. His characterisation is defined by his role in Genesis, but Milton's portrait shows him to be sufficiently intelligent to have implemented an alternative solution to Eve's request to leave. Milton cannot allow him to make a different decision, so we are left with an Adam who falls for love, and not for being careless about Eve's safety, while Eve's arguments raise serious questions about God and his desire for obedience. By allowing Adam to articulate his love for Eve at the conclusion of their conversation Milton concentrated the reader's attention on love. Human love has overcome reason and obedience to God. In attempting to negotiate the clash between the human and divine Adam becomes a tragic hero.

It is too easy to say that Adam's reason should have controlled his love for Eve. There may well be situations in Milton's world where thinking through reasoned points is successful but here reason is not enough to help Adam through his dilemma. Milton demonstrates the complexity of human relationships and adds a further layer of meaning in the spirit of Eve's endeavour, which we have otherwise only seen in Satan. It is hard to condemn Eve's subsequent thirst for knowledge, given that she is motivated by her desire to support Adam. By attributing to Eve such thoughts Milton unwittingly leads us to weigh the competing concepts of obedience to a God who does not fully explain his reasons for the rules, against Eve's desire to use her brain in a good cause. She should unquestioningly obey God's command but her motivation and reasoning carry

---

213 On Eve as a character in her own right rather than just a part of Adam see 'The Renaissance Idea of Androgeny,' by Marilyn Farwell in *Milton Studies 1982*. Also 'Feminism and Paradise Lost,' by Joan Malory Webber in *Milton Studies 1980*

huge weight. In her desire to think through how better they might manage their lives Eve's creative instincts are superior to Adam's.

Eve's lack of sufficiently robust reasoning skills lets her down in the end. That Adam was correct in believing there is safety in numbers is confirmed when Satan cannot believe his good fortune in finding Eve alone: "Beyond his hope, Eve separate he spies," (IX 424). Satan rates Adam's intellect higher than Eve's, but Eve's resistance is stronger than he expected. Satan has to lead her through a series of trials before finding the key to unlock her compliance. Subconsciously Eve may have been swayed by parts of the dream but in the final moment it is hunger that finally tips the balance: "the hour of noon drew on, and waked/An eager appetite, raised by the smell/So savoury of that fruit," (IX 739-741).

Satan's first temptation, that Eve deserves to be seen by more than just one man: "Who shouldst be seen/A goddess among gods, adored and served/By angels numberless, thy daily train" (IX 546-548), falls on deaf ears. Eve is not vain, and is more surprised that a serpent can talk: "What may this mean? Language of man pronounced/By tongue of brute, and human sense expressed?" (IX 553-4). Satan is characteristically quick to use this opportunity to lie about the effect of eating fruit from the Tree and linking this with his first point, because speech allows him to say how wonderful Eve is: "gaze, and worship thee of right declared/Sovereign of creatures, universal dame" (IX 611-12). Eve resists this too: her excellent reply is that they are spoiled for choice in the garden, given the multitude of fruits available to them, and though she makes the mistake of following the serpent to the location of the Tree of Knowledge she is quick to say all the right things, particularly in her reference to God's rule: "we may not taste nor touch;/God so commanded," (IX 651-2) and the importance of using their reason: "our reason is our law" (IX 654). She even repeats that she will obey God's law that: "Ye shall not eat/Thereof, nor shall ye touch it, lest ye die" (IX 662-3). Satan is getting nowhere, but raises himself up to his full magnificence for the final push: God's death threat is empty because he, the serpent, survived eating the fruit, and anyway, why would God wish to deny you this fruit:

> *Why but to awe,*
> *Why but to keep ye low and ignorant,*
> *His worshippers;*
>
> (IX 703-5)

His final points are good ones; if God is just he will not do you harm: "God therefore cannot hurt ye, and be just;" (IX 700) and God simply wants to keep you down: "Why but to keep ye low and ignorant," (IX 704). Finally, he tempts Eve with the notion that God wants to retain knowledge because he would otherwise be envious: "What can your knowledge hurt him, or this tree/Impart against his will if all be his?/Or is it envy, and can envy dwell/In heavenly breasts?" (IX 727-730). By giving these words to Satan Milton weakened his justification of God. These are important and complex theological concepts, worthy of pages in an academic justification of God's ways. In a dramatic poem with invented dialogue, what happens is that Milton raises queries about God's ways which are never fully answered. There is no convincing evidence in Fish's analysis[214] to suggest that this is contrived in order to test the reader by tempting him or her to read the wrong poem, by questioning God. *Paradise Lost* was conceived by Milton as an epic narrative and executed along the lines of a verse drama, which must stand or fall by the power of it own presentation, not sleight of hand.

Therefore, in the first of two soliloquies given to Eve (IX 745-79) and in a daring stream of consciousness, we eavesdrop on her reasoning. Even before Eve commences she seems ready to believe that the serpent has made reasonable points: "Yet rung of his persuasive words, impregned/With reason,

214 Op cit

to her seeming, and with truth;" (IX 737-8). This may not be what God wishes to hear, nor what he expects by way of unquestioning obedience but Satan had made points which deserve an answer and Eve is not unreasonable in trying to analyse them for herself, concluding that if appearances mean anything then what the serpent has said is credible.

And this is the point. Eve judges the merits of Satan's case only on their surface appeal. She does not consider alternative explanations for his points, neither does she test their validity by questioning Satan further about them. The fruit allows a serpent to speak, "Gave elocution to the mute," (IX 748): even though there may be other reasons for this strange power she does not consider them, partly because they would be outside her experience. God could surely not forbid the desire for wisdom: "what forbids he but to know,/Forbids us good, forbids us to be wise?" (IX 758-759). Here Milton is forced to ascribe to Eve some sophistry, or in his view, defective reasoning. Essentially she argues that God's forbidding them from eating fruit of the Tree of Knowledge actually commends it to them:

> *his* (God's) *forbidding*
> *Commends thee more, while it infers the good*
> *By thee* (the serpent) *communicated, and our want:*
> *For good unknown, sure is not had, or had*
> *And yet unknown, is not had at all.*
>
> (IX 753-757)

Lack of information about an unknown good means that good is not possessed, or if it is possessed unwittingly it is not properly owned. Certainly something unknown cannot be used but how is it possible to possess an unknown good? Indeed Adam and Eve do not possess an unknown good, as Eve thinks she knows it will arrive in the form of fruit. In Eve's conclusion: "Such prohibitions bind us not"(IX 760) it is the word 'prohibitions' which is key. Eve decides to disobey God because she cannot work out what is wrong with possessing a thirst for knowledge, which is central to the problem that God's ways are incapable of being fully understood. Her final thought is that death cannot be designed only for humans, given that the snake is still alive; it would simply not be 'just': "For us alone/Was death invented?" (IX 766-767). This is a good question, but she fails to grasp that Satan may have been lying about it.

Eve may not pursue this analysis owing to Milton's need to maintain the dramatic momentum of the narrative as it approaches the climactic point. Deeper insight into Eve's mind might be achieved through soliloquy but it would slow the pace. Milton brought his characters to life but lacked space to elaborate on the additional theological or practical aspects of the question in hand. He was also bound by historical church teaching concerning the wickedness of Eve.

The turning point in the temptation is when Satan opens the possibility of Eve widening her horizons: what harm can there be in knowledge? Consequently Eve ignores her rule of submission to God and Adam and fails to ask Satan for proof. Her ambition to be something greater than she is leads to her downfall. She is not as clever as Adam, but tries to do the correct Miltonic thing and use her brain; this much Milton acknowledges.[215]

Eve's thought processes after eating the fruit show another aspect of her attempt to use reason. To her credit she grapples with the temptation to keep secret from Adam the fact of her eating the fruit in order that she may have control over him:

> *So to add what wants*
> *In female sex, the more to draw his love,*
> *And render me more equal, and perhaps,*
> *A thing not undesirable, sometime*
> *Superior; for inferior who is free?*
>
> (IX 821-825)

215 Eve has no direct contact with God, unlike Adam, and so does not feel the power of his commands in the same way. See 'Civil Society and the Abstract Individual in *Paradise Lost*,' by Carrol B Cox in *Milton Studies 1987*

We are now on a different psychological level from the Eve of the Bible. What Eve reveals here is no desire for vain self-aggrandisement but her insecurity. She wants to find a way of improving herself in order to keep hold of Adam, and believes that by eating the fruit she will be able to communicate with Adam as an equal. Eve's thoughts relate to her private feelings of insecurity and her desire to be loved and valued more as an equal, whereas Satan has a superior view of himself and an ambition to rival God in the heavenly hierarchy.

A further point in defence of Eve is that she genuinely loves Adam and cannot bear the thought of him with another woman if she were to suffer God's punishment of death. Therefore, she concludes that sharing the fruit with Adam will mean:

> *Adam shall share with me in bliss or woe:*
> *So dear I love him, that with him all deaths*
> *I could endure, without him live no life.*
>
> (IX 831-833)

This is the second of Eve's soliloquies (IX 795-833) and concludes with a similar dependence on Adam as he has expressed for her. As with Satan soliloquy is the form of fallen internal monologue, and is the most successful of Milton's dramatic techniques in revealing anguish, remorse or here a half-fallen mind wondering how to act. Eve's questioning some fundamentals of God's plan demonstrates that obeying God involves either unthinking obedience or thoughtful anguish.

Eve's downfall derives from her ambition and love. By dramatising her thought processes Milton revealed the tension between his analytical portrait of Eve and his need to follow the plot. She should, of course, have asked the serpent for proof of his identity, about the exact origin of his ability to speak, the precise meaning of death and the nature of God's injunction regarding knowledge of good and evil, but if he had her do this, Milton would have written a treatise rather than a dramatic poem. In addition, we know that humans cannot detect hypocrisy. The dialogue between Satan and Eve is not a fair fight, given mankind's difficulty in distinguishing appearance from reality, suggesting that a flaw or deliberate weakness in God's creation has played a significant part in the Fall.

In Milton's dramatisation of the plainly told Genesis account it was necessary for Eve to have a second-class mind, ("in outward show/Elaborate, of inward less exact" (VIII 538-9), but he went as far as he dare in portraying her capacity to think and act rationally. All the discussions regarding Milton's view of women stem from this.[216] Eve has to shoulder the blame. God demands of Adam: "Was she thy God that her thou didst obey" (X 145); on behalf of God Michael comments: "a brutish vice,/Inductive mainly to the sin of Eve" (XI 518-9); and Adam concludes: "still I see the tenor of man's woe/Holds on the same, from woman to begin" (XI 632-3). Eve's reasons for going off alone are not all bad and she has a brain, but in a poem where reason is everything, Eve has to be made intellectually inferior to Adam. Not only disobedient, Eve needed to appear stupid. The added danger is that Eve's spirit of pushing back the boundaries, of flying too close to the sun, theologically flawed though it may be makes Adam seem unambitious. Possibly more than any other character Eve gains in stature as a result of Milton's dramatic technique. Conversely, she is the victim of his need to adhere to the biblical narrative.

Eve's love for Adam is overwhelming; meanwhile, in the time Eve has been away, Adam has been expressing his love for Eve by making her a garland. Adam must face another choice. Throughout Adam has been a stickler for the rules, and we might expect that with his superior intellect and the reminders he received he would respond more easily to the situation in which he finds himself. However, love again holds sway.

On her return Eve appears almost drunk: she is "heightened as with wine," (IX 793) and: "in her cheek distemper flushing

216 See Diane McColley's *Milton's Eve*, University of Illinois Press, 1983 and Joseph Wittreich's *Feminist Milton*, Cornell, 1987

glowed," (IX 887), none of which does her cause much good. In Milton's dramatisation Adam allows Eve to leave because he loves her; he wants her to know that he trusts her and that she is not a prisoner. Significantly on her return and with the garland he has prepared for her as a love token, on hearing what has happened the garland falls and "horror chill/Ran through his veins," (IX 890-1) but his first thought is not of obedience but of love:

> *How can I live without thee, how forgo*
> *Thy sweet converse and love so dearly joined,*
> *To live again in these wild woods forlorn?*
>
> (IX 908-10)

At the opening of Book IX Milton's impassioned tone was accusatory:

> *I now must change*
> *Those notes to tragic; foul distrust, and breach*
> *Disloyal on the part of man, revolt,*
> *And disobedience: on the part of heaven*
> *Now alienated, distance and distaste,*
> *Anger and just rebuke, and judgment given,*
> *That brought into this world a world of woe,*
> *Sin and her shadow Death, and Misery*
> *Death's harbinger:*
>
> (IX 5-13)

Yet his dramatisation of the Fall demonstrates that human love involves allowing the freedom to stray, forgiveness and if required death. Contrary to the poem's intention *Paradise Lost* shows that love is a complex emotion where it may be preferable to allow the beloved freedom, perhaps incurring some risk, to being kept prisoner.

How does all this influence our view of God? This test of Adam and Eve's obedience lacks any middle path by way of resolution. Obedience and faith become synonymous, allowing limited scope for challenging reasoning: faith is obedience without question. By portraying a complex drama of human love Milton left us a different message from the Genesis account. On behalf of the human race Adam cries: "Why should not man,/Retaining still divine similitude/In part, from such deformities be free," (XI 511- 513) yet ultimately acquiesces with an echo of Eve's earlier "submiss": "I yield it just, said Adam, and submit" (XI 526). In another world Milton might have taken as his subtitle for the poem *All for Love*, Dryden's title for his account of Anthony's willingness to risk status and achievements for love of Cleopatra, which was written three years after Milton's death.

Their language

Milton's treatment of Adam and Eve was central to his personal *Midrash* on the Genesis account of the Fall. From the simplicity of the biblical account of straightforward disobedience we are led into identifiably human territory, parts of which easily sound familiar to modern readers. The questioning of a seemingly strange rule, the trust between man and woman, how we choose between obeying a law and love for a partner, allowing that partner to have independence, none would be out of place in contemporary literature.

Eve's concern that after she has gone Adam might take another woman, and Adam's evolving reaction to her sin, from anger at Eve's action to sorrow at their loss of innocence, are among Milton's credible images of human behaviour, which draw us to empathise with Adam's plight to the point where we may begin to stray from the path Milton intended for his readers. "That willing suspension of disbelief for the moment, which constitutes poetic faith"[217] which underpins great drama here draws the reader into seeing the situation from Adam's viewpoint.

217 Coleridge, *Biographia Literaria* Chapter 12

Neither merely a weak husband nor a one-dimensional sinner Adam struggles with the contradictions of human existence. Genesis simply concludes with the hardships of human existence and expulsion from Paradise, together with another rule that they should not eat from the Tree of Life.[218] God's plan for Christ's atonement of mankind's sins is in the distant future; Adam and Eve only have themselves to rely upon, and the path to redemption is portrayed as a long and potentially treacherous journey.

The inclusion of dialogue is the single most important element in Milton's narrative. Add to this his use of soliloquy[219] and herein lies the secret of his success in writing a poem about the human condition, and an explanation for his difficulty in justifying God's ways. Eve's language is a telling example of Milton's ability to differentiate between characters. In Genesis she speaks eight words: "The serpent beguiled me, and I did eat."[220] Milton has her tackling complex subjects but her language remains simple, though not necessarily less coherent than Satan's or Adam's, despite the fact that she has the unenviable task of rebutting Satan's persuasive tongue and confronting her husband with what she has done. Eve's language is plain, partly to maintain the biblical position that she is not as clever as Adam or Satan but she makes frequently powerful observations.

An initial tone of acquiescence and calm surrounding Eve is established as she summarises her position and attitude to her situation in Eden:

---

218 "Therefore the Lord God sent him forth from the garden of Eden, to till the ground from whence he was taken. So he drove out the man: and he placed at the east of the garden of Eden Cherubims, and a flaming sword which turned every way, to keep the way of the tree of life." *Genesis* 3: 23-24

219 See Broadbent (op cit) page 80: "the characters of *Paradise Lost* do not soliloquize until they have fallen; unfallen speech and gesture are directed always to another person."

220 *Genesis* 3:13

God is thy law, thou mine: to know no more
Is woman's happiest knowledge and her praise.

(IV 637-638)

Here is a tone of willing acceptance which has the simplicity and rhythm of an aphorism. The balance achieved in the first six words is supported by eleven words reinforcing the statement emphasising happiness, knowledge and thankfulness.

As she recounts her dream[221] Eve is clearly concerned by what she experienced but expresses it in a steady, direct and precise manner:

O sole in whom my thoughts find all repose,
My glory, my perfection, glad I see
Thy face and morn returned, for I this night,
Such night till this I never passed, have dreamed,
If dreamed, not as I oft am wont, of thee,
Works of day past, or morrow's next design,
But of offence and trouble, which my mind
Never knew till this irksome night;

(V 28-35)

A long, calmly expressed sentence, which continues to line 38, is given breathing space by the pauses achieved by commas denoting her emotion though she never loses her composure. Later as she attempts to convince Adam that she should go off alone she never allows her emotions to overflow, even while she is explaining her inventive plans to improve their work in the garden. It is steadily argued and quietly assured:

Thou therefore now advise
Or hear what to my mind first thoughts present,
Let us divide our labours, thou where choice
Leads thee, or where most needs, whether to wind

---

221 V 28-93

> *The woodbine round this arbour, or direct*
> *The clasping ivy where to climb, while I*
> *In yonder spring of roses intermixed*
> *With myrtle, find what to redress till noon:*
> *For while so near each other thus all day*
> *Our task we choose, what wonder if so near*
> *Looks intervene and smiles, or object new*
> *Casual discourse draw on, which intermits*
> *Our day's work brought to little, thou begun*
> *Early, and the hour of supper comes unearned.*
>
> (IX 214-225)

Here Eve is measured in pace and tone as she articulates a plan in logical steps. It is straightforward, deals with practicalities, provides examples and gives a reason (to avoid the distractions which working alongside each other bring) for her suggestion. A fourteen-line sentence, it is fluently expressed, using only two commas at the ends of lines, the pauses in the middle of lines adding to the air of calm expression and a persuasively argued case.

Adam's response typifies his more verbose and circuitous manner. He opens in a gentle tone, the pauses around 'associate sole' attempting to adopt a sense of the calm which Eve adopts. There follows a long section of flattery, praising her initiative. However, the tone centres on Eve's submissive status, she is praiseworthy not particularly because of her inventive ideas but because she is concentrating on 'household' matters for the benefit of her husband: this might even be called patronising:

> *Sole Eve, associate sole, to me beyond*
> *Compare above all living creatures dear,*
> *Well hast thou motioned, well thy thoughts employed*
> *How we might best fulfil the work which here*
> *God hath assigned us, nor of me shalt pass*
> *Unpraised; for nothing lovelier can be found*

In woman, than to study household good,
And good works in her husband to promote.

(IX 227-234)

He does, however, suggest that delight and relaxation are acceptable to God, and that work should not be all consuming (IX 235-243), though this may elevate Eve in our estimation, since she appears more creatively ambitious for improvement in their duty to tend the garden. His only effective repost is to cling to the notion of obedience: "for thou know'st/What hath been warned us," (IX 252-3). Eve is the creative partner, Adam the stickler for the rules: herein lies the dilemma of the entire poem.

Adam's instinct is to greet others in a humble tone. On meeting Raphael he adopts a "submiss approach and reverence meek" (V 359). Adam's opening words to Raphael[222] demonstrate a natural feel for getting off on the right foot, again by flattery – their guest must come from heaven since he has such a "glorious shape" (V 362). It is hard to fault Adam's initial approach to others. He proceeds to show a commendably inquisitive tone "to know/Of things above his world" (V 454-5) utilising the language of astonishment at any suggestion that he and Eve would disobey God's commands, reaffirmed later.[223] His language later demonstrates a keenness for knowledge: "The thirst I had of knowledge" (VIII 8); he has a genuine desire to know more about the size of stars and their purpose[224]though his subsequent continuation of the language of food and drink suggests he is more easily placated than Eve with what he is told: "How fully hast thou satisfied me," (VIII 180), reflecting the narrator's comment: "Adam cleared of doubt," (VIII 179). Adam shows that he prefers not to handle concepts which are too difficult or disturbing to him by using words such as

222 V 361-370

223 V 514-5 and V 544-553

224 VIII 15-38

perplexing, anxious cares, molest us.[225] His attitude to forbidden knowledge is not to ask why it is forbidden but to express gratitude that he may avoid anything obscure or subtle, which is "fume, emptiness and fond impertinence."[226] In contrast Eve later pursues her questioning of the serpent about the constraints placed on them by God, though fatally she neglects to ask the key question concerning the serpent's ability to speak and how this might link to a possible intruder in Eden.

In responding to the serpent she begins straightforwardly: "How camest thou speakable of mute, and how/To me so friendly grown above the rest/Of brutal kind," (IX 563-565). Despite the image of Eve as less able than Adam, so far she is the character with ideas and asks the serpent questions in a logical order. Her soliloquy contains the turning point in the history of Christianity but Eve proceeds with care through the arguments and does not become carried away:[227]

> *his* (God's) *forbidding*
> *Commends thee more, while it infers the good*
> *By thee communicated, and our want:*
> *For good unknown, sure is not had, or had*
> *And yet unknown, is as not had at all.*
> *In plain then, what forbids he but to know,*
> *Forbids us good, forbids us to be wise?*
> *Such prohibitions bind not.*
>
> (IX 753-760)

The punctuation here breaks up Eve's speech, as in the central lines concerning 'good unknown' she carefully attempts to make sense of the situation step by step. It is the link between this section and her following words "In plain then" that causes the difficulty.

Milton alerts us to what he would term false reasoning,

225 VIII 183-197

226 ibid

227 IX 745-779

as in the Fallen Angels debating philosophy "in wandering mazes lost".[228] Eve's key omissions are Adam's reminder to her concerning an unknown enemy and the requirement not to eat the fruit from the Tree of Knowledge. However limited the quality of Eve's thinking, she strives to work her way through the issue, though this exposes the difficulty of measuring the quality of reasoning.

Later Adam and Eve spend hours in "mutual accusation" (IX 1187) but from what is reported of Eve's speech she was correct when making a crucial point: "thou couldst not have discerned/Fraud in the serpent, speaking as he spake;/No ground of enmity between us known," (IX 1149-1151). Up to a point this is true; if she had known what the reader is told, that neither angels nor humans can detect hypocrisy, though Adam is likely to have chosen obedience to the rule above all else.

Even when she suggests suicide Eve retains her composure:

> *Restored by thee, vile as I am, to place*
> *Of new acceptance, hopeful to regain*
> *Thy love, the sole contentment of my heart*
> *Living not dying, from thee I will not hide*
> *What thoughts in my unquiet breast are risen,*
>
> (X 971-975)

Her words seek to placate Adam; she shows faith in Adam and uses emotive words such as 'restored', 'vile', 'new acceptance', 'thy love, the sole contentment of my heart,' in an effort to persuade him. Adam, however, shows more passion, is more excitable, and cannot contain his emotion as he considers what has happened to Eve: "How art thou lost, how on a sudden lost,/Defaced, deflowered, and now to death devote?" (IX 900-901). Repetition and alliteration here help him to communicate his overwrought state. This is quickly replaced not by calm reason but by an equally passionate conclusion expressed with repetition and alliteration, when he offers to join Eve in

228 II 561

whatever fate may befall them: "How can I live without thee, how forgo/Thy sweet converse and love so dearly joined,/To live again in these wild woods forlorn?" (IX 908-910).

The development of and contrast between their diction and tone add to the power of their characterisation. Though Eve speaks simply it is not to suggest she lacks a brain or imagination. She disobeys God's command but unlike Satan not from selfishness, ambition or pride. Her reasoning was flawed but it was an attempt to prove herself useful to and not merely an adjunct to Adam. She raises questions concerning reason, ambition, love and obedience which recur and are central to our response to the poem.

Repentance

A significant example of Milton's originality in *Paradise Lost* is the inclusion of Adam and Eve's repentance. There is no mention of this in Genesis and Milton may have been influenced by *Midrash.* Werman points out: "In *Pirkei de-Rabbi Eliezer*, Adam is portrayed as a sorrowful penitent who prays for the removal of his sin and is forgiven by a merciful God; his repentance is the paradigm for all future generations whose atonement will be accepted by the Creator".[229] Furthermore: "The centrality of repentance in Jewish theology is expressed in a *Midrash* that assigns to atonement a role in God's original plan – 'Adam was created from dust of the place where the Temple was to rise for the atonement of man's sins'."[230] This may be so but there was another arguably stronger incentive, as Milton wished to portray the whole range of Adam and Eve's experiences and emotions.

His presentation of Adam and Eve's capacity to repent only works because they are portrayed as complex characters,

229 Op cit page 131. See Chapter 7 for a detailed analysis of Milton's position and debt to *Midrash*

230 From *Genesis Rabbah* 14.8 quoted by Werman page 141

displaying qualities as well as defects, and therefore possess the ability to recognise their sin and be penitent. They do this with some assistance from the Son, though he can only be a hidden intercessor on their behalf and a sign of what is to come in the future. Adam and Eve even grow in our estimation, since they have only their commitment to God to rely upon, and he is punishing them. They may gain the reader's respect because God's manner has not always deserved their penitence, yet they still acknowledge their disobedience. There may be hope for the future, and Milton clearly desired a gentler tone with which to conclude, but we may wonder whether we love God any more at the end of the poem than we did at the beginning. Milton stresses the free will Adam and Eve were given, which enables them to show repentance, itself based upon their innate goodness. Milton's decision to include repentance was a significant attempt to present fully worked-out characterisations, portraying the capacity for good as well as evil, though it also secured a stronger position for his justification of God in one respect which is the manner of his accepting the sinners' penitence.

Primarily, however, Milton portrayed a very human image of repentance. Adam and Eve are thrown back on each other for support. Adam's pain leaves him: "to sorrow abandoned, but worse felt within,/And in a troubled sea of passion tossed," (X 717-8). He begins with self-loathing and despair at what he has done[231] and questions God's purpose in creating him[232] to the point that "Inexplicable/Thy justice seems;" (X 753-55). He wishes he had rejected the terms of his existence (X 756-59) but to his credit realizes he would not accept that complaint from his own son, concluding: "Be it so, for I submit, his doom is fair," (X 769). His sorrow extends to the effect his decisions will have on future generations "On me, me only, as the source and spring/Of all corruption, all the blame lights due;" (X 832-3).

Eve begs Adam's forgiveness and accepts total responsibility:

---

231 X 720-27

232 X 744-46

"On me, sole cause to thee of all his woe,/Me, me only, just object of his ire" (X 935-36), admitting she "became thy snare" (XI 165). It is when Adam accepts Eve's forgiveness and is reminded of his love for her that he finds the strength to go on in the hope that God will relent and "turn/From his displeasure" (X 1093-94). Adam makes her feel valued and eternally important: "Mother of all Mankind," "since by thee/ Man is to live," (XI 159-61). It is the love they have for each other that saves them; love will "light'n/Each other's burden" (X 960-1) and in sharing their burden they will cope.

The final two books of the poem are neither the most lyrical nor the most exciting. There is a requirement for a muted, tragic tone but simultaneously there is man's repentance and God's forgiveness. However, the recounting of future events is as much a rebuke to mankind as a harbinger of hope. Murder, disease, war, intemperance and old age are set against agrarian plenty, wedded bliss and God's covenant following the flood. Milton does not seem to have been able to resist the stern teaching which dulls the earlier brighter tone of tender togetherness. The future is easily summarised: "so shall the world go on,/To good malignant, to bad men benign," (XII 537-538) and the promise of salvation from "thy saviour and thy Lord" (XII 544) a distant prospect of hope.

God's mood continues to sound self-pitying; look what I gave them and this is how they repay me is the tone:

> *I at first with two fair gifts*
> *Created him endowed, with happiness*
> *And immortality: that reality fondly lost,*
> *This other served but to eternize woe;*
> *Till I provided death; so death becomes*
> *His final remedy, and after life*
> *Tried in sharp tribulation, and refined*
> *By faith and faithful works, to second life,*
>
> (XI 57-64)

Hereafter, redemption will be a long, hard road.

Unsurprisingly Adam does not seem confident of God's continuing support: "But prayer against his absolute decree/ No more avails than breath against the wind," (XI 311-312). Significantly, it is the overarching grip of obedience which dominates Milton's presentation of the expulsion from Eden. Adam follows his previous comment with: "Therefore to his great bidding I submit" (XI 314). God will allow forgiveness but it is conditional, since he stated at the very beginning:

> *I will clear their senses dark,*
> *What may suffice, and soften stony hearts*
> *To prayer, repentance, and obedience due,*
>
> (III 188-191)

Adam and Eve duly comply:

> *prostrate fall*
> *Before him reverent, and there confess*
> *Humbly our faults, and pardon beg, with tears*
> *Watering the ground, and with our sighs the air*
> *Frequenting, sent from hearts contrite,*
>
> (X 1087-91)

What they do not know is that this has been predetermined at worst or foreknown at best and will rest upon one thing – their obedience:

> *Henceforth I learn, that to obey is best,*
> *And love with fear the only God, to walk*
> *As in his presence, ever to observe*
> *His providence, and on him sole depend,*
>
> (XII 561-564)

In presenting the repentance of Adam and Eve Milton was at odds with Protestant thinking which ascribed to God the gift of repentance and salvation, based on faith in Christ's atonement for man's sins. In theory Milton gave to Adam and Eve the gift of free will, either to choose repentance or not: we read a very human description of Adam and Eve's repentance. Eve's words to Adam provide the one certain and very human hope for the future: "thou to me/Art all things under heaven, all places thou," (XII 617-618). They seem repentant but what is the relationship between true repentance and submission? It is obedience to the rules that would have saved them in Eden, which is a very different kind of salvation from that portrayed in the New Testament. God and his world might disappoint or confuse us but in searching for something positive Milton's emphasis on the life of the mind hints at the consolation gained from inner peace, as Michael says: "then wilt thou not be loath/ To leave this Paradise, but shalt possess/A paradise within thee, happier far" (XII 585-587).

By filling in the gaps in the Genesis narrative Milton unleashed some of the most potent questions about our creation and where our priorities lie with regard to God, other people and ourselves. Did Milton intend this to be a temptation for us to resist or was it the result of his dramatic visualisation of the story? Milton was unlikely to allow things to happen by accident; despite his pleas for tolerance his was a personality marked by control and argument, but are we intended to ignore Adam and Eve's conversations and simply obey? Should Milton's Adam have just stopped Eve in her tracks and allowed things to carry on as before?

Milton included as much personal defensive insurance as possible to rebuff any accusation of blame falling on God. Insufficient and contradictory though that defence may be, we are exhorted to push aside rebellious thoughts and consider our duty of obedience to God. It is tough, uncompromising religious teaching, rather than a spiritual journey of temptation and redemption for the reader. This is Protestant England in the seventeenth century, not a mystical experience of the fourteenth or fifteenth century.

However, in the vastness of Milton's epic, Adam and Eve

stand out. It is the very domestic relationship between them that the reader relates to in what may otherwise seem removed, foreign or too big to grasp. If Milton was reminded of former comrades of the revolution in his portrait of Satan then it is just as likely that the portraits of Adam and Eve were coloured by his domestic experiences. He had a wife who went off and then returned; following the onset of blindness with his next two wives he knew about dependency; he had written extensively about divorce[233] but he also knew about the value of marriage and sexual relations. Milton created an intimate and immediate drama about the Fall; a very human drama which sends the reader off in directions which do not assist Milton's intentions. In seeking a comprehensive exposition of all the arguments surrounding the Fall, Milton let loose ideas which it was hard for him to contain. It is when we examine its dramatic characterisation that the poem's inventiveness, energy and immediacy erupt, forcing us to confront awkward questions.

---

233 Much of the material according to Werman (op cit) being based upon an inadequate understanding of Hebraic sources

VI

Unintended Consequences

23

Love

Milton's dramatisation of Genesis does not provide the straightforward conclusion that Adam was a weak husband who should have controlled his wife. Love plays an important role in the development of the Genesis story as the Son is willing to die for mankind (though he knows he will not really die) and for love of Eve, Adam would die with her. Confusingly God's attitude towards love seems lukewarm when compared to his concern for obedience. Raphael's words to Adam: "Him whom to love is to obey" (VIII 634) suggest that love between humans takes second place. Through empathetic characterisation Milton charts the unfolding drama of their love following Eve's sin. Milton is bound by the Genesis narrative but his account struggles to convince us that love between humans is inferior to love for God, which veers towards subservience. The reader may be forgiven for wondering if love between humans was another of God's tests for us, if it is to be discarded in favour of love for God. Allowing Eve some independence of thought and action need not be a bad thing, since their relationship was strengthened by Adam's trust in Eve. Milton's perception of the complexity of human love when under pressure massively complicates our reading of mankind's Fall, complicated as it already is by his determination to stress the inequality between Adam and Eve.

A close examination of Adam and Eve's conversation as Adam has to decide whether to take the fruit encapsulates the dilemma. On hearing of Eve's disobedience loss of Eve is

Adam's first thought, only his second concerns disobedience:[234]

> *O fairest of creation, last and best*
> *Of all God's works, creature in whom excelled*
> *Whatever can to sight or thought be formed,*
> *Holy, divine, good, amiable or sweet!*
> *How art thou lost, how on a sudden lost,*
> *Defaced, deflowered, and how to death devote?*
> *Rather how hast thou yielded to transgress*
> *The strict forbiddance, how to violate the sacred fruit forbidden*
> (IX 896-904)

Here the accumulation of adjectives in line 899, the repetition of 'how' in the following, and the emphatic rhythm created by alliteration in line 901 build the emotion.

His first spoken words to Eve are of praise: "Bold deed thou hast presumed, adventurous Eve," (IX 921) though we sense he is trying to convince himself that this is so. He then displays a pragmatic approach: "But past who can recall, or done undo?" (IX 926) and (wrongly) rationalises the situation, as Eve had done, regarding God's reaction to their sin, concluding: "I with thee have fixed my lot, /Certain to undergo like doom, if death/ Consort with thee, death is to me as life;" (IX 952-4). Both would rather be together in death than live without each other. "Adam shall share with me in bliss or woe:/So dear I love him," (IX 831-2) is Eve's rationale for involving Adam which is tinged by a hint of jealousy at the thought of him with another woman. Milton's drama is again rooted in credible human responses. This is one of the most difficult moments in the poem for Milton, faced as he is by his characters choosing between obeying God's law and following the God-given instinct of love for a fellow human.

Milton attempts to build a case against Adam through Adam's self-analysis. Adam tries to use reason; he accepts that Eve is intellectually his inferior and outwardly is less an image of

234 Adam's later soliloquies are also in his fallen state at X 720-844 and 854-862

their maker, implying he is aware that he should have forbidden Eve's departure:

> *For well I understand in the prime end*
> *Of nature her the inferior, in the mind*
> *And inward faculties, which most excel,*
> *In outward also her resembling less*
> *His image who made both, and less expressing*
> *The character of that dominion given*
> *O'er other creatures;*
>
> (VIII 540-546)

Yet even before the Fall, he knows he could be "fondly overcome" by her ability to persuade, rendering sense powerless:

> *yet when I approach*
> *Her loveliness, so absolute she seems*
> *And in her self complete, so well to know*
> *Her own, that what she wills to do or say,*
> *Seems wisest, virtuousest, discreetest, best;*
> *All higher knowledge in her presence falls*
> *Degraded, wisdom in discourse with her*
> *Looses discountenanced, and like folly shows;*
> *Authority and reason on her wait,*
> *As one intended first, not after made*
> *Occasionally; and to consummate all,*
> *Greatness of mind and nobleness their seat*
> *Build in her loveliest, and create an awe*
> *About her, as a guard angelic placed.*
>
> (VIII 546-559)

To be fair Satan was equally captivated by Eve:

> *her heavenly form*
> *Angelic, but more soft, and feminine,*
> *Her graceful innocence, her every air*

> *Of gesture or least action overawed*
> *His malice, and with rapine sweet bereaved*
> *His fierceness of the fierce intent it brought:*
>
> (IX 457-462)

Small wonder Raphael's brow knits at this point: how is it possible to differentiate between true love and being "fondly overcome"? We know of course that neither man nor angel can detect hypocrisy and so using reason would seem to be a somewhat weak weapon to deploy. Cleverly Eve presents the whole episode as a test of Adam's love: "This happy trial of thy love," (IX 975), knowing that he will find it hard to resist. Ironically the test presented by God in Eden was intended as a trial of their 'love' for him.

Milton's narration of the final stages shows his complete grasp of the way human love works and evolves:

> *he scrupled not to eat*
> *Against his better knowledge, not deceived,*
> *But fondly overcome with female charm.*
>
> (IX 997-999)

They both seem drunk. Milton cannot be on their side but he understands their dilemma. The tenderness of the relationship and the clash between obedience and love are the messages of the characterisation. It turns out that Reason must be a gruesome virtue if it involves watching your beloved die.

Although love for Eve is part of Adam's nature he is also aware of what they have lost, torn as he is between love of Eve and of God. In his confused state his lovemaking becomes desperate: "he on Eve/Began to cast lascivious eyes," (IX 1013-13) and the retributions begin as Adam reminds Eve about the warnings they had received, followed by regret and shame as he remembers what they have lost:

cover me ye pines,
Ye cedars, with innumerable boughs
Hide me,

(IX 1088-1090)

and blame: if Eve had followed instructions, all would have been well: "Would thou hadst hearkened to my words, and stayed/With me, as I besought thee," (IX 1134-5). Once again, however, obedience is paramount and Milton's emphasis on the inequality of Adam and Eve's roles surfaces.

However, Eve demonstrates her persistence in a debate. From IX 1143 she makes a spirited defence – it could have happened even if Adam had been there: "But might as ill have happened thou being by," (IX 1147) which is a weak point, for we know Satan fears Adam more – "Whose higher intellectual more I shun" (IX 483); even Adam could not have detected the serpent's lies: "thou couldst not have discerned/Fraud in the serpent, speaking as he spake;" (IX 1149-50). This is a fair point, because even though Adam is intellectually stronger he could not have detected 'hypocrisy'. Was Eve never to leave Adam's side? "Was I to have never parted from thy side?/As good have grown there still a lifeless rib" (IX 1153-4). This is a good point. In desperation she uses her most contradictory argument: "Being as I am, why didst not thou the head/ Command me absolutely not to go," (IX 1155-6). Forgetting that she previously claimed the issue of her working alone was a test of Adam's love for her, what she says highlights the tension between obedience and exercising freedom of choice.

The domestic quarrel continues apace with Adam's self defence and mutual accusation as they run the gamut of negative emotion:

Love was not in their looks, either to God
Or to each other, but apparent guilt,
And shame, and perturbation, and despair,
Anger, and obstinacy, and hate, and guile.

(X 111-114)

When he is confronted by God Adam will not accept the whole blame: "She gave me of the tree, and I did eat" (X 143), and to her credit Eve confesses. Adam is concerned about his reputation in the future, when he will be blamed for the ills of mankind; at first he thinks this is unfair, "Inexplicable/ Thy justice seems;" (X 754-5) then recognises his guilt: "O conscience! Into what abyss of fears/ And horrors hast thou driven me;" (X 842-3). Running out of ideas he longs for death and finally lashes out at Eve, accusing her of pride and vanity, of being a "fair defect/Of nature,"(X 891-2). At his low point Adam's anger prevents him from recalling that God made Eve for him; anger overtakes both love and reason. Love and hate seem bound together in his attitude towards Eve.

Following Eve's final confession, and a stronger analysis of the situation:

> *both have sinned, but thou*
> *Against God only, I against God and thee,*
>
> (X 930-1)

Adam is reminded of the depth of his love for her, which is the concluding emotion of the poem, to: "strive/In offices of love, how we may lighten/Each other's burden" (X 959-61).[235] Milton clearly understood the course of a domestic quarrel, producing one of the most concisely expressed but credible stages of an argument in which there are so many conflicting emotions. From line 947 onwards the tone reverts to softness and unselfishness, of a quarrel made up, suicide having been considered and rejected:[236]

---

235 Love is a different quality from the 'uxoriousness' that CS Lewis describes in *Preface to Paradise Lost*

236 On Adam and Eve's simpler and more direct speech patterns after the Fall see 'Was Paradise Well Lost?' in EE Stoll's *Poets and Playwrights 1930*. Also 'Speech in *Paradise Lost*,' by Beverley Sherry in *Milton Studies 1975*

If prayers
Could alter high decrees, I to that place
Would speed before thee, and be louder heard,
That on my head all might be visited,
Thy frailty and infirmer sex forgiven,
To me committed and by me exposed.

(X 952-957)

Adam is sufficiently shrewd to realise they could not escape God even in death, and recalls there had been mention: "that thy seed shall bruise/The serpent's head;" (X 1031-2) and that God has been merciful towards them:[237]

in whose look serene
When angry most he seemed and most severe,
What else but favour, grace, and mercy shone?

(X 1094-6)

Love is both the cause of the Fall and the basis of hope for the future. Eve's words: "thou to me/Art all things under heaven, all places thou," (XII 617-18) are some of the most powerful in the poem.

Where then, in the scheme of things does love fit, if it can be both the source of disgrace and the redeeming feature of man? It is a God-given source of joy and goodness but it can have disastrous consequences. How love can be controlled is one of the key questions in the poem. Love may overturn a rational mind but can a rational mind overturn love so easily? Adam's revolutionary realization is that love which depends on inequality between partners does not have to be stultifying for true love does not mean imprisoning the beloved; on the contrary true love presupposes allowing freedom (Adam's point when he allows Eve to go off) and trust (Eve's point). Confusingly, however, in Milton's presentation of God's creation human love

237 See 'Repentance in *Paradise Lost,'* Golda Werman, *Milton Studies 1986,* for a discussion of repentance

and obedience to God do not sit comfortably together. Adam is understandably confused when attempting to understand their predicament, as he has said earlier to Raphael: "To love thou blamest me not, for love thou say'st/Leads up to heaven, is both the way and guide;" (VIII 612-13). Their experience suggests it is not as straightforward as this sounds. How exactly does love lead to heaven if it involves such terrible choices to be made?

Overcome as he is by remorse Adam's love for Eve means he cannot let her die alone, but love hardly seems to be leading to heaven. This trial of love was not to be the last described in the Bible, as the story of Abraham and his son Isaac testifies.[238] Abraham's successful negotiation of God's trial of his love for and obedience to God is shown in his willingness to sacrifice his only son at God's command. This parallels the test of Adam when confronted by Eve's suggestion that she should go off to work alone in the garden. Adam fails the trial but the immediacy and realism of Milton's depiction of the human love between Adam and Eve is likely to remain more powerfully in our minds than the expectation of submissive 'love' demanded by a God whose manner as shown in the poem does little to endear him to us. Biblically we are wrong to think this but the power of Milton's writing is hard to resist.

238 Genesis 22: 1-19

24

Ambition

Milton is at his most observant when portraying love and ambition in all their complexity. Confusingly we are frequently drawn into admiring a sense of adventure, courage and desire for self-improvement in characters we should be criticising. Among these is Satan's ability to create a plan, his mental agility in knowing when to seize an opportunity and his oratory in furtherance of his ambition, whilst Eve's inventiveness in promoting ways to further her ambition of increasing efficiency may seem praiseworthy.

Ambition appears in several guises throughout the poem, but may be summarised as either selflessly doing good for others or attempting to make improvements by changing things. It is, however, the moral purpose behind these ideas and actions which determines their worth, though we must also accept that there exists a tension between the spirit of human endeavour and what has to be described as Milton's dulling emphasis on obedience, which appears to stultify any ambition to change the established order. In short, a character's ambition is likely to highlight the chasm which exists between the imperative to obey God and the human desire to use God-given talents creatively.

The desire to do good for others is morally praiseworthy, though its presentation is not necessarily straightforward. The Son is quick to offer himself as mankind's intercessor and saviour, willing to sacrifice himself to redeem man. Our wonder at this ambition is, however, dulled by our knowledge that the Son is aware he will not die, together with the fact that God is shown to have preordained this. The Son does not appear spontaneously selfless and his ambition to save mankind is consequently tarnished.

From the start Satan's ambition is proclaimed to be wrong: "with ambitious aim/Against the throne and monarchy of God/Raised impious war in heaven" (I 41-43). However, in offering himself to undertake a perilous journey on behalf of the Fallen Angels Satan appears to them the epitome of selfless heroism. The reader is, however, aware of the manner in which he and Beelzebub manipulated the debate in Pandemonium, and understands that the entire enterprise is designed to fulfil Satan's personal plan to match if not overcome God, all of this being founded on his insecurity, envy, and vindictiveness. In a positive and stirring mood he claims that we can achieve whatever we wish, for:

> *The mind is its own place, and in itself*
> *Can make a heaven of hell, a hell of heaven.*
>
> (I 254-5)

This may be true; it is the ultimate rallying cry to promote ambition and endeavour and the poem closes with the consolation that there is a "Paradise within". However, while we may sympathise with some of his criticisms of the manner in which God conducts himself and manages his creation, Satan's is ambition disguising self-aggrandisement.

Eve's desire to work alone to fulfil her ambition to improve gardening efficiency is offset by her ignoring Adam's warning about a hidden enemy and the sense we have that it may also be a trial of the quality of Adam's love for her; will he trust her sufficiently to grant her leave to go? However, Eve is less at fault than Satan. She has constructive plans to divide hers and Adam's labour to ensure greater productivity. Showing admirable confidence, though without any hint of ego, she rejects the suggestion she needs Adam's help and can manage alone. She is proved wrong in this but not as culpably as Satan who is motivated by his ego in his attempt to destroy God's latest creation. We can certainly accept the narrator's comment that he is "aspiring/To set himself in glory above his peers," (I 38-9).

Satan further undermines his case as he demonstrates acute self-knowledge in accepting that ambition was the source of his downfall but in a spiteful exclamation he wonders what God ever did for him:

> *pride and worse ambition threw me down*
> *Warring in heaven against heaven's matchless king:*
> *Ah wherefore! He deserved no such return*
> *From me*
>
> (IV 40-43)

However he realises "nor was his service hard" (IV 45) and with astonishing self-awareness concedes "Yet all his good proved ill in me,/And wrought but malice" (IV 48-9). Even now there are vestiges of his angelic status.

Satan's mistake was not to submit to God: "is there no place/ Left for repentance, none for pardon left?/None left but by submission; and that word/Disdain forbids me," (IV 79-82). He cannot go back but is left with feelings of inadequacy: "Under what torments inwardly I groan;/While they adore me on the throne of hell," (IV 88-9). He understands that "I sdeigned subjection" (IV 50) and that when things go wrong: "Which way I fly is hell; my self am hell;" (IV 75). It is easier to distance ourselves from Satan when we understand his motivation: "To do aught good will never be our task" (I 159) and: "To reign is worth ambition though in Hell:" (I 262). He concludes that to share power with God may provide some satisfaction: "Divided empire with heaven's king" (IV 111). Morally clear water is established between Satan's desire for power, adoration and motivation to destroy and Eve's desire to improve herself in Adam's eyes through creative planning. However, the place of ambition in God's universe remains confused by obedience.

We can only assume that selflessly doing good for others is acceptable to God because we do not see it in any of the protagonists but ambition for self-improvement seems doomed. Adam and Eve's interdependence as ordained by God collides with Eve's desire for independence and the drive (could it ever be described as an instinct?) to grow as an individual. Eventually Adam's anguish gives way to benign acceptance through love, yet the fact that he had to examine his feelings for Eve as well as the merits of her plan to make improvements in Eden which expose her to a danger she could not handle, all bring to the surface the complexities of living productive and fulfilling lives on earth. Having eaten the fruit, not unreasonably, Eve wonders:

> *So to add what wants*
> *In female sex, the more to draw his love,*
> *And render me more equal, and perhaps,*
> *A thing not undesirable, sometime*
> *Superior; for inferior who is free?*
>
> (IX 821-825)

Eve questions the God-given hierarchy. We might wonder whether God had given any thought to the possibility of a dynamic rather than a static universe. Satan's ambition in wishing to overthrow God is wrong because he is motivated by resentment and discontent and is distinct from Eve's desire to improve herself. Is there any reason why humans should not have aspirations? Perhaps Adam should have been educating Eve more effectively, better to satisfy her hunger for self-improvement, but what would be allowed on the syllabus and how much more than Eve does Adam really know?

Paradoxically education does not seem to be highly regarded by God. As Raphael says to Adam:

> *Solicit not thy thoughts with matters hid,*
> *Leave them to God above, him serve and fear;*
>
> (VIII 167-8)

"Be lowly wise" (VIII 173) is the aphorism coined by Raphael to guide Adam and Eve in their earthly state. The spirit of enquiry on earth is forbidden, or at least severely rationed:

> *But knowledge is as food, and needs no less*
> *Her temperance over appetite, to know*
> *In measure what the mind may well contain,*
> (VII 127-8)

Sooner or later all the protagonists hit the buffer of obedience. Eve disobeys Adam, who in turn disobeys God and allows Eve to leave. Eve's ambitions were conceived in a spirit of creative management and a desire to seek his approval by coming out of his shadow. It was a reasoned plan which, by comparison, made Adam appear dull and lacking imagination. Eve's eating the fruit was disobedient but motivated by a wish to improve herself, suggesting that God's test of obedience is effectively a test of mankind's willingness to remain as he is. By contrast Satan misuses his inventiveness and leadership qualities in order to satisfy a thirst for revenge through wilful destruction. Unless ambition is given by God as a temptation, never to be used and constantly resisted, it is a strange attribute. Without energy and creativeness what can be achieved in the world unless God has ordained only a static world?

Reason should assist us to know when to exercise ambition, but what about Eve's request to be allowed space to grow as a person? Must Adam's superiority always limit Eve's ambition to progress? The universe is based on a static state, at best moving only according to God's timescale. Seeking to obey God and the warnings concerning imminent danger lurking in the Garden, Adam is initially minded to object to Eve's suggestion about dividing their labours. It is through love for Eve that he gives way to her ambition by allowing her the freedom to fail, though he was unaware of the possible universal consequences of his actions. In so doing he disobeys God while acknowledging that Eve is trying to use her creative intelligence to benefit their work. In contrast to the Son Adam, not knowing what death is, demonstrates heroic ambition in being prepared to die for Eve.

In appearing to deny ambition to men and angels by prescribing a scheme of progression, God's creation seems limited in what it can achieve. Despite free will mankind has such severe boundaries placed around him that Eve's attempt to accelerate the progression of her place in creation by eating the fruit is ruled out of order. If no questioning of God's plan is allowed, if obedience is everything and God is infallible, what is the point of the angels' adoring chants if not driven by God's egoism? The idea of ambition needs to be reconciled with the divine plan. Milton convincingly demonstrates the troubled minds of characters wrestling with moral dilemmas with great delicacy but he runs the risk that, in seeing things from their point of view, we will accept their views. Milton had to follow the Genesis line that Eve's sin was disobedience but by presenting such a detailed picture of the Fall Milton's inventiveness encourages us to think the unthinkable, and to ask questions which go well beyond his message of obedience.

25

Reason

Milton intended to demonstrate the need for our rational minds to control not only our passions but all aspects of our being. In particular good behaviour, by which he means obedience to the law of God, should be founded on well-reasoned actions enabling us freely to accept responsibility for our own lives. The complex relationship between a faith founded on obedience, love and even democracy did, however, require a deeper treatment than could be achieved in a verse drama. Faith, for example, may well involve obedience but it comprises other elements and emotions which Milton neglected to include, the consequence being that his justification has a lopsided dependence on obedience which generates too many questions and negative responses.

What exactly is Reason?

We are told that "our reason is our law" (IX 654) and the overriding impression in *Paradise Lost* is of the massively moral and rational founded on temperance, the bedrock of Puritanism:

> *There is said Michael, if thou well observe*
> *The rule of not too much, by temperance taught*
> *In what thou eat'st and drink'st, seeking from thence*
> *Due nourishment, not gluttonous delight,*
> *Till many years over thy head return:*
>
> (XI 530 – 534)

Food, drink and sex all require self-control. The tents of wickedness described in this vision of the future contain women:

> *Of lustful appetance, to sing, to dance,*
> *To dress, and troll the tongue, and roll the eye.*
> (XI 619-20)

The earth comprises all God's bounty towards us, but everything seems designed to test us to the point that life is wearingly envisaged as a long trial:

> *for the earth shall bear*
> *More than enough, that temperance may be tried:*
> (XI 804-5)

Man's powers of reasoning therefore have a tough job, comprising responsibility for controlling our senses, imagination and opinions. These topics were to become central elements in eighteenth and nineteenth century thinking among writers and philosophers, though Milton is unable to include sufficient depth of analysis:[239]

> *But know that in the soul*
> *Are many lesser faculties that serve*
> *Reason as chief; among these fancy next*
> *Her office holds; of all external things,*

239 See for example the neoclassical belief in the mind and reason as seen in Pope's *Essay on Man*: "Reason alone countervails all other faculties" compared with the Romantic view of inspiration. As early as 1739 Hume maintained that "reason is, and ought only to be the slave of the passions." (*Treatise of Human Nature*, Book II, part iii, section 3) and Hazlitt (op cit) analysed how the imagination operated in drama. The poetry of Gray, Wordsworth and Coleridge and later Romantics elevated the place of emotion, spontaneity, the influence of nature, even the supernatural. For discussion of the place of the imagination see Coleridge's *Biographia Literaria* (1817) and for a wider analysis MH Abrams, *The Mirror and the Lamp*, OUP 1953

Which the five watchful senses represent,
She forms imaginations, airy shapes,
Which reason joining or disjoining, frames
All what we affirm or what deny, and call
Our knowledge or opinion;

(V 100-108)

Reason is even able to provide victory in battle, should the cause be just:

nor is it aught but just,
That he who in debate of truth hath won,
Should win in arms, in both disputes alike
Victor: though brutish that contest and foul,
When reason hath to deal with force, yet so
Most reason is that reason overcome.

(VI 121-126)

Here again there is no opportunity for Milton to investigate the concept of a just war. Similarly he oversimplifies the emotion of love, which he assumes should be under the controlling hand of reason, though Adam's response to Eve's ideas demonstrates that it is not so straightforward:

love refines
The thoughts, and heart enlarges, hath his seat
In reason, and is judicious

(VIII 589-591)

Humour and 'delight' (IX 239-240 and IX 242-3) should also be managed by reason but without explanation, and 'true liberty,' which is not defined, is 'always' founded on 'right reason':

Since thy original lapse, true liberty
Is lost, which always with right reason dwells

(XII 83-4)

The political and philosophical principles of the English Revolution are here summed up in ten words without further investigation.

Responsibility for imagination, force, love, humour and liberty is crowned by the seemingly harder task of controlling the passions:

> *take heed lest passion sway*
> *Thy judgement to do aught, which else free will*
> *Would not admit*
>
> (VIII 635-637)

Eve's appetite overcomes her 'sovereign reason' when she finally takes the fruit (IX 1127-1131) and Milton later describes the process in terms of a battle with government:

> *Reason in man obscured, or not obeyed,*
> *Immediately inordinate desires*
> *And upstart passions catch the government*
> *From reason, and to servitude reduce*
> *Man till then free.*
>
> (XII 86-90)

Reason is man's distinguishing feature, for unlike the animals he is "endued/With sanctity of reason," (VII 507-8), the epitome of creation: "growth, sense, reason, all summed up in man"(IX 113). So much of our nature rests on our powers of reasoning, but so little analysis of its working and the complexities of using it in situations comprising multiple, frequently competing alternatives is possible. There is the occasional gnomic statement: "great/ Or bright infers not excellence:" (VIII 90-1), but such admonishments are rare. The majority of exhortations concern the use of our brains to obey God in a world bursting with temptations, though there are insufficient examples to show how hard it can be to come to a correct decision. There is just the one example of man's Fall and this catastrophe is reduced to the single command of obedience to God over and above the many strands of morality and philosophy which in fact envelop the situation.

Education lay at the heart of Milton's belief in the importance of reason in making correct moral choices: "The end then of Learning is to repair the ruines of our first Parents by regaining to know God aright, and out of that knowledge to love him, to imitate him, to be like him, as we may the neerest by possessing our souls of true vertue, which being united with heavenly grace of faith makes up the highest perfection."[240] He was by no means unique in thinking this way; it was standard Protestant ideology, as seen, for example, in Whichcote: "To go against Reason, is to go against God; it is the self same thing, to do that which the Reason of the case doth require; and that which God Himself doth appoint: Reason is the Divine Governor of Man's life; it is the very Voice of God."[241] Reason must control passion: spiritual death or alienation from God is, "slavish subjection to sin and the devil, which constitutes as it were the death of the will," and "obscuration to a great extent of that right reason which enabled man to discern the chief good, and in which consisted as it were the life of the understanding."[242] "Reason also is choice," says God in self-justification, (III 108). Somewhat alarmingly, Milton at times regarded books as being more important than people: "Who kills a man kills a reasonable creature, God's image; but he who destroys a good book, kills reason itself, kills the image of God, as it were in the eye."[243] However, the relationship between education and morality and how one influences the other (or not) are given no space. Questions such as how exactly education can make us more morally good beings, given that highly

240 *Of Education* iv 277

241 *Moral and Religious Aphorisms,* Ed Inge, 1930 Aphorism 76 of 1200. Note number 647: "If the Passions be not under the government of Reason, the Man is under the government of his Passions; and lives as if he had no Reason. Passion ungoverned by Reason is Madness."

242 *De Doctrina Christiana* xv 207

243 *Areopagitica* iv 298

educated people are capable of wickedness, and what comprises that education, deserve to be answered. Milton's prose may assist us to some extent, yet it is difficult to understand how the school curriculum he outlines in *Of Education* will necessarily help us to become better people. Reading the works of great writers, learning many languages, considering the philosophy of ancient thinkers and appreciating the principles of logic may be useful but no link is made with the impact of all this on whether we live our lives in unselfish and moral ways. Milton's mantra that in order to act correctly man must be a walking brain begs many questions.

Reason, Obedience and Faith

There have been attempts to deny Milton's own use of reason and logic in the poem[244] but such arguments ignore the lengths Milton went in order to "justify the ways of God to men." Scholars have sought to clarify the efforts which Milton made to present a tidy argument,[245] while Maurice Kelley[246] demonstrated the theological parallels between *De Doctrina* and his poem. But why then may we be left with doubts, unconvinced by his defence of God's actions?

Milton would have assisted his cause if he had confronted the tension between faith and reason, since not everything about God is capable of satisfactory proof. In addition, not everyone is blessed with identically strong intellectual abilities with which to arrive at correct decisions logically.

244 For example WS Worden in 'Milton's approach to the story of the Fall.' *English Literary History* XV 1948

245 Dennis Burden *The Logical Epic,* Routledge 1967; Leon Howard 'The Invention of Milton's Great Argument, A Study of the Logic of "God's ways to men,"' *Huntington Library Quarterly IX* 1945 and JM Steadman's reply in 'Man's First Disobedience,' *Journal of the History of Ideas* 21, 1960

246 *This Great Argument – A Study of De Doctrina as a Gloss on Paradise Lost*, Princeton 1941 though note the debate concerning the authorship of *De Doctrina* mentioned earlier in Chapter 15

Furthermore, there are situations in which mankind does not know what is best for him and has to accept the incomplete, possibly unfathomable workings of God's ways, trusting in faithful obedience rather than attempting to reason things out. One such issue is the test of obedience he gives to Adam and Eve, where the apparently reasonable questions raised by Satan and Eve remain unanswered, throwing mankind back to faithful obedience when reasoning fails to provide answers.

What, for example, is the status of reasoning if we arrive at a result with which God disagrees? Is disagreeing with God then defined as unreasonable thinking? Milton's belief was that mankind possesses the power of reason in order to exercise free will in choosing to do the right thing:

> *take heed lest passion sway*
> *Thy judgement to do aught, which else free will*
> *Would not admit; thine and of all thy sons*
> *The weal or woe in thee is placed; beware.*
>
> (VIII 635-638)

Right and wrong here are absolutes – black and white with no room for grey. As the senior partner Adam must not allow Eve to use her so-called freedom of choice lest he be labelled as uxorious. Either we are correct if we use reason to make what God deems the correct decision, or we are disobedient because we have reasoned inadequately, perhaps allowing passion to overrule reason, but significantly we may just unearth additional layers of morality which could have competing claims to be followed. These are some of the questions which succeeding philosophers have considered and which arise from Milton's insistence on obedience as a matter of faith in a God we cannot fully understand.

God for his part places responsibility for actions squarely in the hands of men and angels by emphasising that the test he set allows freedom of choice. Of Satan he says:

> *I made him just and right,*
> *Sufficient to have stood, though free to fall.*
> *Such I created all the ethereal powers*
> *And spirits, both them who stood and them who failed;*
> *Freely they stood who stood, and fell who fell.*
> *Not free, what proof could they have given sincere*
> *Of true allegiance, constant faith or love,*
> *Where only what they needs must do, appeared,*
> *Not what they would? What praise could they receive?*
> *What pleasure I from such obedience paid,*
>
> (III 98-107)

These are fair points since puppets with no minds of their own would be meaningless, particularly for a creator who seems to crave willing obedience from his creation. However, choice presupposes valid options from which to select. Does free will truly exist in a form that allows us the freedom to act in a different manner from the one required by God without incurring his wrath, leading to death, which therefore seems the only alternative? From the evidence of the examples in the poem (Satan, Adam and Eve) it seems that it is impossible to reason differently from God and therefore obedience is the one way forward.

What God appears not to take into account is that Adam faces an identical predicament with regard to Eve's desire to work alone, as God does in his relationship with his creation. Eve must be allowed the freedom to fail by being allowed to go off alone. Behaving as God desires implies we must think like God, since it is impossible to argue with him. Usefully, those not lucky enough to find such thinking easy are blessed with a conscience, and encouragement: "To pray, repent, and bring obedience due," (III 190) though there is no definition of conscience or from where the encouragement will come.

The reality of the situation is accurately spoken when Raphael warns Adam:

Attend: that thou art happy, owe to God;
That thou continuest such, owe to thyself,
That is, to thy obedience; therein stand.

(V 520-522)

This echoes God's earlier warning to Adam[247] and Eve's acquiescence: "God is thy law, thou mine:" (IV 637), Milton being careful to allow no excuses for their subsequent behaviour. Specifically Raphael warns Adam about Satan: "Who now is plotting how he may seduce/Thee also from obedience" (VI 901-2). Raphael's statement is God's best defence against subsequent criticism. Similarly, when Adam reminds Eve about not eating from the Tree Of Knowledge there is a long headmasterly lecture about school rules:

needs must the power
That made us, and for us this ample world
Be infinitely good, and of his good
As liberal and free as infinite,
That raised us from the dust and placed us here
In all this happiness, who at his hand
Have nothing merited, nor can perform
Aught whereof he hath need, he who requires
From us no other service than to keep
This one, this easy charge, of all the trees
In Paradise that bear delicious fruit
So various, not to taste that only tree
Of knowledge, planted by the tree of life,

(IV 412-424)

This is a reductive not creative or dynamic view of living on earth since, though the description of a bountiful earth with just one rule makes Eden sound idyllic, it is made clear by Raphael that he is confined in what he can tell Adam and Adam is similarly reluctant to allow Eve to put into practice her ideas to develop their gardening.

---

247 Related in VIII 323-327

Later, after Eve has had her dream about the Tree, Adam consoles her with the idea that: "Evil into the mind of god or man/May come and go, so unapproved, and leave/No spot or blame behind:" (V 117-119). There is, however, no explanation as to how or why this works. Are we to suppose that reason is working undercover, or that conscience (whatever it is and from wherever it comes) operates on a different plane?

There were occasions when Milton showed the limitations of reason and not simply its misuse. The Lady in *Comus* criticises the use of reason by Comus:

> *Enjoy your dear Wit, and gay rhetoric*
> *That hath so well been taught her dazzling fence.*
> (789-80)

Is there, therefore, a limit to the intellectual sophistication that is allowable? Certainly the disputes of the Fallen Angels are mocked:

> *Others apart sat on a hill retired,*
> *In thoughts more elevate, and reasoned high*
> *Of providence, foreknowledge, will and fate,*
> *Fixed fate, free will, foreknowledge absolute,*
> *And found no end, in wandering mazes lost.*
> (II 557-561)

Just as he had done when a Cambridge student Milton dismisses empty, theoretical disputes which lead nowhere, presumably preferring debate relating to practical matters of morality and action. We are to understand that the Fallen Angels are misusing reason, as does Satan when he tells Eve that God deliberately keeps man down, despite the fact that the point is not an illogical one, since we are given no reason for this: "Why then was this forbid? Why but to awe,/Why but to keep ye low and ignorant,/His worshippers;" (IX 703-705). The Chorus in *Samson Agonistes* declares: "Down Reason then, at least vain reasonings down," (l. 322), when the ways of God do not seem to square with human powers of understanding. We can only conclude that God's ways are unknowable and not subject to 'reasoned' analysis. At this point the reader may be forgiven for having serious problems with the logical basis of Milton's defence.

What exactly is 'vain reasoning' and what is wrong with it? Perhaps it is wrong because the reasoning process is taking place outside the boundaries of God's law and is therefore faulty. The devils have lost their way because they turned their backs on God and were therefore lost in 'wandering mazes,' which is different from the 'intuitive' reasoning of the angels:

> *Fancy and understanding, whence the soul*
> *Reason receives, and reason is her being,*
> *Discursive, or intuitive; discourse*
> *Is oftest yours, the latter most is ours,*
> *Differing in but degree, of kind the same.*
>
> (V 486-490)

Raphael's point to Adam highlights the limitations of untidy reasoning in man, which does not reach the symmetry of heavenly reasoning, though Milton provides no definition of 'intuitive reasoning'. Is it reasoning at all or simply instinct or a level of spiritual elation which the medieval mystics were seeking, which caused them to be so sceptical about the use of human reason?

The "sanctity of reason," (VII 508) will only come to Adam and Eve when they reach Heaven. In the meantime they must be like the Fallen Angels, lost in 'intricate mazes,' or perhaps they should stop trying to think too hard and simply obey God in all things, even when it involves placing obedience to God above love for each other. Abdiel receives the greatest plaudits from God for his opposition to Satan and the rebel angels "who reason for their law refuse" (VI 41). Abdiel concludes that Satan's "reason I have tried/Unsound and false; (VI 120-

1). This may work for an angel's 'intuitive' reasoning but how should mankind cope with the weaker powers of reasoning we have been granted?[248]

Human powers of reasoning are insufficiently robust. If we get something wrong having used our powers of reasoning, have we been unreasonable? If "vain" reasoning is poor reasoning (and against God's commands) what are we supposed to do when there are imposed limitations on man's capacity to understand? This does not only apply to man. We are told explicitly that Uriel too is susceptible to Satan's lies:

> *For neither man nor angel can discern*
> *Hypocrisy, the only evil that walks*
> *Invisible, except to God alone,*
> *By his permissive will, through heaven and earth:*
> *And oft though wisdom wake, suspicion sleeps*
> *At wisdom's gate, and to simplicity*
> *Resigns her charge, while goodness thinks no ill*
> *Where no ill seems:*
>
> (III 682-89)

Eve is deceived by lies, led even to thinking that animals have brains: "for in their looks/Much reason, and in their actions oft appears" (IX 558-559), but we are told again that man is unable to detect hypocrisy:

> *Since reason not impossibly may meet*
> *Some specious object by the foe suborned,*
> *And fall into deception unaware,*
>
> (IX 360-2)

It seems that anyone would therefore find it difficult, if not impossible, to see through Satan's arguments when he

---

248 It is worth noting that Milton overlooks Abdiel's 'intuitive' power which seems superior to the inability of men and angels to detect 'hypocrisy' mentioned with regard to Uriel

speaks through the serpent. Eve insists to the serpent that "our reason is our law" (IX 654) but it seems to be flimsy protection, especially when Adam refers to the way "sensual appetite" holds sway over "sovereign reason," (IX 1129-30). If human reason is not infallible where does that leave Adam and Eve? God gives man an intellect with which to work out the truth but if we fail God's test, using the powers we have been given, it seems we have been unreasonable. Adam followed the rules until he did not insist on Eve staying with him. If he had put his foot down, he would have been obeying one law, but his love for Eve overcomes other considerations and he allows her to exercise free will. It is a stern religion that forces humans to make such choices. Milton's Eve and Satan, like Marlowe's "overreachers," fly too close to the sun, Eve less culpably than Satan. The force of ambition and love against the rule of obedience and the complications they cause for Adam cannot be ignored.

If using reason simply leads us to obey God, then it is a strange faculty whereby the dice are loaded against Adam and Eve, for in their situation nothing less than unthinking obedience will suffice. Under the circumstances in which they found themselves there was no necessity for Adam and Eve to think at all. However, they each attempted to navigate their way through related issues arising from the situations they had to confront, and despite the 'reasonableness' of the points they addressed, whether of their own making or Satan's, they should both have said a resounding 'NO!' Trying his best to use reason in an effort to allow Eve genuine free will and the opportunity to grow Adam allows her to leave, yet it is regarded as defective thinking. What to Adam was a reasoned course of action did not accord with God's will. God can never be wrong but far from supporting this given, the additional thinking by Adam and Eve complicated Milton's defence of God. The fact is that Milton appears not to display any sympathy for Adam's plight and faithful obedience overrules the use of reason.

Reason and Love

At the beginning of Book IX Milton unambiguously sets the tone:

> *I now must change*
> *These notes to tragic; foul distrust, and breach*
> *Disloyal on the part of man, revolt,*
> *And disobedience: on the part of heaven*
> *Now alienated, distance and distaste,*
> *Anger and just rebuke, and judgement given,*
>
> (IX 5-10)

Disobedience, alienation, anger and just rebuke are the consequences for Adam of being provided with the emotion of love for Eve by God. What are the differences between unreasonable behaviour, the misuse of reason, a weak or uneducated mind and wilful disobedience? These are the layers of meaning consequent on Milton's treatment of Adam and Eve because God appears not to have thought through how his creation might develop. He unleashed the power of love on humans and although he could foresee the future he oversimplified Adam's dilemma when faced with choosing between love for God and love for Eve. Adam chose to eat the fruit for love of Eve, not for hatred of God. Milton's God's seems to lack an understanding of human feelings: free will is a chimera and it is all too easy for the reader to conclude that we should behave like emotionless automata. Pascal, Milton's contemporary, had taken a different stance when he wrote: "Le coeur a ses raisons que la raison ne connait pas."[249]

Adam, not God or the Son, becomes the centre of the poem's focus. Placed in a situation where he must choose between love for Eve and obedience to God he bears in mind everything he has been told concerning the forbidden fruit and a lurking

---

249 'The heart has its reasons which reason knows nothing of' *Pensees iv 277*

enemy but does not wish to overrule Eve's freedom to choose. Eve has to be allowed the opportunity to fail. Although he has been warned about an enemy lurking in the garden, he does not know who or what this is or that they are ill-equipped to deal with hypocrisy. But in allowing Eve to develop as a person Adam disobeys God's command.

The theological problem is that where there is a command not to do something, the power of reasoning may scarcely be required because the thing to do is obey. On a theoretical plane reason should control Adam's love for Eve; it was, after all, the simplest of instructions to follow. There may be other circumstances where deciding how to act might demand more analysis but this situation was clear-cut, except that Milton's dramatisation of the story allowed so many perspectives on the situation to emerge that he lost his grip of the main point, thereby raising doubts about the very morality of God for putting Adam and Eve into this predicament.

This conclusion is reinforced through the presentation of Adam in particular. Despite using his brain to consider what he should do, he is forced to choose between love of Eve and obedience to God. Milton's powerful dramatisation of Adam's moral dilemma touches the reader and highlights the problem Milton faced when employing a dramatic medium to convey what is a complex theological argument. Either Milton misjudged our reaction to his picture of human love or (as Milton's defenders would have it) we may simply be finding difficulty with the concept of God itself. Either way Milton's justification had problems.

The clashes between reason and obedience, and reason and love result from Milton's development of the characters found in Genesis and his point becomes distorted through the lens of his dramatic reconstruction. If ambition and love clash with obedience to God (which in God's view is linked to reason), where do these other feelings fit into the scheme of things?

Reason and Democracy

If the argument is that Eve was not clever enough to deal with the situation, then is the implication that only the 'bright' people should be allowed to make decisions? What is the status of those who do not possess strong mental faculties or who have not benefitted from an education which would support their powers of reasoning? Milton does not define what is meant by the cleverest human beings, and there is no idea of the measure.[250]

In *Of Education* and *Areopagitica* Milton optimistically believed in the capacity of all people to grow in spiritual awareness, but later he became less sanguine. In *The Ready and Easy Way to Establish a Free Commonwealth* Milton argued for a republic, but showed more impatience than tolerance: "And if the people, laying aside prejudice and impatience, will seriously and calmly now consider their own good, both religious and civil,… and will elect their knights and burgesses able men…" (VI 125). He lays great store by the notion of 'able' men, to the point that: "only those of them who are rightly qualified," and "of a better breeding," should choose a council. "To make the people fittest to choose, and the chosen fittest to govern, will be to mend our corrupt and faulty education, to teach the people faith, not without virtue, temperance, modesty, sobriety, parsimony, justice" (VI 131-2). There is no definition or test of 'able', and one wonders how much cleverer than Eve the people will need to be.[251]

The consequence is that the not-so-bright are doomed to fail, or live in subjection to their leaders regardless of their ability to lead responsibly and accept unthinking obedience to

250 On order and hierarchy see CS Lewis, 'The Doctrine of the Unchanging Human Heart,' in *Preface to Paradise Lost* (op cit). On the issues of 'ignorance' and 'innocence' see Jun Harada 'Temptation and Anti Christ in the English Revolution', *Milton Studies 1986*. EMW Tillyard accuses Eve of "mental levity," and consequently Adam is guilty of "uxoriousness," in *Milton,* Part III, chap 3

251 On Milton's 'elitist' politics see Andrew Milner op cit

God, taking their chances like the rest of us when confronted by hypocrisy. Here is another example of the enormity of Milton's task in justifying God's ways to us. It was a harder task than simply providing some dialogue to the Genesis narrative: a Pandora's Box is open: once again Milton loses control of his argument.

The difficulties of believing in Milton' God

The complex realities of life would appear to change the status of reason. If mankind's capacity to reason is secondary to obedience then faith becomes obedience without question. Milton overcomplicated his own faith, which seemed to involve the use of reason on some occasions but not others. Milton argued in *De Doctrina Book I Chapter II* that faith was a matter of obedience and that obedience was freedom.[252] In his dramatisation of the Fall, however, reason and human experience do not sit comfortably alongside faith in God. A good parent explains why the rules of the house exist and why it is dangerous to put one's hand in the fire but God provides no explanations for his tests of obedience. God inhabits a plane which is above and beyond reason, making the task of justifying him impossibly difficult. Milton attempted to persuade the reader that obedience is the only way to know God but, for example, while it is possible to obey the rules of the road because they are usually demonstrably sensible and justifiable, religion is founded on a belief in what cannot be seen, explained or fully understood and God's presence may

252 Milton writes that eating the forbidden fruit: "comprehended at once distrust in the divine veracity, and a proportionate credulity in the assurances of Satan; unbelief; ingratitude; disobedience; gluttony; in the man excessive uxoriousness, in the woman a want of proper regard for her husband, in both an insensibility to the welfare of their offspring, and that offspring the whole human race; parricide, invasion of the rights of others, sacrilege, deceit, presumption in aspiring to divine attributes, fraud in the means employed to attain the object, pride and arrogance." *Columbia xv*

be felt in many different ways such as nature, beauty, music, art and literature. To persuade the reader of God's justice simply by insistence on obedience reduces faith to a single formula and narrows the diversity of means by which faith may be experienced.

In order to convince the reader of the justice of God's actions Milton needed to broaden the scope of his justification. Love of God is dismissed in favour of a reductive obedience, which seems neither a loving action on the part of God nor to bring joy to Adam and Eve. The reality is more akin to submission, suggesting that man is under an authority, may not stray beyond boundaries and is unable to develop. The Fallen Angels will not "adore" God;[253] Mammon cannot bear the thought of subservient "bowing" to God[254] yet the devils "bend" to Satan[255] just as the angels bow to God,[256] who gains pleasure from the obedience of others: "What pleasure I from such obedience paid," (III 107). Submission is the only answer for Satan's rehabilitation: "None left but by submission;" (IV 81) and Abdiel is the only figure to challenge Satan: "Canst thou with impious obloquy condemn/The just decree of God," (V 813-4).

Adam's original acceptance of things as they are and his acquiescence regarding the limits placed on him by God are challenged by Eve's creative plans: they are not set free by obedience but incarcerated by it. The instruction not to eat the fruit is undemanding: "This one easy charge," (IV 421) and Raphael explains to Adam that human existence is but part of a longer journey, culminating in the discovery of heavenly grace and fuller knowledge. Yet Milton's picture of pre and post lapsarian human life is claustrophobic; a world where there are limits to allowable knowledge and the gift of reason has limited

253 I 323

254 I 434-5

255 I 616 and II 477

256 III 350

use. Intended to be reassuring Raphael's words are disarmingly simplistic:

> *That thou art happy, owe to God;*
> *That thou continuest such, owe to thyself,*
> *That is, to thy obedience;*
>
> (V 520-522)

Endurance of such an existence certainly does deserve a final reward. Raphael's accusation: "that sole command,/So easily obeyed" (VII 47-8) neglects other ways for example, through love for others, endeavour, loyalty and self-sacrifice, in which man may fulfil God's hopes for his creation. In reality the comment: "Him whom to love is to obey, and keep/His great command;" (VIII 634-5) is the only way in which the relationship between God and man is defined in the poem. Indeed Eve's punishment is that she will be ruled by her husband: "to thy husband's will/ Thine shall submit, he over thee shall rule" (X 195-6). This suggests that the relationship between man and woman will replicate that between man and God in its feudal submission. As God commands Michael to expel the pair from Eden, "For I behold them softened and with tears/Bewailing their excess" (XI 110-11) he is pleased with their submission, adding that should they continue to behave Michael may: "Dismiss them not disconsolate;" (XI 113). Even the poem's close restates the theme of obedience. When God is reassured he has regained control he allows himself to be generous, as when his Tabernacle is set up: "such delight hath God in men/Obedient to his will," (XII 245-5), and even the future saving grace of Christ will rest on the Son's "Obedience to the law of God" (XII 397).

We only have to compare Christ's parable of the talents[257] with the Genesis account of the Fall to discover that a faith

257 St Matthew's Gospel 25: 14-30 The servant who hid the money given to him by his master to make more money because he was afraid of his master's anger should an investment go wrong, is castigated for his timidity and lack of imagination

conceived of more richly encourages mankind to be inventive whilst accepting responsibility for his actions. Using reason involves fully considering all aspects of a situation, its competing options and priorities, but Milton's God appears dull and selfish, his only gratification being derived from observing his creation follow the one way prescribed by him. Milton's presentation of obedience implies living in a world where there are just two responses: in practice real life is not so straightforward and Milton knew this when he wrote of the need to tolerate the opinions of others, though in practice he was not always so accommodating.

In trying to know and understand God's mind, to comprehend the nature of his command regarding the forbidden fruit, and to do so in the form of a dramatic poem Milton proved to be unsuccessful. He confused the ideas of reason and obedience, forcing us back onto simple obedience over reason because it seems all too easy to reason incorrectly and it is certainly impossible to argue with God. There is no overt evidence to suggest that Milton was using sleight of hand in order to lead the reader through a personal redemption as argued by Stanley Fish. We have to take the poem for what it is, its strengths and weaknesses. Milton believed he could justify God, acting as barrister for the defence; possibly he felt he had to in order to bring people to their senses, perhaps even to convince himself that there was after all a guiding hand at work behind the disappointments he experienced, though we cannot be sure about the autobiographical dimension. Whether or not Milton realised that in what he created he had raised more questions than he answered about God's ways we do not know, though we should be eternally grateful to him, for his attempt forces us to face the nature of our own existence and our relationship with a creator.

26

Free Will, Foreknowledge and Predestination

All literary and theological study of *Paradise Lost* eventually leads to a consideration of free will, foreknowledge and predestination. Mankind's free will is repeatedly the underlying principle of God's self-justification and Milton's belief as outlined in *De Doctrina*. However, God indicates on a number of occasions that he has ordained or decreed certain events and these 'decrees' are regarded as commands by his angelic emissaries.

Milton's theodicy creates its own confusion, though he faced the enormous task of presenting God which involved incorporating some theological and philosophical concepts into a verse drama. God had to be shown to allow free will, otherwise he would appear to be a dictator, though he had to remain a strong and decisive figure who would warrant our faith in him. He attempted to crush what he regarded as the negativity of Calvin's theology of predestination, but he allowed too many competing contradictory ideas about free will and predestination to permeate the poem. To be fair there were many interpretations of this theological conundrum in existence, including those of Boethius, the Compatabilists and the Incompatabilists among the most important, as we shall see, but Milton seems to have found it difficult to maintain consistency in his presentation of God, sending confusing messages to the reader.

Milton attempted to resolve the tensions between free will, foreknowledge and predestination by replacing it with a model consisting of the Arminian concept of free will for man and foreknowledge, but not predestination, on the part of God, complemented by the granting of God's grace to the penitent believer in Christ. However, the already muddy water is stirred further by references to God's decrees and his apparent habit of intervening in order to implement his grand design. References to foreknowledge, decrees and free will abound while Milton relies on Arminianism to resolve the tensions.

Was it possible to persuade us that the free will granted to us to use in voluntary obedience to God is the true state of mankind, when Milton provides evidence of God's management of affairs? We may reasonably wonder whether a verse drama was the most suitable vehicle for a minute and technical theological analysis of all this, but it is the most important area of the poem where theology and philosophy cannot be avoided since they determined Milton's presentation of God's nature. We need to establish whether there is a connection between the references to foreknowledge and predestination, whether they are distinct or identical, and in light of this ask how genuinely free mankind is in Milton's account of the Fall and thus how it affects our view of God.

Foreknowledge and Predestination

Alongside *The Westminster Confession*, the Westminster Divines produced the *Larger* and *Shorter* Catechisms.[258] *The Shorter* is explicit about God's control over man:

> ***Q. 7. What are the decrees of God?***
> *A. The decrees of God are, his eternal purpose, according to the counsel of his will, whereby, for his own glory, he hath foreordained whatsoever comes to pass*

In putting the opposing view Milton's difficulty is that he appeared to wish for two contrasting versions of events. On one hand God transfers blame for the Fall squarely on Adam, Eve and Satan by allowing them free will, while simultaneously

258 *The Shorter* completed in 1647 and presented to Parliament in April 1648

taking credit for events designed to lead to mankind's redemption through the Son. In an attempt to absolve God from accusations that he had preordained events leading to the Fall Milton regarded foreknowledge as being distinct from predestination.[259] However, use of the word 'decree' and indications that the angels too believe events and actions have been commanded force us to question the veracity of God's statements concerning free will.

From the first description of Satan chained on the burning lake there is confusion as to whether it is God's will or his foreknowledge that is at work as he 'allows' Satan to proceed with his sin, which will end in his damnation:

> *nor ever thence*
> *Had risen or heaved his head, but that the will*
> *And high permission of all-ruling heaven*
> *Left him at large to his own dark designs,*
> *That with reiterated crimes he might*
> *Heap on himself damnation, while he sought*
> *Evil to others, and enraged might see*
> *How all his malice served but to bring forth*
> *Infinite goodness, grace and mercy shown*
> *On man by him seduced, but on himself*
> *Treble confusion, wrath and vengeance poured.*
>
> (I 210-220)

The confusion here between 'the will/And high permission' of God and 'left him at large' does not help us clearly to understand Milton's point. Similarly, in what has become a cause célèbre among critics,

259 1619, Fotherby: "All things are praedecreed unto man by God." The word predestination is used in this sense by Hampole (1340), Wyclif (1380), in *The Articles of Religion* (1562) and W Wilkinson (1579). In 1648 *The Westminster Assembly's Larger Catechism*, Question 12 states: "God's decrees are the wise, free and holy acts of the counsel of his will, whereby from all eternity, he hath, for his own glory, unchangeably fore-ordained whatsoever comes to pass in time." (All examples cited in the *Oxford English Dictionary*)

inexplicably and almost laughably[260] an omnipotent God claims to the Son that Satan is at large: "whom no bounds/Prescribed, no bars of hell, nor all the chains/Heaped on him there, nor yet the main abyss/Wide interrupt can hold;" (III 81-84). This is special pleading by God at its worst given his omnipotent status and undoubted power to imprison Satan at will.

Milton provides God with opportunities to deny involvement in the Fall of Adam and Eve: "if I foreknew,/ Foreknowledge had no influence on their fault,/Which had no less proved certain unforeknown"(III 117-19).Clearer evidence of God's directly determining hand in events is seen, however, when Sin and Death follow Satan to Earth:

> *Sin and Death amain*
> *Following his track, such was the will of heaven*
>
> (II 1024-5)

On the other hand Milton's Arminian credentials sound loudly in the statement:

> *Man shall not quite be lost, but saved who will,*
> *Yet not of will in him, but grace in me*
> *Freely vouchsafed;*
>
> (III 173-175)

However, only one line prior to this statement God has said to the Son:

> *All hast thou spoken as my thoughts are, all*
> *As my eternal purpose hath decreed:*
>
> (III 171-172)

It is hard to reconcile a decree from God with free will in man. Further problems arise when we consider that on the basis of

260 William Empson (op cit) claimed this was the first of God's 'grisly jokes'

either foreknowledge or predestination it is surely unnecessary for God ever to ask a question, such as when he asks for a volunteer to die in redemption of mankind.[261] Even the Son knows in advance that he has been granted eternal life and therefore has nothing to fear from death.

Confusion between predestination and foreknowledge continues when God knows that Adam will not find companionship among the animals, "the brute":[262]

> *I, ere thou spakest,*
> *Knew it not good for man to be alone,*
> *And no such company as then thou saw'st*
> *Intended thee, for trial only brought,*
> *To see how thou could'st judge of fit and meet:*
>
> (VIII 444-448)

and has already decided to create a "help meet." Is this foreknowledge or predestination? God tells the angels not to be dismayed at man's Fall because it was "foretold"[263]and denies any decree of his had influenced matters: yet speaking to the Son God reassures him that "all thy request was my decree:"[264]

Despite the impression given by these examples, which was supported by the determinist theological context within which Milton wrote, he had wished to present a different view of God. The contemporary Protestant standpoint, as confirmed by the Westminster Assembly, followed Calvin's concept of double predestination: God pre-elects both those who will accept God's grace and be saved and those who are to suffer reprobation. But Milton would not accept such an inactive role for mankind. It viewed man as a pawn to be manipulated by a God who did not allow him the freedom to influence his own destiny. Jacobus Arminius

261 III 209-216

262 VIII 441

263 X 34-44

264 XI 47

on the other hand argued that man could choose or reject salvation offered by God through Christ, though God did possess foreknowledge of which individuals would be open to divine grace. This allowed mankind free to make good the depravity of the original sin he inherited. For Milton the attraction of Arminianism lay in the fact that both man and God had active roles. Man had the freedom to choose the way of Christ or not, while God had to open the door for him to grant man that grace.

The question raised by Arminius' view concerns the precise nature and status of God's foreknowledge. It seems unlikely for a careful thinker and writer to allow such confusion in his greatest work. Perhaps the most generous response is to acknowledge that Milton's poetic ambitions did not afford him the opportunity to examine the terms he used, to the detriment of both Milton's portrait of God and the persuasiveness of his justification.

There are, however, numerous divine decrees, and for God to say: "what I will is fate," (VII 173), seems incompatible with the concept of freedom of action. Similar doubts arise from the use of 'decrees' by the heavenly chorus, suggesting that God's hand is behind everything:

> *Just are thy ways,*
> *Righteous are thy decrees on all thy works*
>
> (X 643-4)

An example of God's intervention is Satan's argument with Gabriel about their relative strength of arms; indeed Paradise and "the starry cope/Of Heaven" might all have been at risk without the presence of God's golden scales of justice:

> *now dreadful deeds*
> *Might have ensued, nor only Paradise*
> *In this commotion, but the starry cope*
> *Of Heaven perhaps, or all the elements*

At least had gone to wrack, disturbed and torn
With violence of this conflict, had not soon
The eternal to prevent such horrid fray
Hung forth in heaven his golden scales, yet seen
Betwixt Astrea and the Scorpian sign,
Wherein all things created first he weighed,
The pendulous round earth with balanced air
In counterpoise, now ponders all events,
Battles and realms: in these he put two weights
The sequel each of parting and of fight;
The latter quick up flew, and kicked the beam;

(IV 990-1004)

This prompts Gabriel to point out to Satan the might of God's will:

what folly then
To boast what arms can do, since thine no more
Than heaven permits, nor mine, though doubled now
To trample thee as mire: for proof look up,
And read thy lot in yon celestial sign
Where thou art weighed, and shown how light, how weak,
If thou resist.

(IV 1007-1013)

God's hand is clearly at work in his manipulation of the heavenly battle:

Had not the eternal king omnipotent
From his high strong hold of heaven high overruled
And limited their might;

(VI 227-9)

and:

Two days are therefore past, the third is thine;
For thee I have ordained it, and thus far

Have suffered, that the glory may be thine
Of ending this great war,

(VI 699-702)

Words such as 'overruled' and 'ordained' are unarguably God at work in his own creation. Satan's 'escape' from Hell is, therefore, improbably weak compared with God's ability to fix the earlier fight, though he uses every opportunity to give an impression of his foreknowledge rather than intervention. A statement made by God moments later gives it all away:

For man will hearken to his glozing lies,
And easily transgress the sole command,
Sole pledge of his obedience: so will fall,

(III 93-95).

In seeking to demonstrate foreknowledge we may be justifiably wary of God's use of such phrases as 'will fall' given the elastic meanings behind these words.

Adam is unexpectedly astute in showing his awareness of the closeness of the two concepts when he responds to the vision of the future with which he is presented at the end of the poem:

Let no man seek
Henceforth to be foretold what shall befall
Him or his children, evil he may be sure,
Which neither his foreknowing can prevent,

(XI 770-773)

This takes us to the heart of the problem. To Adam foreknowledge is inseparable from predestination. In practice knowledge of what the future holds is identical to predestined events because what is foreseen cannot be changed. On the other hand God could change things and should accept some responsibility for events which he foresees but claims not to have caused. Knowing about terrible things which will occur in the future yet not be willing to change them becomes the same as having predestined them, unless God himself is not free and there are other factors at work in the causation of events, otherwise inaction on the part of God may be as potent as action. All God's action and inaction have consequences; the primary example being the origin of evil. If God is determined to place before mankind a genuine test of obedience or goodness then he has to create, or at least allow the alternative, which is evil. This might be the wickedness of Satan or more generally death, war, famine and any of the future events shown to Adam.

Milton's prose might offer clarification on these matters. However the confusion between predestination and foreknowledge in *Paradise Lost,* highlighted by God's use of the expression "high foreknowledge," a new and intriguingly novel plane of foreknowledge, is not helped by reference to *De Doctrina Christiana*. Milton's use of the words predestination and foreknowledge excluded the possibility of any predetermined actions, although: "Future events which God has foreseen will certainly happen." This is clear, because an omniscient God may not be wrong. Milton goes on to write: "but they will not happen necessarily, because prescience can have no influence on the object foreknown, inasmuch as it is only an intransitive action."[265] Foreknowledge to Milton is seeing into the future but having no influence upon it: "So without least impulse or shadow of fate,/ Or aught by me immutably foreseen,/They trespass, authors to themselves in all/Both what they judge and what they choose;" (III 120-123). Milton was determined to separate foreknowledge and predestination in *De Doctrina* I 3: "God is not mutable, so long as he decrees nothing absolutely which could happen otherwise through the liberty assigned to man; he would indeed be mutable, neither would his counsel stand, if he were to obstruct by another decree that liberty which he had already decreed, or were to darken it with the least shadow of necessity."[266]

---

265 *De Doctrina* I 4, Columbia xiv 85

266 Columbia xiv 77

If God's foreknowledge is restricted to what will happen according to the free will of man what is the significance of God's decrees and the actions he sanctions in the poem? God cannot merely enact man's decisions as the pawn of man's choices? God's authority and power thus diminished, it seems hardly likely. What is clear is Milton's insistent belief in God's foreknowledge and man's free will: "they themselves decreed/ their own revolt, not I" (III 116-117) echoing the earlier use of "not me." The problem of God's decrees and references to the will of God remains unanswered and there is a gaping canyon between what he says and what he does, which does nothing to strengthen Milton's justification.

Free will

Even if predestination is set aside then, foreknowledge complicates the concept of free will, and Milton confuses the issue by ascribing to God speeches containing words inconsistent with the notion of foreknowledge without predestination. Verse drama clearly limited Milton's ability to delve into philosophical subtleties. The Genesis account of the Fall in its sparseness does not hint at such matters, allowing the narrative to retain the power of simplicity. Milton filled his poetic drama with God's references to man's free will and denials of his own responsibility but which was confused by the many instances of his intervention in affairs through 'decrees'. The matter is further complicated by the conclusion that if the power of reason[267] is insufficient for the task of understanding God's ways, then what is the option other than to surrender reason and commit ourselves to him in a way similar to the emotional approach of the medieval mystic?

The theory of free will sounds straightforward enough but it is not so simple in practice, two issues in particular standing out. Firstly, God repeatedly confirms that mankind, as well as angels, possesses the gift of freedom to choose the path he takes:

267 Reason is always equated with choice in Milton's mind. See III 108

"I made him just and right,/Sufficient to have stood, though free to fall./Such I created all the ethereal powers" (III 98-100). However, when instructing Raphael about what should be said to Adam God warns that this is not necessarily an easy quality to manage:

> *advise him of his happy state,*
> *Happiness in his power left free to will,*
> *Left to his own free will, his will though free,*
> *Yet mutable; whence warn him to beware*
> *He swerve not too secure:*[268] *tell him withal*
> *His danger, and from whom, what enemy*
> *Late fallen himself from heaven, is plotting now*
> *The fall of others from like state of bliss;*
>
> (V 234-241)

Free will is a fragile gift or 'mutable', which is to say that those who possess it may easily falter and should not allow themselves to fail through overconfidence. Milton duly made Adam sound overconfident regarding the one rule he and Eve had to obey.

Secondly, if God gave to the 'ethereal powers' the same freedom of choice this has consequences for understanding the origin of evil within Heaven itself. Werman[269] cites the *Midrash* of *Ze'enah U-Re'enah* where, in creating man in his own image, God ascribes to man free will, explaining to the angels that man is better than they can ever be. Angels are intelligent and desire to be good but man may be tempted by wickedness and thus God argues his free choice of virtue is the more valuable. Not only did this absolve God of responsibility for man's behaviour but acted as a catalyst for the heavenly rebellion by angels envious of man's status. By contrast Milton's angels also possess free will and though God will not help the Fallen Angels to repent he will help man: "Mine ear shall not be slow, mine eye not shut" (III 193). This

268 'Secure' in the sense of overconfidence

269 Op cit pages 113-4

is because man was deceived, whereas the rebel angels "by their own suggestion fell,/Self-tempted, self-depraved" (III 129-30). Whichever of these readings is true (and we do not know how much of this *Midrash* Milton knew, though he is likely to have been familiar with the point) this raises awkward questions concerning the origins of evil in God's creation and is, therefore, not a comprehensive explanation of the process by which the good angels turned bad.

Milton's God warns man that free will is not the gateway to godhead which the *midrashists* indicated the Fallen Angels thought it might be. As a result of his free will man's moods and thoughts are changeable; as Raphael dutifully tells Adam later: "God made thee perfect, not immutable;" (V 524) and "ordained thy will/By nature free, not over-ruled by fate (V 526-527)[270]. Free will becomes a potentially explosive quality with which to be endowed. It may lead to complacency and its possession entails constant vigilance; nor is it helped by the fact that man lacks the ability to detect hypocrisy, leaving him exposed to deception and evil intentions; the source of evil in the universe, however, remains unclear.

On a positive note, just as man was free to sin he was also free to choose sorrow and repentance. Milton's description of this process is given in graphic, human terms, and is one of the most significant additions to his dramatisation of the Genesis story. It is all the more important in that it denies the Calvinist view of man as a hopelessly wicked creature and espouses the value of good works, opposing the Calvinist belief in justification by faith alone: "By faith not void of works:" (XII 427). Werman[271] points out that the emphasis on Adam and Eve's repentance as part of their free will is found also in *midrashic* sources.

Milton's characters are fully human, capable of repentance as well as sin. It is the Son as intercessor who reports to the Father:

---

270 See V 520-527 for the complete passage

271 op cit page 139

See Father, what first fruits on earth are sprung
From thy implanted grace in man, these sighs
And prayers, which in this golden censer, mixed
With incense, I thy priest before thee bring,
Fruits of more pleasing savour from thy seed
Sown with contrition in his heart, than those
Which his own hand manuring all the trees
Of Paradise could have produced, ere fallen
From innocence.

(XI 22-30)

For the Son to say that this penitence is a finer fruit than anything Adam and Eve could have grown in the garden sounds awkwardly contrived, nevertheless this penitence enhances the tone of the poem's closing stages and was to become a useful link with *Paradise Regained*.

Ultimately we face the task of placing Milton at a point on the spectrum of thinking between at one extreme man's ability to have freedom of action and at the other a determinist position denying that we have complete control over our actions. On the philosophical plane the 6th century writer Boethius had long been an influence on English writers before Milton.[272] In his *Consolation of Philosophy*[273] Boethius attempted to reconcile human freedom and divine foreknowledge. God has a timeless knowledge of events because he is aware simultaneously of all things that have happened and will happen and cannot intervene in events. For God there is no past, present and future but a simultaneous vision of events through all time, as it were a never changing present. Milton was particularly influenced by Boethius' insistence that reason was the means by which man could avoid any form of determinist view and retain control of his actions. In this way the greater the power of reasoning a man possesses the freer he or she is: God does

272 *Consolation of Philosophy* had been translated by Chaucer for example, possibly King Alfred and certainly Elizabeth I

273 Book V, chapters 2,3 and 6

not intervene, merely sees events taking place. Future events, including actions in the future resulting from individual free will, are therefore necessary only because of the condition of their being known by God through his ability to see all events.

Knowledge of this reconciliation of free will and foreknowledge must have been in Milton's mind as he wrote, but we do not see this in his presentation of God which seems contradictory. His intention to defend God's position inevitably drove him to this Compatabilist standpoint, which favours the view that free will and infallible foreknowledge may coexist.[274] Milton certainly did not favour the Incompatabilist view which is one of theological fatalism. Here infallible knowledge of a human act, thereby making the act necessary and thus unfree (the view which Milton has Adam observe in the closing stages of the poem), would not square with God's allowing free will.[275]

Within the context of contemporary religious thinking Milton's position was most straightforwardly encapsulated in the teaching of Jacobus Arminius[276] who set himself against the determinist outlook of Calvin. In Arminianism God's grace could only be received through man's free will, by following the example set by Christ of how to live out our earthly lives.[277] God's grace would only be received by the believer who turned to Christ for salvation. In so doing man was to employ powers of reasoning to make choices about how to live. Following the Compatabilist ideas concerning God's foreknowledge, but

274 For example the Aristotelian, Boethian, Ockhamist, Molinist and Augustinian/Frankfurtian solutions

275 See *The Significance of Free Will* by Robert Kane, Oxford University Press, 1998. A useful account of the arguments may be found in 'Foreknowledge and Free Will' by Linda Zagzebski in *The Stanford Encyclopedia of Philosophy*, Fall edition 2011, edited by Edward N Zalta and available online: http:plato.stanford.edu./archives.fall2011/entries/free-will-foreknowledge/

276 1560-1609

277 See some of the other references to free will at III 98-9, IX 351, IX 1174, X 9, X 46

without his intervention, supported by the Arminian position on man's active role in the use of reason to guide his actions and willingness to turn to Christ as the way to salvation and receive God's grace, Arminianism seems to be the means by which Milton brought together the separate strands of his thinking.[278]

A further issue which complicates the debate on free will, and embedded in a belief and trust in God, is the number of options genuinely available to man in the decision-making process. From the standpoint of moral philosophy a choice made voluntarily requires credible and fully understood options from which to select. Milton's religion provides just two options, representing extremes of good and evil. There is Satan's way, which means death and exclusion from heaven, or there is faithful trust in God. Just how free can Adam and Eve be in their decision-making when, if they disobey God they do not know what their punishment (i.e. death) means? Without genuine choice between known alternatives free will is a reductive gift, limiting man to faith and obedience. Free will becomes a chimera; in the context of deciding whether or not to obey God there really is no such thing as freedom of thought owing to the lack of alternatives. Suppressing reason in favour of belief without evidence, illustrates that once again that the problem with Milton's God is the problem of God.

Faith is about the willingness of a believer to submit and to trust. In so doing it is necessary to understand that some freedoms are being surrendered, such as the freedom to disagree, to create alternative moral principles, to question, to use imagination and to mark out a future with ambition and enterprise. In his presentation of Adam and Eve Milton came close to producing a working example of the concept that character is destiny. Adam falls for love of Eve, while Eve

278 For a discussion of all these ideas see *Milton's Good God: A Study in Literary Theodicy* by Dennis Richard Danielson, Cambridge, 1982 especially p 82ff

falls because of ambition and her questioning attitude to God, as well as for love of Adam through her fear that Adam would take another wife. Intellectual freedom carries significant risks and the poem shows many times that the power of reason may turn out to be a flimsy tool; ironically it is especially in matters of religious faith that reason demonstrates its fallibility.

What are we left feeling at the end of the poem? Firstly, our sense of God's hand influencing events in the poem is hard to escape. Secondly, through Arminianism Milton attempted a reconciliation of the competing concepts of free will, foreknowledge and predestination but his confusing portrait of God does not lie comfortably alongside the theory. Thirdly, the textual issues in Genesis surrounding the nature of God appear to have been difficult to reconcile. Lastly, by introducing the Son Milton attempted to engender hope for Adam and Eve and the human race concerning man's salvation[279] but the implications for their faith of belief in the power of Christ's future sacrifice was hampered by the apparent role played by God's role in the prior planning of everything from the Fall to the crucifixion and resurrection.

In deciding to follow God or any being claiming to be the creator and ruler of the universe we should ensure that the duty to obey is worthy of the sacrifices it entails: Milton surely intended this as the next step for the reader to take. In failing to convince us about God's ways, we must be content with the conclusion that there are questions Milton did not help us to resolve. He placed before us two extremes of obedience and disobedience, representing good and evil. But in dramatising the complex predicaments life is likely to place before us as we attempt to understand our relationship with the creator and how we should behave, he exposed the possibility of other options. At times there may be just two possible alternatives from which

279 Protevangelium is the term for the first declaration of the gospel in Genesis 3:15. It is a prophecy that Christ will overcome the devil and redeem mankind. It comes immediately after the Fall of Adam and Eve and shows God's intention of saving men from sin

to choose when making a moral decision but there may also be a wider range of solutions, including the 'least worst' option. Lest we worry that this is a postmodern secular interpretation, we need only recall what was to be written about these matters in the 18th century to appreciate that these are among the perennial concerns of mankind.

VII

The Paradox of Milton's Dramatisation of The Fall

27

Assertion rather than justification

Readers always remember that Milton aimed to "justify the ways of God to men." But he prefaced this with his intention to "assert divine providence." It is likely that by 'assert' he meant to champion and affirm God's nature and care for us, but given the unanswered questions arising from his defence of God the justification of God flounders, enveloped by massively important questions about God and his ways, to be overtaken by repeatedly asserted exhortations that we must be obedient. Milton's plan required that God should be presented as a reasonable deity whose ways were capable of acceptance by man. The intense emotions of love and ambition inherent in mankind have serious provisos attached to them, and although Milton may say that reason should control emotions such as love the difficulties of dealing with such a dilemma become self-evident.

Tensions between reason and faith, reason and love, democracy and autocracy, together with questions regarding the duty of obedience to God, the status of human love and the freedom to be inventive and ambitious, tumble from the page. Milton's democratic spirit allowed them all, though the tensions frequently betray ambivalence within Milton himself, as has been shown regarding his attitudes to democracy and equality. Satan is also spectacularly filled with tensions: he hates God but loved heaven and speaks well of God at times; he hates Adam and Eve because he is jealous of them but would work with them and enjoy Eden with them; he hates Eden but admires it as superior to heaven. These are credible human thoughts and it is therefore unsurprising that Milton did not illuminate or open God's grace to all readers. The more his characters raise questions about God's actions, the more Milton resorted to insistence on God's ways.

The angry God of the Genesis P source could not be sufficiently countered by that of either the J source or a gentler presentation of the Son who, certainly in the early stages of his inclusion, is too thinly drawn and anxious to please to provide consoling or inspirational warmth. Milton was therefore left 'asserting' divine providence and God's actions. Submission, obedience, acceptance and hierarchy stand as the cornerstones of Milton's justification of God where they did not (at least in theory) in his contentious involvement in such issues as the monarchy and parliamentary and church organisation. He had always disliked extreme Protestant authoritarianism, yet however much Milton's characters articulated other viewpoints individualism did not appear to have a place in Milton's understanding of God. His God expects crushing sacrifices to be made, including the death of a loved one in the name of obedience, but without explanation. In God's universe there is no room for democracy. The wicked too have the power of reason, but misuse it by disregarding obedience as the primary rule. Obedience will never be a popular concept, it has dull and negative connotations, but it could be made more palatable if God's motives were clearer and he seemed less egotistical. Ultimately, God's ways cannot be understood. Ironically it seems we can only accept God if we ignore some of the evidence of our senses, resist using our powers of reason in certain situations and simply trust in him. God's position is weakened rather than strengthened by Milton; belief and trust in God remain as they always have, an act of faith not of reason.

Milton's God enjoys setting tasks in order to test his creation's obedience. The notion of an arbitrary test of obedience was a well-known Renaissance phenomenon[280] and mentioned by

280 See '*Paradise Lost* and the Myth of Prohibition' by Michael Lieb in *Milton Studies 1975*

Milton in *De Doctrina Christiana*: "(not to eat the fruit of the tree) would not have been obligatory on anyone, had there been no law to enjoin or prohibit it."[281] It is a matter for the individual how to respond to the command,[282] but if obedience becomes blind, suppressing both the faculty of reason and the emotion of love, then we may be left with a dangerously bleak world view. Milton's missionary zeal could never carry every reader with him, but Milton's forensically subtle portraits of the protagonists surely refute Dr Johnson's complaint that the poem: "comprises neither human actions nor human manners. The man and woman who act and suffer, are in a state which no other man or woman can ever know," and that "the reader finds no transaction in which he can be engaged; beholds no condition in which he can by any effort of imagination place himself."[283] What Adam and Eve have to face may be unique but the issues underlying the decisions they must take are surely common to dilemmas facing humans in their domestic and public lives.

Certainly not everyone could agree with AN Wilson's statement that the poem is a: "serene testament to the brightness and sureness of Milton's own religious faith."[284] In contrast a frequent response will be of protest at the contradictions and complexities which make the poem more assertion than justification. Milton could not escape the requirement for obedience and justification (in the sense of receiving God's grace by faith alone, as opposed to justification through good works), which were at the heart of Protestant thinking. *The Westminster Confession of Faith* was sternly authoritarian on the matter of obedience:

> *CHAPTER XIX. Of the Law of God.*
> *I. God gave to Adam a law, as a covenant of works, by which he bound him and all his posterity to personal, entire, exact,*

281 XV 117

282 See David Weisberg's 'Rule, Self, Subject: The Problem of Power in *Paradise Lost*,' in *Milton Studies* 1993

283 'Life of Milton' in *Lives of the Poets*

284 *The Life of John Milton* Oxford, 1983

> *and perpetual obedience; promised life upon the fulfilling, and threatened death upon the breach of it; and endued him with power and ability to keep it.*

The Shorter Westminster Confession is similarly explicit:

> *Q. 39. What is the duty which God requireth of man? A. The duty which God requireth of man, is obedience to his revealed will.*

In his insistence on the power of reason Milton was writing in the context of his times, yet the question remains as to whether the reader's experience of the poem is sufficiently uplifting and reassuring concerning God's compassion and grace.[285]

Milton of course did not intend obedience to be seen as unthinking, negative dullness but as liberating freedom based on the rational. Whilst a contented believer might engage with this concept, the unconvinced or a reader looking for reassurance, some reaffirmation of faith, an uplifting explanation of God's ways is as likely to wonder at God's pronouncements and the associated ideas of free will, foreknowledge and predestination, concluding that the questions and complications raised by Adam, Eve and Satan have substance. Milton's ambition to present the mind of God appears all the more audacious when so many believers had stressed the importance of setting aside reason, focussing on the experience of God, which was just as likely to be a physical rather than a mental one, as it had been

285 In contrast the Roman Catholic Church commissioned *The Catechism of Trent*, published in 1566, containing a section entitled *Faith Excludes Curiosity:* "From what has been said it follows that he who is gifted with this heavenly knowledge of faith is free from an inquisitive curiosity. For when God commands us to believe He does not propose to us to search into His divine judgments, or inquire into their reason and cause, but demands an unchangeable faith, by which the mind rests content in the knowledge of eternal truth." Further sections include ***Knowledge Of God More Easily Obtained Through Faith Is Clearer***.

for the early English mystics. This would account for the way Milton appears to have drifted into assertion.

Milton's insistence on the power of faith set against the limitations of reason exposed in the poem underlines the difficulty of Milton's self-imposed task as God's spokesman. The definition of Faith in *Hebrews II: 1* summarises the issue: "Faith is the assurance of things hoped for, the conviction of things not seen." Freely listening to the word of God and submitting to it grows from a personal relationship between created and creator; it is obedience willingly given, but in the belief, not absolute or factual knowledge about God. Acceptance that faith is located on a different plane from reason is a given across time and religions. In the event, it was as a result of his artistic ambitions regarding poetry and drama, founded on a habit of mind that was used to recognising and enumerating different points of view, that Milton demonstrated the difficulty of relying on reason, despite his intentions and Protestant roots. In *Paradise Lost* he veered towards the human rather than the divine as his artistic mission overwhelmed its theological foundations.

Milton closed the poem with the loose ends tied up; Dr Johnson was right: "Adam's deceiver was at last crushed; Adam was restored to his maker's favour, and therefore may securely resume his human rank."[286] In III 134 "But mercy first and last shall brightest shine" Milton confirmed he wished to convey the joy of reconciliation, God with man and man with woman. It is, however, a bitter-sweet sensation rather than one of glorious worship of God. Adam and Eve are closer than they have ever been, humanly and convincingly stronger after what they had experienced. Facing problems together strengthens their relationship. Michael presents Adam with a vision of ultimate victory for good and personal happiness with Eve:

> *The world was all before them, where to choose*
> *Their place of rest, and providence their guide:*

286 See III 129-134

> *They hand in hand with wandering steps and slow,*
> *Through Eden took their solitary way.*
>
> (XII 646-649)

Despite this emotional outpouring, the "sum/ Of wisdom," which Adam takes with him is starkly: "that to obey is best," (XII 561). That is Milton's intended message but if it were the only message we took away from *Paradise Lost* it would be a meagre diet. What has been learned in addition is more complex than this, and it comes about as a result of Milton's success as a creative artist. Yvor Winters notoriously claimed: "It requires more than a willing suspension of disbelief to read Milton, it requires a willing suspension of intelligence."[287] If all that had been proved in the poem was that obedience is everything, he might have been correct: thankfully Milton achieved more. There is much in the poem that elevates the human.[288] In his studies and travels Milton was exposed to the art and literature of Renaissance Humanism, and although his writing pointed to an unflinching Protestant faith in God he did not ignore the human dimension. The success of *Paradise Lost* derives from the human drama it depicts; it is the poem's artistic power and quality which captures our imagination and engagement.

What is revealed through Milton's dramatic imagination is liable to make the reader howl in protest at what we witness in terms of 'God's ways'. Adam and Eve are shown in the reality of the domestic situation: the closeness we feel towards them exposing deeper aspects of what it is like to be a human being.[289] Milton unwittingly encouraged us to see things from the human (fallen) view, which raises more questions than it answers about God's justice.

---

287 *The Function of Criticism* 1957

288 For an example of an investigation into Milton's place in humanist thinking see David Reid's *The Humanism of Milton's Paradise Lost*, published Edinburgh, 1993

289 John R Mulder in 'The Lyric Dimension of *Paradise Lost,' Milton Studies 1987,* is good on the "absence of human certainties."

Paradise Lost does not work on the level of an uplifting sermon or mystical experience and will be read in different ways by readers holding widely differing views about faith. However, as a tool for converting unbelievers or reassuring the faithful it leaves much to be desired. The broad cosmic canvas of the poem, traversing time and space, the spectacular scenes, the sense of history and literature, the imaginative presentation of characters struggling to make sense of their place in the scheme of things marked out Milton as a great poet and dramatist. A proper appreciation of his importance in the development of verse drama and characterisation should place him higher in our understanding of the English dramatic tradition, and the evolution of the novel with its focus on the internal lives of characters responding to the challenges of human relationships and the pressures of the world in which they live.

28

A great poem in spite of itself

Paradise Lost satisfied Milton's ambition to be remembered as a great epic poet but there was more. The Book of Genesis became just the starting point for Milton's descant on the Fall: when it came to the execution of his greatest poetic project his habits of mind and vision of biblical figures as human beings gave birth not only to a supreme literary achievement but a catalyst to existential thinking through succeeding centuries. Far from being the hard, puritan and impenetrable epic poem of the caricature *Paradise Lost* became a drama for all time, raising questions about the human condition which have preoccupied mankind ever since.

In an age when we are fascinated by the vastness of space and the wonders of the cosmos Milton's picture of Adam and Eve in all their untidy humanity forces us to confront (within the context of the 17th century) the spiritual dimension, mankind's relationship with a creator and our place in the scheme of things. Who we are, where we come from and whether we are alone are questions which continue to haunt modern man. During our lives we inhabit a space frequently described by theologians as a permanent Holy Saturday, in a state of waiting, questioning and uncertainty, caught between Christ's crucifixion yet unsure about the resurrection on Easter Sunday and anxious to know for sure. The questions asked by Milton's characters are therefore likely to be our questions.[290]

---

290 See for example *Between Cross and Resurrection: A Theology of Holy Saturday* by Alan E Lewis, published by Wm. B. Eerdmans Publishing Co, 2003

In addition Milton provokes us to evaluate the philosophy and morality underlying marriage, issues of equality between men and women, the nature of democracy and hierarchy (secular and religious), the role of education and the place of ambition. Reading *Paradise Lost* involves teasing out moral and existential issues, confronting the idea of godhead and understanding conflicting options for action, which may result not in simple conclusions but in 'least-worst' choices. By writing the poem he did, laying bare the dilemmas facing human beings, Milton's achievement was all the greater, as our probing and questioning reflect the importance and complexity of what Milton placed before us.

Milton provided a link between medieval mysticism and the Age of Enlightenment where the battle between faith and reason was fought in the open. The questions he provoked in *Paradise Lost* set the agenda for the following four centuries. 18th century philosophy was less preoccupied with sectarian struggles and more with the issue of how to reconcile faith and reason. Milton had asked the question but his answer of obedience was insufficient in the Age of Enlightenment, to the extent that philosophers attempted to replace formal religion with reason. There was an attempt to create a theory of everything comprising theology, philosophy, politics and science. Thinkers such as Newton and Priestley retained a Christian perspective whilst Deists such as Locke and Theists such as Rousseau were strongly influential. In attempting to create a moral structure based solely on reason, Christian roots were frequently hard to sever; as Eagleton writes: "The God of Scripture has the distinct advantage of being in some sense personal, whereas reason is distinctly un-godlike in its impersonal hauteur."[291]

During the 19th century religious believers as well as philosophers were forced to confront advances in scientific thinking and discoveries which raised questions about the nature of our origin and therefore of the place of faith. The world

291 Page 33 in a survey of thinking about reason and Christian belief: *Culture and the Death of God* by Terry Eagleton, published Yale 2014

was buffeted by Darwin's theory of evolution[292] and Charles Lyell's observations about geology.[293] The latter questioned the very creation of the earth by its claim that the earth was much older than had first been thought, whilst Darwin's theory that mankind evolved from the apes provoked condemnation from the church and contributed to the crisis of faith which was encapsulated in Arnold's poem *Dover Beach*.[294] Contemplating the comforting sight of a calm full tide Arnold contrasts it to the sea of faith, which is going out:

> *The Sea of Faith*
> *Was once, too, at the full, and round earth's shore*
> *Lay like the folds of a bright girdle furl'd.*
> *But now I only hear*
> *Its melancholy, long, withdrawing roar,*

Arnold was writing two hundred years after the publication of the first edition of *Paradise Lost* in 1667; the two poems about religion could not be further apart in style or sentiment, or are they? Milton had left so many unanswered questions, had raised so many uncertainties about the nature of God and faith that we should acknowledge his contribution to setting an agenda for the debate which continues in our own times.

During the 20th and 21st centuries these concerns have been augmented by massive disagreements and developments over the implementation of new forms of democracy, changing views on sexuality and marriage, social mobility, the encouragement of ambition and what constitutes an education. Crucially there is the expansion of our knowledge about a cosmos in which we appear to play a much smaller part than Milton could have imagined, and would have made Arnold even more pessimistic.

In *Paradise Lost* Milton did not set out to write a theological treatise, even though matters such as foreknowledge and

292 *On The Origin of Species*, published 1859

293 *The Principles of Geology*, published 1830-33

294 Published 1867

predestination surface, but the human tragedy of Adam and Eve contains so much that begs questions about God's justice that its themes are relevant to any and every age. We may not need to go quite as far as Feisal G Mohamed[295] who in considering ethical and political engagement grounded in belief likens Samson to a 21st century suicide bomber[296] but we should appreciate the link he is making between violent action and strongly held beliefs. Milton was composing his epic within the era of a brutal sectarian struggle with its roots in the English Reformation, which had been enacted by Henry VIII and delicately held together by Elizabeth I. He had witnessed the massive lurches in democracy and governance from Charles I to the Protectorate and back to the Restoration of Charles II. Different times from ours certainly, but not so different regarding the morality, ideals and beliefs which lay behind them, and which in varying degrees Milton reveals in *Paradise Lost*.

In trying to write a theological justification of God's actions in the form of a poetic drama within an epic structure, Milton created one of the greatest literary conundrums. With an ostentatious belief in his own powers he strove to achieve nothing less than knowing, explaining and portraying the mind of God. It is hardly surprising that this is the weakest aspect of the poem. What happened instead was that this public relations professional for God drew back the curtain to reveal just how hard it is to be human. We are encouraged to empathise with the protagonists and to understand the number and difficulty of the choices they (and we) have to make. Frequently we are forced to question the sternness of Milton's religion, which he planned should have assisted us to resist such thoughts. However, due to God's unprepossessing manner and some of his egotistical characteristics we cannot easily dismiss the reasonable questions posed by Satan and Eve. They are fundamental questions which have stood the test of time, finding new answers with each generation.

---

295 *Milton and the Post-Secular Present: Ethics, Politics, Terrorism,* published Stanford University Press, 2011

296 *Samson Agonistes*

Milton wanted the English people to turn to God and obediently trust in him, in the spirit of Christ's words: "the truth shall make you free" (John 8:32). In Milton's case the message was 'obedience will make you free'. But the act of composition unleashed in Milton his instinct to allow freedom of speech and debate, just as he had spent all those years writing pamphlets, examining all sides of an argument. We should remember that prior to *Paradise Lost* much of his writing had concerned radicalism and rebellion, but in his verse drama unusually he was defending orthodoxy. The truth is that Milton was an iconoclast by nature but in *Paradise Lost* he found himself defending not prosecuting and this seems to have forced him back to conservative obedience. He did not satisfactorily conclude his dilemma because he seemed unable to do otherwise than allow his characters to have their say. Milton's political dilemma, never completely resolved, was that he wished to give people their voices, to have democratic choices, but he also knew that they were frequently weak and needed to be told what to do. His art too was caught between democracy and autocracy. In placing mankind centre stage in his drama Milton examined how we should behave as responsible human beings living in a Christian context: he opened a debate which was taken up by subsequent generations of novelists and playwrights, philosophers and theologians.

It may be argued that Milton's treatment of the Genesis story reflected his inner turmoil at the failure of the English Revolution and a need to convince himself that obedience to the will of God should be patiently borne. The comfort of faithful certainty was possibly important to him during the period of composing his poem but how far autobiographical elements in the poem are significant is a matter of speculation. What we can say with more certainty is that the characters unbalance his argument. We are more inclined to recognize and understand Adam and Eve's reasoning, Satan's strengths and God's shortcomings than Milton intended. The puppets controlled the puppeteer. If it had been Milton's intention deliberately to tempt us into accepting the implied questions about God raised by his characters, he was in the impossible predicament of neither fully nor satisfactorily being able to defend an unknowable God.

Paradise Lost feels like the product of real life experiences, as much as of literary precedents and theology. Milton's investigations into faith, reason, love, and ambition speak to the revolutionary while his orthodoxy speaks to the faithful, conservative believer. But we know that he was not naturally an orthodox man; he would constantly find ways to argue a case differently from others. Milton is not the dry and dusty Puritan of the modern caricature. Through his experiences as a scholar, traveller, writer, revolutionary politician, radical Protestant, prisoner, father and husband he developed a detailed insight into the challenges and setbacks, high points and low points, the exhilaration and exasperation of human existence. It is no surprise that, Dr Johnson aside, readers in every century have discovered that Milton succeeded in his presentation of humanity. He wrote a powerful human drama while simultaneously attempting to write an *apologia* for God.

Milton was one of the cleverest, but also one of the least reliable of poets. He twisted and turned Houdini-like, the greatest literary illusionist, struggling with his presentation of reason and obedience through characters who are given compelling reality. The simplicity and flatness of the characterisation in Genesis carries its own special power and authority, managing the burden of conveying the relationship between mankind and God in a more straightforward way than the complex characterisation in *Paradise Lost*. But Milton achieved something different: he opened the book of life to reveal its messiness. *Paradise Lost* is the most enigmatic long poem written in English: readers may love it, hate it or hold both views simultaneously but it always provokes a response.

It is a drama of the human condition, more successfully about what it is to be human than what it is to be God. It is also a tragedy about errors of judgment leading to disobedience but where hope is promised but a long way off. God's cause was to be better served in *Paradise Regained*, where we read the New Testament elements of Christianity, an image of God coming to us as a man, relating to people, showing mercy, bringing salvation and completing the narrative. The Son's arrival on earth makes God's justice, forgiveness and grace more comprehensible than appears in *Paradise Lost.* But Milton gave mankind a platform from which to shout loudly questions concerning the complex and confusing mire in which we appear to live, and where submission seems an unsatisfactory but the only way through. Calling this 'faith' would appear to be taking the line of least resistance for a writer whose preference was for strong arguments and proofs.

We leave the poem our minds still brimming with questions about God's nature and purposes. From the beginning Milton had been determined not to write a traditional epic consisting of chivalry and knights but a poem of Christian heroism. Whilst the Son's feats and willingness to save mankind through death might seem to qualify him for the title of hero it is mankind's heroism in managing a relationship with God which has the stronger claim. Milton's investigation of Christian heroism elevated human endeavour, Adam holding the more robust claim to be called a hero. Milton's artistic method undermined his project to the point where our focus is on mankind's struggle to understand a God whose ways cannot be understood.

For if Milton failed to "justify the ways of God to men," then happily he created a great poem in which he justified 'the ways of men to God'. It contains man's reply to God: though Milton could not master the mind of God he was triumphant in displaying the mind of man. Milton's insistence on the intricacy, responsibility and drama of working out our destinies created a deeply moral energy, which carries a resounding resonance for every reader in every age.